MAKING THE AMERICAN MIND

SOCIAL AND MORAL IDEAS IN

THE McGUFFEY READERS

Making the American Mind

Social and Moral Ideas in the McGuffey Readers

RICHARD DAVID MOSIER

*Submitted in partial fulfillment
of the requirements for the degree of Doctor of Philosophy,
in the Faculty of Philosophy, Columbia University*

KING'S CROWN PRESS
Columbia University, New York
1947

Preface

A STUDY of the main currents of thought in the McGuffey readers may legitimately hope to embrace some of the ideas which lie at the heart of American civilization. There is indeed a direct and intimate relation between the curriculum and the culture which students of American civilization have only recently come to investigate. A study of the basic pattern of ideas in the McGuffey readers will be concerned to point out, accordingly, the role education has played in the development of American civilization; and it will therefore attempt to describe the basic values and ideas which the McGuffey readers, and through them American education, put before American youth. Such a study must of course deal with the traditions and perspectives of generations older than the readers themselves, and it must grasp the broader currents and eddies in American thought, if the pattern of ideas in the McGuffey readers is to be placed with proper historical perspective against the broader background of American culture.

In carrying out the present study, I have become indebted to numerous persons who gave unstintingly of their time and criticism in the forwarding of so difficult an undertaking. Among those who deserve generous thanks are several to whom I should like to address a note of appreciation. I am particularly indebted to Professor George S. Counts, Teachers College, Columbia University; to John A. Krout, Professor of History, Columbia University; to Professor Edward H. Reisner, Teachers College, Columbia University; to J. H. Randall, Jr., Professor of Philosophy, Columbia University; and to Professor Donald Tewkesbury, Teachers College, Columbia University. And I owe an incalculable debt to my wife, Rosalind A. Mosier, who assisted me at every stage of the inquiry.

For permission to quote copyrighted material, I am indebted to the American Book Company, successors to the parent companies that published the McGuffey readers. For quotations from Carl Russell Fish, *The Rise of the Common Man,* from Hamlin Garland, *Son of the Middle Border,* from Charles A. Beard, *An Economic Interpretation of the Constitu-*

tion, and from J. S. Bassett, *The Life of Andrew Jackson,* by permission of The Macmillan Company, publishers, I am also indebted. For an excerpt from *One Man's Life* by Herbert Quick, copyright 1925, used by special permission of the publishers, The Bobbs-Merrill Company, I am deeply indebted to the latter publishers. For permission to quote from Mark Sullivan, *Our Times,* I am indebted to Charles Scribner's Sons. For permission to quote from James Fenimore Cooper, *The Redskins,* I am indebted to G. P. Putnam's Sons. For permission to quote from Merle Curti, *The Growth of American Thought,* I am indebted to Harper and Brothers. For permission to quote from John Clifton, *Ten Famous American Educators,* I am indebted to Long's College Book Company. For permission to use material from *Samuel F. B. Morse: His Letters and Journals,* from Beveridge, *Life of John Marshall,* and from Henry Cabot Lodge, *Works of Alexander Hamilton,* I am indebted to Houghton Mifflin Company. For permission to quote from Ralph W. Gabriel, *The Course of American Democratic Thought,* I am indebted to the Ronald Press Company. For permission to quote from Vernon L. Parrington, *Main Currents in American Thought,* I am indebted to Harcourt, Brace and Company. For materials from Ralph L. Rusk, *The Literature of the Middle Western Frontier,* I am indebted to Columbia University Press. For excerpts from Arthur M. Schlesinger, Jr., *The Age of Jackson,* and William Kent, *Memoir and Letters of James Kent,* I am indebted to Little, Brown and Company.

R. D. M.

Contents

1

The Struggle for Political Power

AT THE CLOSE of the Revolution the most urgent problem was the creation of a new political state. The debates occasioned by this venture into republicanism revealed the concern of men of property for established institutions, should popular vote bring into positions of power radicals and democrats. The conservative fear for established institutions led the advocates of Federalism to a system of checks and balances, which was to protect minorities from the tyranny of majorities in the inevitable political struggles of the Republic. Opposed to this conservative group were the economic liberals who rejected middle-class conservatism, and inclined increasingly to the radical democracy of the French Enlightenment. The Hamiltonian tradition in American politics, while no doubt conceived in liberty, was hardly dedicated to the proposition that all men are created equal. The Jeffersonian tradition, on the other hand, sought a more liberal conception of government in an agrarian paradise of freeholders. In a very broad sense, one can say that the struggle between these two opposing traditions has absorbed American politics since the founding of the Republic, though, of course, with assorted issues and changing arguments suited to the economics of each situation.

If the struggle for political power be thus broadly conceived in terms of the ideas of the opposing Hamiltonian and Jeffersonian traditions, the position of the McGuffey readers with reference to these traditions may be charted with a fair degree of success. Though succeeding chapters give a more detailed account of the various phases of this continuing struggle, the present chapter is concerned to seek the origins and the advocates of the basic ideas which have become absorbed by these two great traditions. In pursuing this task we have sought to follow the ideas wherever they lead, and they lead inevitably to the great debate over the Constitution, and thereby, to the basic conflicts between the Hamiltonian and Jeffersonian traditions. The conflicting ideas of these two traditions define the political philosophy of the McGuffey readers.

I

In Daniel Webster, able Whig attorney from Massachusetts, the Mc-
Guffey readers found a remarkable spokesman for their political link
with a Hamiltonian past; for it is from Harrington, Locke, Blackstone,
Hamilton, and Webster that the political philosophy of the McGuffey
readers is ultimately derived. The premises of Webster's logic bear the
imprint of a Federalist past, derived by the strict laws of primogeniture
and entail from the English classical theorists and constitutionalists,
though sufficiently modified by the ambitious logic of Hamilton to suit
the needs of a developing American economy. It was Webster who suggested that the stake-in-society principle of the constitutionalist fathers of
this Republic was not without application in the nineteenth century; for
when the advancing cohorts of democracy and radicalism were demanding
nothing more radical than the right to vote, and nothing more revolutionary than a just place in the determination of policy, he agreed:

I take the principle [of stake-in-society] to be well established, by writers of the
greatest authority. In the first place, those who have treated of natural law have
maintained, as a principle of law, that, as far as the object of society is the protection of something in which the members possess unequal shares, it is just that
the weight of each person in the common councils should bear a relation and
proportion to his interest.[1]

The argument that men who have a stake in society should have a
voice in the common council proportionate to their share of the social
order was hardly, as Webster pointed out, a new idea. Economic power,
Webster argued, is the real criterion of political power; and the authority
for this economic determinism is the great English theorist, Harrington,
from whom the fathers of the Republic drew so generously to embroider
their arguments:

It is his leading object, in his *Oceana,* to prove, that power *naturally* and *necessarily* follows property. He maintains that a government founded on the disregard of property is founded in injustice, and can only be maintained by military
force. "If one man," says he, "be sole landlord, like the Grand Seignior, his empire is absolute. If a few possess the land, this makes the Gothic or feudal constitution. If the *whole people* be landlords, then it is a commonwealth." "It is
strange," says an ingenious person in the last century, "that Harrington should
be the first man to find out so evident and demonstrable a truth as that property
being the true basis and *measure* of power." In truth, he was not the first. The
idea is as old as political science itself. It may be found in Aristotle, Lord Bacon,
Sir Walter Raleigh, and other writers. Harrington seems, however, to be the first
writer who illustrated and expanded the principle, and given to it the effect and
prominence which justly belong to it. To this sentiment, Sir, I entirely agree. It

seems to me to be plain, that, in the absence of military force, political power naturally and necessarily goes into the hands which hold the property.[2]

This is the principle which underlies Webster's remarks in the Mc-Guffey readers. In one of the lessons, for example, he notes the importance of the American experiment in government, which has been founded on just principles of political science, and from which innumerable benefits flow to the masses. He enumerates the blessings that have come to the American people, and notes with pride that

with America, and in America, a new era commences in human affairs. This era is distinguished by free representative governments, by entire religious liberty, by improved systems of national intercourse, by a newly awakened and unquenchable spirit of free inquiry, and by a diffusion of knowledge through the community, such as has been before altogether unknown and unheard of.[3]

These benefits and blessings have been granted us by the wisdom of the founding fathers of the Republic who, with heavenly guidance, erected the structure of the most beneficent government on earth.[4] The gentlemen assembled at Philadelphia to frame and adopt a Constitution for the government of this new enterprise were superior to all groups of assembled legislators in the long course of human history, and none "can stand in preference to the general Congress assembled at Philadelphia."[5] Thus the McGuffey readers agreed with Webster in his estimation of the assembled patriots who framed this government and its laws, and they would stand with him in maintaining that the Constitution is the legal embodiment of the machinery of a most beneficent government, to which all should give the last full measure of devotion.[6] When the farmer-labor coalition was pressing the demand to number among the benefits of this just government the right to vote, however, Webster would argue in quite other quarters that:

The English Revolution of 1688 was a revolution in favor of property, as well as of other rights. It was brought about by men of property for their security; and our own immortal Revolution was undertaken, not to shake or plunder property, but to protect it. The acts which the country complained of were such as violated the rights of property. An immense majority of all those who had an interest in the soil were in favor of the Revolution; and they carried it through, looking to its results for the security of their possessions.[7]

But it was hardly on the basis of the security and sanctity of property that Tom Paine had awakened the patriots to shed their blood in a cause of doubtful outcome. They believed with Paine that the Revolution was being fought to secure the inalienable rights proclaimed by the Declaration, rights which Webster dismissed as "other rights." In the writings of Paine and the other propagandists of the Revolution it appeared that the war was being fought for natural and inalienable rights of life, liberty, and the pursuit of happiness. As for the pursuit of private property and personal gain, we may take the word of Paine that:

> Personal property is the *effect of society:* and it is as impossible for an individual to acquire personal property without the aid of society, as it is for him to make land originally. . . . All accumulation, therefore, of personal property, beyond what a man's own hands produce, is derived to him by living in society; and he owes on every principle of justice, of gratitude, and of civilization, a part of that accumulation back again to society from whence the whole came . . . if we examine the case minutely it will be found that the accumulation of personal property is, in many instances, the effect of paying too little for the labor that produced it; and the consequence of which is, that the working hand perishes in old age and the employer abounds in affluence.[8]

This is Paine's answer to a sermon by Watson, Bishop of Llandaff, entitled *The Wisdom and Goodness of God in having made both Rich and Poor.* And it is likewise a reply to the contention of the McGuffey readers that God "made the poor man, as well as the rich man."[9] Not without reason, then, did the politicians of the conservative cause brand Paine as "a filthy little atheist."[10] Not without cause did the orthodox of Harvard College present a copy of Watson's *Apology for the Bible* to every undergraduate as a counterblast to Paine's *Age of Reason.*[11] And not without reason did the good advocates at the trial of Thomas Williams for publishing Paine's *Age of Reason* declare that such atheistical tracts should be restricted because, "the poor stand most in need of the consolation of religion, and the country has the deepest stake in their enjoying it. . . ."[12] Nor was it without cause that the McGuffey readers devoted a lesson to Paine's atheism, declaring that Paine had said that "the Christian fable is but the tale of the more ancient superstitions of the world, and may easily be detected by a proper understanding of the mythologies of the heathen."[13]

Well might the forces of conservatism and established institutions oppose this "dirty little atheist," for it was he who declared that:

> The first principle of civilization ought to have been and ought still to be, that the condition of every person born into the world, after a state of civilization commences, ought not to be worse than if he had been born before that period.[14]
>
> It is not charity but a right, not bounty but justice, that I am pleading for. The present state of civilization is as odious as it is unjust. It is absolutely the opposite of what it should be. . . . The contrast of affluence and wretchedness . . . is like dead and living bodies chained together.[15]
>
> It is the practice of what has unjustly obtained the name of civilization . . . to make some provision for persons becoming poor and wretched only at the time they become so. Would it not, even as a matter of economy, be far better to adopt means to prevent their becoming poor?[16]

These are good questions, but of course they were raised by one not qualified to speak on so delicate a subject; for Paine was reputedly an atheist,[17] and the McGuffey readers are inclined to put the question to Mr. Locke, who, fortunately enough, had declared that, "The great and chief end, therefore, of men uniting into commonwealths and putting themselves under government is the preservation of their property."[18]

Let the question be answered by Mr. Locke, who was to the highest pitch of devotion and adoration, a Christian. Mr. Locke whose office was to detect the errors of thinking, by going up to the fountain of thought, and to direct into the proper track of reasoning the devious mind of many, by showing him its whole process, from the finest perceptions of sense, to the last conclusions of ratiocination; putting a rein besides upon false opinion, by practical rules for the conduct of human judgment.[19]

By leaving the question to Mr. Locke the McGuffey readers were enabled to disassociate themselves from the principles of the author of the *Age of Reason*. Whereas Webster found that the American Revolution had been "brought about by men of property for their security,"[20] Paine found the great lesson of the Revolution in the awakening of people to the "imposition of governments."[21] He had no great fear of popular government; he did not feel that demagogues would arouse the people to acts of violence and revolution. "As far as my experience in public life extends," he declared, "I have ever observed that the great mass of people are always just, both in their intentions and their arguments. . . ."[22]

One of the great advantages of the American Revolution has been, that it has led to a discovery of the principles, and laid open the imposition of governments. All the revolutions till then had worked within the atmosphere of a court, and never on the grand floor of a nation. The parties were always of the class of courtiers. . . . In all cases they took care to represent government as a thing made up of mysteries, which only themselves understood; and they hid from the understanding of the nation the only thing that was beneficial to know, namely, *That government is nothing more than a national association acting on the principles of a society.*[23]

These arguments, but principally his remarks on the fables of religion, the McGuffey readers could hardly accept:

It seems, gentlemen, this is an age of reason, and the time and the person are at last arrived, that are to dissipate the errors that have overspread the past generations. The believers in Christianity are many, but it belongs to the few that are wise to correct their credulity! Belief is an art of reason; and superior reason may therefore dictate to the weak! In running the mind along the numerous lists of sincere and devout Christians, I cannot help lamenting that Newton had not lived to this day to have had his shallowness filled up with this new flood of light![24]

Paine's claim that religion was but myth and superstition could not be understood by those who numbered among their intellectual forebears the great Puritan, the poet who sang of a glorious *Paradise Lost:*

Did Milton understand those mythologies? Was he less versed than Mr. Paine in the superstitions of the world? No: they were the subject of his immortal song; and though shut out from all recurrence to them, he poured them forth from the stores of a memory rich with all that man ever knew, and laid them in their order as the illustration of that real and exalted faith, the unquestionable source of that fervid genius, which cast a sort of shade upon all the other works of man.[25]

Moreover, argued the McGuffey readers, even the men of science have been confirmed Christians:

Newton was a Christian! Newton whose mind burst forth from the fetters cast by nature over finite conceptions; Newton whose science was truth, and the foundations of whose knowledge of it was philosophy. Not those visionary and arrogant assumptions which too often usurp its name, but philosophy resting upon the basis of mathematics, which, like figures, cannot lie. Newton who carried the line and rule to the utmost barriers of creation, and explored the principles by which, no doubt, all created matter is held together and exists.[26]

But this extraordinary man, in the mighty reach of his mind, overlooked, perhaps, the errors which a minuter investigation of the created things on this earth might have taught him, of the essence of his Creator. What shall then be said of the great Mr. Bayle, who looked into the organic structure of all matter, even to the brute inanimate substance which the foot treads on. Such a man may be supposed to have been equally qualified with Mr. Paine, to "look through nature to nature's God."[27]

The result of all this scientific investigation, maintained the McGuffey readers, "was the most confirmed and devout belief in all which the other holds in contempt as despicable and driveling superstition."[28] All the great and illustrious men of history have believed in what Paine called a superstition, a fable, a myth; and among these have been the great scientists, poets, and statesmen of all times.[29] Washington and Franklin were Christians. "What other two men whose lives belong to the eighteenth century of Christendom have left a deeper impression of themselves upon the age in which they have lived, and upon all after time?"[30] Hamilton and John Marshall were Christians.[31] Thus, concluded the McGuffey readers,

you find all that is great or wise, or splendid, or illustrious among created beings, all the minds gifted beyond ordinary nature, if not inspired by their Universal Author for the advancement and dignity of the world, though divided by distant ages, and by the clashing opinions which distinguished them from one another, yet joining, as it were, in one sublime chorus to celebrate the truths of Christianity, and laying upon its holy altars the never-fading offerings of their immortal wisdom.[32]

II

Among those who sang "in one sublime chorus to celebrate the truths of Christianity," and laid "upon its holy altars the never-fading offerings of their immortal wisdom," was Alexander Hamilton. To Hamilton the McGuffey readers devote a lesson explaining that he is to be absolved from the criminality of dueling because,

Hamilton yielded to the force of an imperious custom. And yielding sacrificed a life in which all had an interest—and he is lost—lost to his country—lost to his family—lost to us.[33]

Thus do we speak in reverence of the great father of the conservative tradition who, in contrast to Paine, did not believe in the mass of the people.

All communities divide themselves into the few and the many. The first are the rich and well born, the other the mass of the people. The voice of the people has been said to be the voice of God; and, however generally this maxim has been quoted and believed, it is not true to fact. The people are turbulent and changing; they seldom judge or determine right. Give, therefore, to the first class a distinct, permanent share in the government. They will check the unsteadiness of the second; and as they cannot receive any advantage by a change, they therefore will ever maintain good government. Can a democratic assembly, who annually revolve in the mass of the people, be supposed steadily to pursue the public good? Nothing but a permanent body can check the imprudence of democracy. Their turbulent and uncontrollable disposition requires checks.[34]

The overwhelming majority of the men assembled at Philadelphia to draft the Constitution were men who shared the paternalistic outlook of Alexander Hamilton. Not one of the members present represented the small farming or laboring classes of the colonies.[35] The agrarian legislature of Rhode Island refused to attend.[36] Patrick Henry, leader of the populist movement in Virginia and delegate from that state, "smellt a rat" and refused to attend the meeting.[37] Most of the delegates were, like Hamilton, lawyers by profession, and many of them came from the large commercial centers of the Atlantic coast. Forty of the fifty-five members were holders of public securities.[38] Fourteen of the members held lands for speculation, and twenty-four had property in the form of money loaned at interest. Eleven of the attending delegates held interests in mercantile, manufacturing, and shipping lines.[39] Fifteen of the delegates owned slaves.[40] Thus, Professor Beard has contended that

The overwhelming majority of members, at least five-sixths, were immediately, directly, and personally interested in the outcome of their labors at Philadelphia, and were to a greater or less extent economic beneficiaries from the adoption of the Constitution.[41]

Another student of Federalist politics shares this view of the Philadelphia convention:

Too much emphasis cannot be put upon the fact that the mercantile and financial interests were the weightiest of all the influences for the Constitution; the debtor and agricultural interests the strongest groups against it. It deserves repetition, for a proper understanding of the craft and force practiced by both sides in the battle over ratification, that those who owed debts were generally against the Constitution and practically all to whom debts were due were for the new Government.[42]

"Society," declared the McGuffey readers,

is composed of two classes, debtors and creditors. The creditor class has been erroneously supposed the more enviable. . . . The debtor class has the sympathy of mankind. . . . In any case the debtor is safe. He has put his enjoyments behind him; they are safe; no turns of fortune can disturb them.[43]

But the good gentlemen at Philadelphia had no opportunity to read the McGuffey readers, and believed quite the opposite. The chaotic economic conditions following the Revolution convinced them that they needed a strong government to set the house in order.[44] Merchants who had supported the Revolution found the doors of trade with England and the West Indies closed to them. The existence of different currencies hampered interstate trade, and the Revolutionary notes became almost worthless as inflation set in. Large security issues floated by the Revolutionary government depreciated rapidly in value. Depreciating currency was wiping out debts owed to the creditor class. Surely, unless this economic house were set in order those who had invested in government securities and who had speculated in lands and currency would lose their possessions.[45]

Under the pressure of these circumstances, the men assembled at Philadelphia were in no mood for talk of democracy:

Since the victory at Yorktown a serious alteration had taken place in the views of many who had fought hardest for Independence and popular government. These men were as strong as ever for the building of a separate and distinct National entity; but they no longer believed in the wisdom or virtue of democracy without extensive restrictions. They had come to think that, at the very best, the crude ore of popular judgment could be made to enrich sound counsels only when passed through many screens that would rid it of the crudities of passion, whimsicality, interest, ignorance, and dishonesty which, they believed, inhered in it. Such men esteemed less and less a people's government and valued more and more a good government. And the idea grew that this meant a government the principal purpose of which was to enforce order, facilitate business, and safeguard property.[46]

The people, argued Roger Sherman, "want information and are constantly liable to be misled."[47] In a similar manner John Dickinson warned against the "dangerous influence of those multitudes without property and without principle, with which our country like all others, will in time abound."[48] Moreover, suggested Gerry, "The evils we experience flow from an excess of democracy."[49] The time will come, warned Gouverneur Morris, "when this Country will abound with mechanics and manufacturers who will receive their bread from their employers. Will such men be the secure and faithful Guardians of liberty?"[50] Well might McGuffey readers insist, almost one hundred years later, that "A thorough conviction of the difference of men is the great thing to be assured of in social knowledge."[51]

If one looks for the origin of the ideas which the delegates assembled at Philadelphia threw about with such abandon in the great debate over the Constitution, one will find them in the middle-class apologists, in Harrington, Locke, Blackstone, to which Professor Parrington adds Machiavelli, Vattel, Pufendorf, Montesquieu, Milton, Sidney, Halifax, and Hume.[52]

Unhappily for the democrats every one of these great names counted against their aspirations. Hobbes was a state absolutist whose *Leviathan* provided sharp weapons for those who wished to tone the government high; Hume was a Tory who accepted the traditional interpretation of human nature in the light of which democracy was the open door to anarchy; Blackstone was a Tory lawyer, who interpreted the British constitution by a narrow legalism that was obsolete before the *Commentaries* came from the press. Harrington, Milton, and perhaps Sidney, were republicans of strong aristocratic bias, and Halifax and Locke—the latter by much the most influential of all—were constitutional monarchists. Every one of these great authorities either distrusted or violently condemned democracy, yet they provided the major body of theory made use of by the Federalists.[53]

To Blackstone the McGuffey readers give the difficult task of explaining the origins of property. On the whole, Blackstone and the McGuffey readers have done an admirable job in explaining the origins of private property, both to its owners and to the dispossessed. They explain how

in order to secure property, recourse was had to civil society, which brought along with it a long train of inseparable concomitant states, governments, laws, punishments; and the public exercise of religious duties.[54]

Moreover, to the origins of property may be traced the development of a ruling and leisure class, for

it was found that part only of society was sufficient to provide, by their manual labor, for the necessary subsistence of all; and leisure was given to others to cultivate the human mind, to invent useful arts, and to lay the foundation of science.[55]

It is clear, then, that all that is good, beautiful, or noble in man may be traced to the institution of private property; for had not "a separate property in lands as well as movables, been vested in *some* individuals the world must have continued a forest, and men have been mere animals of prey."[56] But property has relieved men of the necessity of preying upon one another, and the accumulation of private property has meant the "ennobling of the human species, by giving it opportunities of improving its *rational*, as well as of exerting its natural faculties."[57] Thus has Divine Providence woven our duty and our happiness together in carrying out His inexorable will to accumulate and to acquire.[58]

Nevertheless, it all began in a kind of primitive communism:

In the beginning of the world, we are informed by holy writ, the all-bountiful Creator gave to man "dominion over all the earth; and over the fishes of the sea, and over the fowl of the air, and over every living thing that moved upon the earth." This is the only true and solid foundation of man's dominion over external things whatever any metaphysical notions may have been started by fanciful writers on this subject. The earth, therefore, and all things therein, are the general property of mankind, exclusive of other beings, from the immediate gift of the Creator. And while the earth continued bare of inhabitants, it is reasonable to suppose that all was in common among them, and that everyone took from the public stock, to his own use, such things as his immediate necessities required.[59]

We are warned not to imagine, however, "that this communism of goods seems ever to have been applicable, even in the earliest stages, to aught but the substance of the thing; nor could it extend to the use of it."[60] This is somewhat contradictory to what has previously been said, and Blackstone found himself in a trap of his own logic. He has said that in the original state of nature "everyone took from the public stock, to his own use, such things as his immediate necessities required," and this, as he himself admitted, was the order of Divine Providence. But now he finds difficulty in rescuing property from this primitive communism. Thus he argues that, "by the law of nature and reason, he who first began to use it, acquired therein a kind of transient property, that lasted so long as he was using it, and no longer."[61] In the end he is forced to admit that

when mankind increased in number, craft, and ambition, it became necessary to entertain conceptions of a more permanent dominion; and to appropriate to individuals, not the immediate use, only, but the very substance of the thing to be used. Otherwise, innumerable tumults must have arisen, and the good order of the world been continually broken and disturbed, while a variety of persons were striving who should get the first occupation of the same thing, or disputing which of them had actually gained it.[62]

Having thus wallowed in his own logic, Blackstone, and thereby the McGuffey readers, was finally forced into the position of covering his lack of exact knowledge by asserting that, "Necessity begat property." Nevertheless, it is clear that the necessity of securing land long enough to profit from its cultivation was part of a divine scheme, and that somehow, though the Sovereign in heaven had originally created a sort of primitive communism in property, He soon found it necessary, in order to insure personal property, to ordain and create, through men, "civil society, which brought along with it a long train of inseparable concomitants, state governments, laws, punishments; and the public exercise of religious duties." The effect of this new ordinance was to create a ruling class.[63]

How practical politics might exploit these ordinances from heaven in an age of Jacksonian radicalism and democracy is the subject of another chapter devoted to the alliance between religion and the conservative tradition. But it is worth noting here that the ordinances Blackstone discovered in searching for the origins of private property are additional pieces in a pattern which condemns Paine for his atheism, praises Marshall and Hamilton for their wisdom and piety, and finds in the institution of property a heavenly ordinance for the creation of a leisure class.

III

Blackstone's arguments were employed to good effect by Hamilton in the great debate over the Constitution. In contrast to the arguments of Hamilton, however, Richard Henry Lee's *Letters from a Federal Farmer* cautioned about too much haste in accepting the Constitution. While admitting that economic conditions demanded some correction and stability, he charged the instrument is in "want of that one important factor in a free government, a representation of the people." The change proposed to be adopted with the Constitution, Lee charged, "is a transfer of power from the many to the few."[64]

To earlier charges from a farmer questioning the advisability of home rule, Hamilton had given the characteristic response by quoting Blackstone:

The true reason of requiring any qualification, with regard to property in voters, is to exclude such persons as are *in so mean a situation*, that they are esteemed to have *no will* of their own. If these persons had votes, they would be tempted to dispose of them, under some undue influence or other. This would give a great, an artful, or a wealthy man, a larger share in elections than is consistent with general liberty. If it were probable that every man would give his vote freely, and without influence of any kind; then, upon the true theory and genuine principles of liberty every member of the community, however poor, should have a vote in electing those delegates, to whose charge is committed the disposal of his property, his liberty, and his life. But since that can hardly be expected, in persons of indigent fortunes, or such as are under the immediate dominion of others; all popular States have been obliged to establish certain qualifications, whereby some, in order to set other individuals, whose wills may be supposed independent, more thoroughly upon a level with each other.[65]

These are familiar arguments to anyone who has studied the debates of the Philadelphia convention. The poor, the propertyless, should not be allowed to vote because, if they did, their votes would inevitably fall into the hands of the wealthy and propertied; therefore, restrict the vote to the wealthy, the propertied, in order to protect the poor from falling in with the rich. This was Blackstone's contribution to the Hamiltonian logic, and it is the unbreakable political link of the McGuffey readers with a Hamiltonian past. In the face of this kind of reasoning, it was no wonder that Jefferson should declare:

Blackstone and Hume have made tories of all England, and are making tories of those young Americans whose native feelings of independence do not place them above the wily sophistries of a Hume or a Blackstone. These two books, and especially . . . [Blackstone], have done more towards the suppression of the liberties of man, than all the million of men in arms of Bonaparte, and the millions of human lives with the sacrifice of which he will stand loaded before the judgment seat of his Maker.[66]

To the McGuffey readers Napoleon was "the man without a model, and without a shadow";[67] while Blackstone, whom Jefferson charged with doing "more towards the suppression of the liberties of man, than all the million of men in arms of Bonaparte," was highly regarded. The fact is that Hamilton and Blackstone were thinking in terms of established institutions; they were opposed to the newer concepts of Jefferson and Paine, who, more responsive to the French revolution, ran quickly to the slogan—liberty, equality, fraternity. But of these new concepts the McGuffey readers will have none. We are told in one of the lessons that, "Men have been warned against old prejudices; I would rather warn them against new concepts. The novelty of an opinion on any moral question is a presumption against it."[68] The political pattern had been set by the Hamiltonian-Federalist-Whig tradition, and the McGuffey readers could see no reason to change it.

Hamilton's great work in putting the young republic on a sound financial and commercial basis won for him the plaudits of the McGuffey readers, which frankly admit that the Constitution had its origin in the necessities of disordered finance, prostrate commerce, and ruined credit. Under its benign influences, these great interests immediately awoke as from the dead, and sprang forth with newness of life."[69]

Under Hamilton's leadership, Federalism triumphed, and the commercial, financial, and creditor classes "awoke as from the dead, and sprang forth with newness of life." These are no doubt splendid achievements in the building of the young capitalist nation, but if we question the McGuffey readers about the sentiments of the Declaration of Independence, we are told that, "The Declaration is necessary to strengthen our position abroad, to raise mere civil war to national war, and to encourage our forces in their endeavor."[70]

It was not surprising, then, that Amos Singletary, agrarian spokesman, should question the sincerity of the men assembled at Philadelphia in their search for new formulae of government.

These lawyers, and men of learning, and moneyed men, that talk so finely, and gloss over matters so smoothly, to make us, poor illiterate people, swallow down the pill, expect to get into congress themselves; they expect to be the managers of this Constitution, and get all the power and all the money into their own hands, and then they will swallow up all us little folks, like the great leviathan.[71]

Now Hamilton was a lawyer, a man of learning, and a moneyed man; he *did* expect to get into public office and "be the manager of this Constitution"; and though he did not "get all the power and all the money" into his own hands, he did think in terms of the leviathan state. A brilliant statesman, a student of Harrington, Blackstone, Hume, and Locke, a dreamer of commercial empires, a strict accountant, and a sound financier, Hamilton literally put the economic house of the new government in order. His dearest project, the Bank, was designed to unite men of wealth and property indissolubly to the government; for Hamilton had discovered in Hume his political psychology, as he had discovered in Blackstone his political philosophy:

Political writers, says a celebrated author, have established it as a maxim, that, in contriving any system of government, and fixing the several checks and controls of the constitution, *every man* ought to be supposed a knave; and to have no other end, in all his actions, but *private interest.* By this interest we must govern him; and, by means of it, *make him co-operate to public good,* notwithstanding his insatiable avarice and ambition. Without this, we shall in vain boast of the advantages of *any constitution.*[72]

"The men of property in America," Hamilton wrote, "are enlightened about their own interest, and would easily be brought to see the advantage of a good plan." The good plan was the United States Bank, presumably inspired by the Bank of England; but it could also be of service in refunding the public debt and in restoring public credit. Hamilton looked forward to the time when the principles of the industrial revolution would be applied more extensively to the United States, and his great *Report on Manufactures* reveals unusual keenness and sharpness of intellect. He saw the importance of the new methods of industrialism, realized how the new methods of manufacture would tap the resources of the nation, and contemplated without emotion the prospect of employing the weak, the helpless, and the young in the great factories of the nation:

> Besides this advantage of occasional employment to classes having different occupation, there is another, of a nature allied to it, and of a similar tendency. This is the employment of persons who would otherwise be idle, and in many cases, a burden to the community, either from bias of temper, habit, infirmity of body, or some other cause, indisposing or disqualifying them for the toils of the country. It is worthy of particular remark, that, in general, women and children are rendered more useful, and the latter more early useful, by manufacturing establishments, than they would otherwise be. Of the number of persons employed in the cotton manufactories of Great Britain, it is computed that four-sevenths, nearly, are women and children; of whom the greatest proportion are children, and many of them of a tender age.[73]

One of the poems in the McGuffey readers tells how:

> 'Mid the dust, and speed, and clamor
> Of the loom-shed and the mill,
> 'Midst the clink of wheel and hammer,
> Great results are growing still!
>
> Though too oft, by Fashion's creatures
> Work and workers may be blamed,
> Commerce need not hide its features,—
> Industry is not ashamed![74]

On the other hand, there is nothing particularly wrong with farm life:

> Since I have learned the ways of man,
> I often turn to these again,
> And feel life wore its highest charm
> When I was living on the farm.[75]
> Let vapid idlers loom in silk,
> Around their costly board;
> Give us the bowl of soup and milk
> By homespun beauty poured.[76]
> Then contented with my state,
> Let me envy not the great;
> Since true pleasure may be seen,
> On a cheerful village green.[77]

These are matters to which we shall return in a later chapter, but let us note here that the tendency to praise farm life is more noticeable in the earlier editions, and in this respect the readers may have been willing to agree with Jefferson: "The mobs of great cities add just so much to the support of pure government, as sores do to the strength of the human body." On the other hand, many of the lessons, as we shall note in a subsequent chapter would agree with the prospects of Hamilton's vision of manufactures. Stories of the elaborate pretensions of machinists and skilled laborers who make inventions that yield them as much as fifty thousand pounds have the dubious distinction of encouraging those laboring in factories in accordance with Hamilton's plan.[78] Jefferson's plans were entirely different, however, for he argued:

> While we have land to labor then, let us never wish to see our citizens occupied at a work-bench, or twirling a distaff . . . for the general operations of manufacture, let our work-shops remain in Europe. It is better to carry provisions and materials to work-men there, than bring them to the provisions and materials, and with them their manners and principles.[79]

Jefferson's simple prescription for government finds no place in the McGuffey readers:

> A wise and frugal government, which shall restrain men from injuring one another, which shall leave them otherwise free to regulate their own pursuits of industry and improvement, and shall not take from the mouth of labor the bread it has earned. This is the sum of good government, and this is necessary to close the circle of our felicities.[80]

Rather, the McGuffey readers were likely to declare, like the widow of Pine Cottage, "God, who sent manna from Heaven, can provide for us as he did for Israel."[81] Contentment, whatever betides, is the price for ascribing the arrangements of society to Divine Providence, as did Blackstone; or for having too niggardly a conception of the resources of the popular intelligence, as did Hamilton. Both were the high tories of the conservative tradition; both desired restriction of the suffrage; both distrusted the people; both believed government instituted for the protection of property; and both sought schemes of protection for a propertied minority from the propertyless majority. In the end, as we shall see in another chapter, the conservatives were forced to seek refuge in the courts and in the churches, and the McGuffey readers were forced to plead for the preservation of "the well-proportioned columns of constitutional liberty . . . the skillful architecture which unites national sovereignty with state-rights, individual security, and public prosperity."[82] Webster was forced to point out the blessings that have been derived from the Constitution.[83] For the days of Jackson, of democracy, of universal suffrage, had finally come upon the old high tories of the conservative tradition, and the McGuffey readers found it necessary to warn: "Let the American dread, as

the archenemy of republican institutions, the shock of exasperated parties, and the implacable revenge of *demagogues*."[84] To the alert democrat these arguments had a familiar ring, a ring heard in the halls of the
Constitutional Convention at Philadelphia, a ring echoed by Hamilton;
it was, in fact, the resuscitation of the old conservative arguments, and it
was wholly within the conservative tradition.[85]

The McGuffey readers might argue that this government had been
founded by revolutionary fathers whose great principle was "the love of
liberty, protected by law," but Jefferson had warned of the "very dangerous doctrine to consider the judges as the ultimate arbiters of all constitutional questions."[86] He was, of course, thinking of that magnificent
Federalist giant, John Marshall:

The great object of my fear is the Federal Judiciary. That body, like gravity,
ever acting, with noiseless foot, and unalarming advance, gaining ground step by
step, and holding what it gains, is engulfing insidiously the special governments
into the jaws of that which feeds them. . . .[87] It is one which would place us under the despotism of an oligarchy. . . . The Constitution has erected no such
single tribunal, knowing that to whatever hands confided, with the corruptions
of time and party, its members would become despots.[88]

It was John Marshall whose,

strategic judicial decisions served as a causeway over which passed the eighteenth-
century doctrine of the sovereignty of the law, to unite with the new philosophy
of capitalistic exploitation.[89]

It was John Marshall in whom the McGuffey readers rejoiced, noting
with satisfaction that he was a good Christian whose wisdom and piety
had brought the nation many of the benefits Webster was so fond of
enumerating.[90] It was John Marshall to whom Federalism, conservatism,
and property turned when the turbulent and changing mobs of Jefferson's
day thrust the great democrat into the presidency:

But to this mandate of the supposedly sovereign people Marshall declined to
yield. Defeated at the polls, no longer in control of the executive and legislative
branches of the government, Federalism found itself reintrenched in the prejudices of John Marshall.[91]

The two fixed conceptions which dominated Marshall throughout his long career on the bench were the sovereignty of the federal state and the sanctity of
private property; and these found their justification in the virulence of his
hatred of democracy. No man in America was less democratic in his political convictions. Underneath the free and easy exterior of the Chief Justice was as stal-
wart a reactionary as ever sat on the Supreme Court bench.[92]

The great legal and clerical synthesis worked out in the days of Jackson, and properly the subject of another chapter, was another step in the

working out of the conservative strategy; and that synthesis identified the law of the courts and the interpretations of Marshall, Kent, and Story with the moral order imposed by the omnipotent will of a sovereign God. In this great conservative and religious synthesis the McGuffey readers played an important, though probably an unconscious, part; and as a result, further identified themselves with the Hamiltonian-Federalist-Whig tradition.

IV

The educational problems set by such basic political concepts as those we have been discussing was whether the spirit and structure of the republic could stand the impact of universal suffrage. To the Beechers, upon whom the compilers of the McGuffey readers drew heavily for educational orientations, the problem of education was to safeguard established institutions from the inroads of Jacksonian hordes. The educational pleas of the McGuffey readers are, therefore, to be taken in their relation to the political concepts already developed. The theory grew that upon school and church had devolved the duty of educating the people in religious and moral culture, for the development of a strong moral character was the only safeguard of republican institutions. The people, declared Catherine Beecher, have become our masters; and consequently,

the education of the common people, then, who are to be our legislators, jurymen, and judges, and to whom all our dearest interests are to be entrusted, this is the point around which the wisest heads, the warmest hearts, the most powerful energies should gather, for conservation, for planning, for unity of action, and for perservering enterprise.[93]

The McGuffey readers looked upon the extension of the right to vote to the common people as a great experiment which entailed numerous threats to republican institutions.[94] There was, then, an intimate relationship between politics and education. The effect of religious and moral culture should be to make the virtuous man, the citizen, the Christian; for moral culture was the base of society, and once freed from that foundation, society would become as animals.[95] Emerson caught the spirit of the same intimate relationship between politics and education, saying:

Let us make our education brave and preventive. Politics is an after-work, a poor patching. We are always a little late. The evil is done, the law is passed, and we begin the uphill agitation for repeal of that which we ought to have prevented the enacting. We shall one day learn to supersede politics by education.

What we call our root-and-branch reforms, of slavery, war, gambling, intemperance, is only medicating the symptoms. We must begin higher up, namely, in Education.[96]

Despite its link with the conservative tradition, no series of textbooks more genuinely accepted and tried to carry out Emerson's educational principle. The intimate relationship between politics and education was grasped in the lessons and stories of the McGuffey readers, and they tried to work at the roots of reform, rather than at the symptoms. The whole project for a universal education was, like that of universal suffrage, a perilous experiment.[97] This view was clearly expressed by the McGuffey readers as a reflection of the troubled career of the church and school in the West:

The great experiment is now making, and from its extent and rapid filling up, is making in the West, *whether the perpetuity of our republican institutions can be reconciled with universal suffrage.* Without education of the head and heart of the nation, they cannot be. . . . And I perceive a spirit of impatience rising, and distrust in respect to the perpetuity of our republic; and I am sure that these fears are well founded, and am glad that they exist. It is the star of hope on our dark horizon.[98]

To those who believed that the Republic had been founded on Hamilton's fiscal schemes, there was indeed cause for alarm. Hamilton desired, as he himself said, to link "the interest of the State in an intimate connection with those of the rich individuals belonging to it."[99] The bank, the funding plan, and the national debt were the means he proposed. "A national debt, if it be not excessive," wrote Hamilton,

will be to us a national blessing. It will be a powerful cement to our Union. It will also create a necessity for keeping up taxation to a degree which, without being oppressive, will be a spur to industry. . . .[100]

But the young republic, founded on such principles of sound finance, seemed now in some imminent danger from an aspiring demagogue. "I am one of those who do not believe that a national debt is a national blessing," said Jackson, "but rather a curse to a republic; inasmuch as it is calculated to raise around the administration a moneyed aristocracy dangerous to the liberties of the country."[101]

The contrast could not have been more striking! It was no wonder that the McGuffey readers warned of the "archenemy of republican institutions, the shock of exasperated parties, and the implacable revenge of *demagogues.*"[102] It was necessary for the McGuffey readers to remind their auditors that "our ablest patriots are looking on the deep, vexed with storms, with great forebodings and failings of heart for fear of the things that are coming upon us. . . ."[103] The demagogues, the shock of exasperated parties, and the ambition of unscrupulous politicians encouraged a secret "distrust in respect to the perpetuity of our republic. . . ."[104] The great dangers arising from demagogues and parties made the McGuffey readers feel that:

No punishments of Heaven are so severe as those for mercies abused; and no instrumentality employed in their infliction is so dreadful as the wrath of man. No spasms are like the spasms of expiring liberty, and no wailing such as her convulsions extort. . . . May God hide from me the day when the dying agonies of my country shall begin. O, thou beloved land, bound together by the brotherhood and common interest and perils, live forever—one and undivided.[105]

In a similar manner the brotherhood of conservatives expired in one horrible groan, and Chancellor Kent, magnificent spokesman of neo-Federalist politics, explained:

There never was such misrule. Our Tory rich men are become startled and alarmed at our downhill course. My opinion is that the admission of universal suffrage and a licentious press are incompatible with government and security to property, and that the government and character of this country are going to ruin. This suffrage is too great an excitement for any political machine. It racks it to pieces, and morals go with it.[106]

"To the ambitious man," declared the McGuffey readers with one eye on the spoils system of Jackson, "an honorable office will appear as beautiful as the apple of paradise."[107] What was needed in the face of these popular infractions of republican rules was a new emphasis on moral courage. One of the lessons takes up that topic with a story of the rebellion of prisoners, who were quelled and led back to their cells by an officer possessing the highest moral courage. "A more impressive exhibition of moral courage, opposed to the wildest ferocity, under the most appalling circumstances, was never seen."[108] The question to be decided in view of the character of the new government under laws of universal suffrage was, "can the nation, or the vast balance of power of it be so imbued, with intelligence and virtue as to bring out, in laws and their administration, a perpetual self-preserving energy?"[109] Moreover, declared the McGuffey readers, "Fear is what we need, as the ship needs wind on a rocking sea, after a storm, to prevent foundering. But when our fear and our efforts shall correspond with our danger, the danger is past."[110] But the danger was hardly past as long as the question of *whether the perpetuity of our republican institutions can be reconciled with universal suffrage* remained in the minds of men.[111]

The first antidote is religion; the next, education:

For next to religion, education is the guardian protector of our liberties, the tutelar genius that is to preside over our destinies, and the spirit that is to scatter intellectual wealth from one end of our country to the other; cold, indeed, must that man be, whose whole soul is not kindled into fervent aspirations for its success.[112]

When education becomes the task of rearing those who will rule the state, when universal suffrage thrusts upon men the necessity of educating their masters, then education cannot be taken lightly, or glossed over, for it is a serious business upon which all else depends.[113] Education, therefore, cannot be conceived without some prior conception of the state; and the state is, after all, merely the men who discharge its functions. If the common people be rulers, then we must be certain that the rulers are righteous. What constitutes a state?

> men, high-minded men. . . .
>   men, who their duties know,
> But know their rights, and knowing dare maintain,
>   Prevent the long-aimed blow,
> And crush the tyrant while they rend the chain:
>   These constitute a state;
> And sovereign law, that state's collected will,
>   O'er thrones and globe's elate
> Sits empress, crowning good, repressing ill.[114]

If, then, the real problem of education is whether universal suffrage may be reconciled with the perpetuity of our republican institutions, it is clear that "the educator is to work by the most refined influence on that delicate, ethereal essence, the immortal soul."[115] Moreover, "it is thought by many, that anyone may become a teacher. The most moderate ability is thought to be competent to fill the most important profession in society."[116] But no longer can the nation afford to be parsimonious in these important matters, for, "There should be no pinching economy in education. Money should never be weighed against the soul of a child."[117] Finally, concluded the author of the lesson, "Much as I respect the clergy, I believe that they must yield in importance to the office of teacher."[118]

The office of the teacher is the noblest on earth. It requires higher ability than any other; for the highest ability is that which penetrates farthest into human nature; comprehends the mind in all its capacities; traces the law of thought and moral actions; understands how the child is roused into the most vigorous and harmonious action of its faculties; and knows how to blend and modify the influences which outward circumstances exert on the youthful mind.[119]

With the devout insistence of their great predecessor, Noah Webster, the McGuffey readers desired that children be made into republican machines:

There is something to be learned and something to be taught in the schools, besides the mere mechanical round of book lessons. There, the mind is to be developed, and the heart corrected; the dispositions modified, and the passions moderated; the habits formed, and the principles fixed; the feeling trained, and the bias given for the residue of existence.[120]

The educational problem had thus been set with the question of "whether the perpetuity of our republican institutions could be reconciled with universal suffrage"; and the educational solution offered in "the bias given for the residue of existence." The solution of this educational problem rested on the inculcation of moral and religious culture; for the perpetuity of republican institutions could only be secured as moral restraints were strengthened at the same time that political freedom was increased. But the remedy must soon be applied, for the demagogues were leading the people on a more and more radical course.

God help the nation where self-government, in its literal sense, exists. . . . When a people that has been properly educated by experience calmly selects the agents, and cooly sets to work to adopt a set of principles to form its fundamental law or constitution, the machine is on the right track, and will work well enough so long as it is kept there; but this running off and altering the fundamental principles every time a political faction has need of recruits, is introducing tyranny in its worst form—a tyranny that is just as dangerous to real liberty as hypocrisy is to religion.[121]

The warning of the McGuffey readers is worth repeating in this connection: "Let the American dread, as the archenemy of republican institutions, the shock of exasperated parties, and the implacable revenge of *demagogues.*"[122] The dangers inherent in excessive democracy, dangers which Hamilton and the Federalists had established as a principle of political science, were echoed by Fisher Ames, who saw in the demagogues of excessive liberty a real threat to the perpetuity of our republican institutions.

For let it be remarked, that a feeble government produces more factions than an oppressive one; the want of power first makes individuals legislators, and then rebels. Where parents want authority, children are wanting in duty. It is not possible to advance further in the same path; the one will conduct us first to anarchy, and next to foreign or domestic tyranny; the other, by the wise and vigorous exertion of lawful authority, will lead to permanent power, and general prosperity. I am no advocate for despotism; but I believe the probability to be much less of its being introduced by the corruption of our rulers, than by the delusion of the people.[123]

As the McGuffey readers looked upon the tyranny of the struggle which had raged about them, they were led, like Fisher Ames, to believe that some defect in our moral culture had brought the calamities of the Jacksonian age upon us. For the tyranny of the demagogue, let it be remembered that "wisdom and laws that prevent tyranny and oppression" are the only recourse of the people of sound principle.[124] Thus, education must give a bias for "the residue of existence," for education "is not the end, but only the means."[125] Moreover, "Youth is not aware, that not for present use is all this designed."[126] The example of Napoleon should be a horrible reminder to all those who believe that institutions founded, like our own Constitution and government, by gentlemen who were rich and well-born can remain safe from the tyranny of an uninformed majority.[127]

Thus the McGuffey readers could agree with Fisher Ames in hoping that some means be found to preserve our government from the licentiousness and demagoguery of factions and majorities, as the political wisdom of the founding fathers, "in framing our constitution, was to guard against licentiousness, that inbred malady of democracies, that deforms their infancy with grey hairs and decrepitude."[128] The elaborate systems of checks and balances, courts, legislatures, and committees was designed to protect our republican institutions from the "implacable revenge of demagogues"; for,

the essence, and almost the quintessence, of good government is to protect property and its rights. When these are protected, there is scarcely any booty left for oppression to seize; the objects and the motives to usurpation and tyranny are removed. By securing property, life and liberty can scarcely fail of being secured: where property is safe by rules and principles, there is liberty.[129]

As the rules and principles of good government safeguarded property, they provided a haven for every man who could rise to high estate. "Knowledge is power," declared the McGuffey readers. "It is the philosopher's stone, the true alchemy, that turns everything it touches into gold."[130] Those who have not risen in society may be pitied, but the fault is their own.

Their hours of leisure are either idled away, or talked away, or spent in some other way equally vain and useless; and they complain, that they have no time for cultivation of their minds and hearts.[131]

But in America there is no class comparable to the European gypsy, for America is a paradise of acquisition, "where property is safe by rules and principles":

Gypsies are a class of people who have no settled place to live in, but wander about from spot to spot, and sleep at night in tents or barns. We have no gypsies in our country for here every person can find employment of some kind, and there is no excuse for idlers or vagrants.[132]

The road to wealth, to honor, to usefulness, and happiness, is open to all, and all who will, may enter upon it with the almost certain prospect of success. In this free community, there are no privileged orders. Every man finds his level.

If he has talents, he will be known and estimated, and rise in the respect and confidence of society.[133]

It is this conception of society and property that makes idleness a crime and education a necessity. "Success in every art, whatever may be the natural talent, is always the reward of industry and pains." If I love to read, says a child in one of the lessons, "I will be wise and good."[134] Moreover, it may be explained that if a man cannot read he is heir to much trouble. One of the lessons explains how a man approached a cross-road at nightfall. He didn't know which road to take, and since no one was at hand, he could not make any inquiries. The signposts were incomprehensible to him, for he had not purchased the McGuffey readers, and thus lost his way on a most important mission. Reading is a prelude to morality, declares the author of the lesson:

I hope my young readers will not forget this story. I know you must study hard, if you wish to learn to read; but the boys and girls who cannot read must go through the world like the man on his journey. They will never know whether they are on the right road or the wrong one."[135]

Averting the wrong road in life, besides being dependent upon the ability to read, is the sacred charge of religious and moral instructors. In the discharge of their heavy responsibilities they must be skillful, for upon them rests the moral character of the American citizen:

How unworthy of one who performs the function of a religious instructor, upon whom depends, in a great measure, the . . . final character of many fellow beings, to imagine that he can worthily discharge this great concern by occasionally talking for an hour, he knows not how, and in a manner he has taken no pains to render correct. . . . Alas! they come ruined and worthless from such a man as this. They lose that holy energy, by which they are to convert the soul, and purify man for heaven. . . .[136]

The emphasis on moral and religious culture in the educational philosophy of the McGuffey readers we shall examine more closely in another chapter; but let us note here both the positive and negative aspects of that philosophy. One lesson makes the distinction very succinctly. The object of education is to enable the citizen "to act rightly, honorably, successfully." On the other hand, "If education has been rightly conducted, it will teach the man to suffer with dignity, with honor, nay with profit."[137] The emphasis on suffering with dignity, honor, and profit is worthy of closer examination. One of the lessons explains how a rich Mr. Lennox spoke to a boy working in the field and found that he worked from six in the morning till late in the evening, sometimes with nothing to eat except a raw turnip pulled from the ground. The boy knew nothing of toys, but his ambition was to get to school. When asked how he could work despite the hunger that must creep over him, the boy replies that he never thinks of food. When asked what he most desires, the boy replies that the other boys at school "have an Eclectic Spelling book and Reader, and a Testament." You shall have them, promised rich Mr. Lennox. "Tell your father so, and that it is because you are an obliging, contented boy."[138]

"O, what a sad, sad sight is this!" exclaims another lesson.

A boy with a dunce-cap on his head! Why does he stand there, in front of the school? What has he done? He is a bad boy. He talks and laughs in school. He loves to be idle, and does not learn his lesson.[139]

Another lesson finds that, "Little Cora is at the head of her class. See, she is standing up, reading to her teacher. Shall I tell you why she is at the head? She always knows her lesson, and never comes late to school. [140] Moreover, "They are all good girls. Will you not try to be good like them? If you are good, all who know you will love you. God loves good girls."[141] It is clear that Robert Raikes, advocate of the Sunday School, would be proud of Little Cora and the contented boy who worked from dawn to dusk without eating. As the McGuffey readers explain, "Mankind may admire and extol LaFayette more than the founder of the Sunday School; but religion, philanthropy, and enlightened common sense, must ever esteem Robert Raikes the superior of LaFayette."[142]

But there were those who, in the nature of things, could not see the safeguards of universal public education unless it be looked upon as one of the checks in the system of checks and balances of a sovereign God:

I sometimes feel a little blue over the outlook here, with our penny-paper universal education and our workingmen's parties, with their tremendous lever of suffrage, decrying brains. . . . But the more I learn, the more am I impressed with the wonderful system of checks and balances which history reveals (our Constitution is a baby-house to it!) and the more my confidence in the general commonsense and honest intention of mankind increases. . . . I take great comfort in God. I think He is considerably amused with us sometimes, but that He likes us, on the whole, and would not let us get at the match-box so carelessly, as He does, unless He knew that the frame of His Universe was fire-proof. How many times have I not seen the fire-engines of Church and State clanging and lumbering along to put out—a false alarm![143]

The cause of education was to be one of the fire-engines of Church and State, for it is known that, "Public will gives law and enforces obedience: public sentiment, then is the unlimited sovereign of the state." Nevertheless, there must be a genuine effort to fight the social distinctions that flow from inequalities of wealth:

Distinction will soon enough find its way into society from considerations of

wealth and influence: it should be the duty of our legislature to provide an antidote against all its evil consequences.[144]

From this objective flows the principle "that society is bound to provide
for its members education as well as protection, so that none may be ignorant except from choice." In the end, this is the principle which must
prevail, for it is "essential to a republican government."[145]

Despite all this crying up of republican principles, however, there is a
strong current Calvinism hidden under a pile of Edwardian rationalism;
and it is to this great source of religious and moral culture that the educational objects of the McGuffey readers always return. The great theological statesmen of an older generation of Puritans rests always in the background of republican protestations. And so the principle that society is
bound to provide education for its members was to the stern generations
of New England nothing that they had not come to accept after decades
of theological inbreeding. In the end, it is the stress on moral culture in
the McGuffey readers that leads through the pronouncements of the
Beechers to the great Calvinists of the Bay colony; and it is this great
metaphysical source that ultimately colors the educational objectives,
however much they may be cried up as republican principles.

Beecher's lesson on the Puritan fathers is hallowed with great names,
and there is a great shouting about the metaphysicians who lie in the dust.

The memory of our fathers, should be the watch-word of liberty throughout
the land; for, imperfect as they were, the world before had not seen their like,
nor will it soon, we fear, behold their like again.[146]

Even Jonathan Edwards, who liked to see children "stirred up mightily
to seek God," is in direct line of descent:

The ministers of the early colonial days of New England, though well-read,
scholarly men, were more statesmen than theologians. Their minds ran upon the
actual arrangements of society, which were in great measure left in their hands,
rather than on doctrinal and metaphysical subtleties. They took their confession
of faith just as the great body of Protestant reformers left it, and acted upon it
as a practical foundation, without much further discussion, until the time of
President Edwards. He was the first man who began the disintegrating process
of applying rationalistic methods to the accepted doctrines of religion, and he
rationalized far more boldly and widely than any publishers of his biography
have ever dared to let the world know. He sawed the great dam and let out the
whole waters of discussion over all New England, and that free discussion led to
all the shades of opinion of our modern days.[147]

For all their bigotry and religious provincialism, the McGuffey readers
argue, the great Puritan divines were God's own statesmen on earth.
"Would to God that the ancestors of all nations had been not only almost, but altogether such bigots as our fathers were."[148] After all, it is

argued, from the great epoch of dizzy metaphysical subtleties "there have gone forth a progress so steady, a growth so wonderful, a reality so important, a promise yet to be fulfilled so glorious. . . ."[149] Projects of change, of reform, come from conceited philosophers who imagine their knowledge transcends that of God; for:

> Projects are, in general, the offspring of restlessness, vanity, and idleness. I am too busy for projects, too contented for theories, and, I hope, have too much honesty and humility for a philosopher.[150]

The soul of the Puritan is not lost in needless projects of reform; for the soul is that which may bear up under any misfortune, drinking from the unbridled source of spiritual power. The heart of the educational scheme is this certain crusty hardness that bears up under misfortune, poverty, death, and disease; and the educational solution is forthcoming in a return to the spiritual hardihood of Puritan forebearers.[151]

> I learnt from it never to repine at my own misfortune, or to envy the happiness of another; since it is impossible for any man to form a right judgment of his neighbor's suffering; for which reason also, I am determined never to think too slightly of another's complaints, but to regard the sorrows of my fellow creatures with sentiments of humanity and compassion.[152]

That is the moral culture to which Dr. Beecher and the McGuffey readers wish to return when they set the problem of reconciling republican institutions with universal suffrage; for, as they tell us, "without education of the head and heart of the nation," they cannot be reconciled. The education of the common people,

> who are to be our legislators, jurymen, and judges, and to whom all our dearest interests are to be entrusted, this is the point around which the wisest heads, the warmest hearts, the most powerful energies should gather, for conservation, for planning, for unity of action, and for perservering enterprise.[153]

For, next to religion, education is the guardian protector of our liberties. . . .[154]

V

The honored position of women in the minds and hearts of most Americans did not thereby assure women of a comparable place in political and civil affairs. This is the paradox of the American conception of women throughout the nineteenth century. Everywhere women were respected and honored; everywhere they were accorded civilities of the most exalted type. But the continued resistance to the entrance of women into political affairs provoked its own reaction in the fair sex and led, eventually, to the declaration of sentiments and the entrance of women into a deliberate movement for the right to vote and to hold office.

In some ways the position of the McGuffey readers with respect to this phase of the struggle for political power is more precise than in the case of other phases that we have been considering. It is perfectly clear from the earlier editions, for example, that it has been "beautifully ordered by Providence" that woman, "who is the mere dependent and ornament of man in his happier hours, should be his stay and solace when smitten with sudden calamity."[155] However much we may decry these convictions, it is evident that they represented the prevailing opinion of American society.[156]

But the reform movements of the thirties and forties no doubt inspired American women to take a more active part in political affairs. This seems to have been the case of the eight women who were sent as delegates to the World's Antislavery Convention in London. When with much debate and much acrimony they were excluded from the convention, they agreed that the time had come to make the position of women hinge on other current reforms.[157] Among these delegates were Lucretia Mott and Elizabeth Cady Stanton, who from that time forward identified themselves with the movement for women's rights. Meantime, however, women like Margaret Fuller were demonstrating the potentialities of women should they be given broader freedom in the working out of their destinies.[158]

Perhaps the case of Margaret Fuller and women like her led one of the lessons to the point of declaring that women appear to best advantage in the domestic scenes of home.[159] The whirl of social activities is not for a woman, for she is most happy and most useful when carrying out her duties in the home.[160] The relative positions of men and women in these delightfully painted domestic scenes makes it clear that the McGuffey readers, perhaps in deference to the prevailing mood, acknowledge that men are the monarchs of the home, while women, however much one may respect them as wives and mothers, are of a subordinate station.[161]

Despite these directives from the McGuffey readers, women continued to make progress in their quest for civil rights. When the first editions of the McGuffey readers were published in 1836 and 1837, women had no legal control over their children or their property, and, of course, they could not vote or hold office.[162] By 1839, however, they had already won from Mississippi some ratification of the laws regarding property; and within a decade Texas, Indiana, Pennsylvania, New York, California, and Wisconsin had followed the precedent set by Mississippi. When, encouraged by these successes, a convention of women was held at Seneca Falls, New York, in 1848, the struggle for the right to vote was organized and a women's declaration of independence asserted that "all men and women are created equal."[163] Though these sentiments somewhat altered the immortal document, they were clearly within the spirit of the Declaration of Independence, and in that sense, presented a strong case for arousing public sentiment in the cause of women.

Despite all this, however, the McGuffey readers continued to describe how man is the monarch of the little kingdom of the home; but at the same time, they accorded the utmost honor to women, particularly when the lessons found them in the roles of wives or mothers. One of the early lessons, for example, tells how

a married man, falling into misfortune, is more apt to retrieve his situation in the world than a single one; partly, because he is more stimulated to exertion by the necessities of the helpless and beloved beings who depend upon him for subsistence; but chiefly, because his spirits are soothed and relieved by domestic endearments, and his self-respect kept alive by finding, that though all abroad is darkness and humiliation, yet there is still a little world of love at home, of which he is the *monarch*.[164]

Catherine Beecher did not hesitate, however, to identify herself with this point of view. "Heaven has appointed one sex the superior, and to the other the subordinate station," wrote Catherine, "and this without any reference to the character or conduct of either." For that reason, she argued, it is "as much for the dignity as it is for the interest of females, in all respects to conform to the duties of this relation."[165] Buttressing this argument were the descriptions given by the McGuffey readers of the stable home life in which the influence of an ever-loving woman, the nurse, the daughter, or the mother, is felt in all relations. "Her smiles call into exercise the first affections in our hearts."[166]

This continued emphasis on the proper home life may have been inspired by the increasing frequency of divorce and the increasing laxity of home discipline over children. Champions of marriage reform felt, like Elizabeth Cady Stanton, that the "whole question of woman's rights" seemed to turn on this pivotal relation between the sexes.[167] It was the irrepressible Mrs. Stanton who introduced a series of resolutions for more liberal divorce laws at the national woman's rights convention of 1860.[168] At the same time, the amazing variety of feminine dress displayed at these conventions could not escape the notice of masculine critics, and the bloomer rage caused some gentlemen to despair of ever returning to the good old days.[169] Even the craze for modish bonnets generously trimmed with "love-ribbon" came under the scrutiny of the critical compilers of the McGuffey readers, and one of their lessons declared that, "There is not so variable a thing in nature as a lady's head dress; within my own memory, I have known it rise and fall above thirty degrees."[170]

In spite of this determined resistance to any change in the relations of the sexes, the McGuffey readers continued to praise the elevated character of women. "The influence of the female character is now felt and acknowledged in all the relations of life."[171] Though the facts are not accurate, the sentiment of the lessons is good. But in all this the readers never let their auditors forget the respect and honor due a woman as a mother, for "in no relation does woman exercise so deep an influence, both immediately and prospectively, as in that of mother. To her is committed the immortal treasure of the infant mind."[172] Moreover,

She watches over us like a guardian angel, and protects us through all our helpless years, when we know not of her cares and her anxieties on our account. She follows us into the world of men, and lives in us, and blesses us, when she lives not otherwise upon the earth.[173]

Another lesson is somewhat insistent that a young bride who lost her first husband was nothing but a good wife to her second, for to him she never "gave her broken heart."[174]

She was an amiable and exemplary wife, and made an effort to be a happy one; but nothing could cure the silent and devouring melancholy that had entered into her very soul. She wasted away in a slow and helpless decline, and at length, sunk into the grave, the victim of a broken heart.[175]

But that experience must have been unusual, for another lesson explains that it has often been observed that women sustain the "most overwhelming reverses of fortune" with great fortitude.[176] Another lesson describes the experience of a famous judge who learned to speak in public and to overcome the most difficult obstacles through the tender influence of his mother.

To her I am indebted, for all my enjoyment of intellect. I have no doubt, that, had a severe and chilling discipline been pursued with me at home, as it was in school, I should always have been a dull and ignorant being, perhaps an idiot. To a good, faithful, intelligent mother, what gratitude and respect do not her children owe. I shall always vindicate the cause of women.[177]

Most of the lessons devoted to the theme of respecting and honoring women, particularly mothers, occur in the editions prior to the Civil War. At no point does there seem to be a direct opposition to the struggle of women for suffrage; but at the same time, the McGuffey readers make it abundantly clear that woman's place is in the home and that her position is subordinate to that of man, who is the monarch of the household. Perhaps the position of the McGuffey readers with respect to women and their rights could be summarized in the words of De Tocqueville, who declared that while Americans

have allowed the social inferiority of woman to subsist, they have done all they could to raise her morally and intellectually to the level of man; and in this respect they appear to me to have excellently understood the true principle of democratic improvement.[178]

VI

The political philosophy of the McGuffey readers rests ultimately on the foundations laid by Harrington, Locke, Blackstone, Hamilton, and Webster. This orientation made the political influence of the readers almost a foregone conclusion, though they speak only rarely of specific political events. But Blackstone and Webster are the most direct links with the Hamiltonian past, and it is their influence which throws the political philosophy of the McGuffey readers wholly within the conservative tradition. For the McGuffey readers accepted the work of the fathers at Philadelphia as the embodiment of all that was good and just in government, remarking that no body of legislators had produced such remarkable political instrumentalities for the direction of domestic affairs.

The acceptance of the work of the legislators assembled at Philadelphia was, however, more than the patriotic gesture of a series of textbooks paying tribute to its political orientations. In matters of political philosophy the McGuffey readers went far beyond what might be considered the conventional tribute to the principles upon which this republic was founded. In denouncing Paine for his atheism and radicalism, in ignoring Jefferson, in praising Marshall and Hamilton for their piety and wisdom, and in quoting at great length from Blackstone and Webster, the McGuffey readers made it clear that in contemplating the opposing political traditions generated by the heat of the Revolution they preferred a Hamiltonian and Federalist past to the radical and revolutionary outlook of a Jefferson or a Paine. There is, moreover, the frank recognition that the revolutionary principles embodied in the Declaration of Independence were meant merely as propaganda to encourage our forces and win support from abroad. In the end, it is the Constitution, not the Declaration of Independence, to which the McGuffey readers return for a definition of republican principles.

When the necessities of Jacksonian democracy called forth the denunciations of demagoguery, radicalism, and excessive democracy, the McGuffey readers warned of the shock of exasperated parties and of the revenge of implacable demagogues. Political morality seemed to crumble under the spoils system and the loud cries of job seekers, and the McGuffey readers warned of the corrupting influence of political jobs on public morals. Dr. Beecher spoke through the McGuffey readers, asking whether the perpetuity of our republican institutions could be reconciled with universal suffrage. He spoke of the dark days that had come upon the land, and of the dark shadow on the horizon. The political and moral principles upon which the republic had been founded seemed to be in great danger. The outlook of the older generations reared on Blackstone, Locke, Hamilton, and John Marshall was ignored by the tumultuous and changing mobs who entered politics with their recently won right to vote.

The antidote for these new forms of demagoguery and radicalism was religion and education, the fire engines of Church and State, to which conservatives turned in their darkest hours. The McGuffey readers hinted that there was more involved in education than merely learning to read, write, and take accounts. One of the great purposes of education was to give a bias to the residue of experience. But the plea for education must be linked particularly with a call to return to the stern moral code of the Puritan fathers, and the objects of education were considered largely in terms of religious and moral culture. Through pleading advocates like Dr. Beecher, the McGuffey readers voiced their fear for the corrupting influences of the new age that had come upon them, and hinted that in the metaphysical subtleties of the great New England theologians lay the appropriate foundations for state, school, church, and society.

This plea for a return to the past, for the security of long established institutions, and for a religious basis of society led to a further identification of the McGuffey readers with the Hamiltonian-Federalist-Whig tradition in politics. The description of Whig principles given by a leading Whig journal in 1847 is an accurate charting of the political position of the McGuffey readers:

The *principles* of the Whig party are well defined; they are *conservative* and inculcate a regard for the laws and support of all established institutions of the country. They eschew *radicalism* in every form; they sustain the constitution and the laws; they foster the spirit of patriotism. . . .[179]

But the spirit of patriotism could also lead to the attitude of the expansionist and militant nationalist who argued, like Henry Clay in the McGuffey readers, that:

An honorable peace is attainable only by an efficient war. My plan would be to call out the ample resources of the country, give them a judicious direction, prosecute the war with utmost vigor, strike wherever we can reach the enemy, at sea or on land, and negotiate the terms of peace at Quebec or at Halifax. We are told that England is a proud and lofty nation, which, disdaining to wait for danger, meets it half way. Haughty as she is, we triumphed over her once, and if we do not list to the counsels of timidity and despair, we shall again prevail. In such a cause with the aid of Providence, we must come out crowned with success; but if we fail, let us fail like men, lash ourselves to our gallant tars, and expire together in one common struggle.[180]

2

Patterns of Nationalism and Patriotism

THE BROAD POLITICAL PATTERN we have been considering would be incomplete without a treatment of the growing nationalism and patriotism in American thought. This phenomenon was reflected in the McGuffey readers and received its appropriate emphasis. But the growing nationalist sentiment of the decades prior to the Civil War seemed to be strengthened rather than weakened by sectional pride and sectional ideals. Though the early editions of the McGuffey readers clearly reflect the sectional pride we noted in an earlier chapter, and though the West found its cultural ideals expressed in the pages of the McGuffey readers, it is true also that the growing nationalism and patriotism of the thirties and forties was reflected. In the decades following the Civil War, however, the sectional emphasis is curiously absent. However that may be, it is within the province of our task to consider the sectional emphasis of the early editions, even if only in contrast to the purer nationalism of later works.

I

We have already given considerable attention to the West, and that emphasis would hardly have been justified were not the sectionalist tendencies plainly in evidence in the McGuffey readers. We saw how men like Lyman Beecher were concerned lest the West grow to maturity without the benefit of the clergy and the moral culture they could impart. "What will become of the West," demanded Beecher, "if her prosperity rushes up to such a majesty of power, while those great institutions linger which are necessary to form the mind, and the conscience, and the heart of that vast world?"[1] Such a vast world, Dr. Drake tells us in one of the lessons of the McGuffey readers, has been bounded by nature and connected by a series of rivers—the Mississippi, the Cumberland, the Missouri, the Illinois, and the Ohio.[2] This was the vast world to which Lyman Beecher would bring moral culture and to which Dr. Drake had staked out his claim, vested in rights derived from nature.[3]

The conception of the West one gets from the early lessons of the McGuffey readers, then, is that of a vast world set apart by nature for the prosperity and culture of the citizens who dared venture into her vast lands.[4] "Everything here is free, open, active," wrote Clark. "To be useful one must lay aside all narrow tastes and exclusive feelings, and from a pure love of humanity, plunge into the life around him."[5] But it was the violence of the plunging that ruffled the souls of the more cautious. Dr. Drake insisted in the McGuffey readers that, "Measures should be taken to mould a uniform system of manners and customs, out of the diversified elements which are scattered over the West."[6] It is of the greatest importance, wrote Samuel Mills, "That the standard of truth should be immediately planted here. . . ."[7]

It was patent that education and the church would be the chief means of implanting the truth, but the McGuffey readers added that, "we should foster western genius, encourage western writers, patronize western publishers, augment the numbers of western readers, and create a western heart."[8] Nor could the publishers of the McGuffey readers find fault with the demand to "patronize western publishers." Competition with Eastern bookmakers was violent, and the creation of an exclusively Western culture would no doubt make the burden of Western publishing somewhat easier. We are thus "connected by nature in the great valley," the McGuffey readers told the young, and "we must live in the bonds of companionship, or imbue our hands in each other's blood."[9] No people, declared a Western editor,

are so ready to make experiments respecting social relations and domestic arrangements, as those of the western country,—none who are so little fettered by established habits, or who are less disposed to consider hereditary prejudices and heirlooms which cannot be parted with.[10]

Perhaps it was this experimental characteristic of the Western citizen that worried old Lyman Beecher and made the McGuffey readers insist that the literature of Ohio be truly American.[11]

Our literature cannot fail to be patriotic, and its patriotism will be American; composed of a love of country, mingled with an admiration for our political institutions. . . . The literature of the whole Union must be richly endowed with this spirit; but a double portion will be the lot of the interior, because the foreign influences, which dilute and vitiate this virtue, cannot reach the heart of the continent where all that lives and moves is American.[12]

It is worth noting, then, that Western sectionalism, being particularly true in its patriotism and nationalism, can only strengthen the patriotic tendencies of the age. This unusual characteristic of Western culture is behind the demand in the McGuffey readers that the "geography of the interior, in truth, admonishes us to live in harmony, cherish uniform plans of education, and found similar institutions."[13] In building the Inland Empire, admonished the McGuffey readers, those "who have moral power, should exert it in concert. . . ."[14] Moreover, some steps should be taken "to mould a uniform system of manners and customs, out of the diversified elements which are scattered over the West."[15]

Sectionalism of quite another type may be exemplified, however, by a lesson on a Virginia gentleman, who sometime after the Civil War, was leading a plantation existence. This type of existence is not, by implication, conducive to deep meditations; nor can the Virginia gentleman distinguish between forms of government.[16]

His opinions respecting forms of government and forms of creeds are not the result of long study or deep meditations, but were inherited with his estate, which passed from father to son by the strictest laws of entail. Whether Catholicism or Protestantism embraced the purer creed or the more divine form of worship, whether nations were wiser, better governed, more prosperous, under hereditary monarchs, electoral princes, or presidents were matters on which it would have puzzled him to give an opinion.[17]

Sectional pride merges almost imperceptibly with nationalism, patriotism, and the worship of the Constitution. We have already seen that the McGuffey readers make it a point to note that their sectional pride and their sectional literature and ideals were more truly American than those of the East. By this means the passing of the sectional interest into a broader patriotism and nationalism is easily managed. The fear that the extreme sectionalism of some sections would draw the nation apart, break asunder the Union, and destroy the everlasting benefits of the Constitution grows stronger as the editions approach the irrepressible conflict. But even an early edition could become alarmed and pray to God for His help in the plea of the West to be united with the East in ties of common brotherhood.

May God hide me from the day when the dying agonies of my country shall begin! O, thou beloved land, bound together by the ties of brotherhood and common interests and perils, live forever,—one and undivided. . . . And let no man at the East quiet himself, and dream of liberty, whatever may become of the West. Our alliance of blood, and political institutions, and common interests, is such that we cannot stand aloof in the hour of her calmity, should it ever come.[18]

II

But this early sectionalism passes by quiet and easy stages into the broader patriotism and nationalism of the whole series. Typical of the patriotism of the McGuffey readers is the speech by Webster on the "Duties of American Citizens," which, by devious routes, found its way into the edition of 1844. "Fellow-citizens," Webster told the young auditors who read the McGuffey series,

let us not retire from this occasion, without a deep and solemn conviction of the duties which have devolved upon us. This lovely land, this glorious liberty, these benign institutions, the dear purchase of our fathers, are ours; ours to enjoy, ours to preserve, ours to transmit. . . . But what are lands, and seas, and skies to civilized man, without society, without knowledge, without morals, without religious culture; and how can these be enjoyed in all their extent and all their excellence, but under the protection of wise institutions, and a free government.[19]

These are cogent arguments, and they establish the theme which, together with the cult of hero worship, marks out the pattern the McGuffey readers follow. Cornelius Matthews noted that by some people

patriotism or love of country is regarded as an airy bubble, raised by cunning statesmen to dazzle and bewilder the multitude. . . . Our country, if we truly love it, evokes our feelings, our judgment, our imagination, and solicits these, by an unforeseen persuasion, to employ themselves in adorning and exalting the object of their regard.[20]

It was the latter view, rather than the former, to which the McGuffey readers held, and with "an unforeseen persuasion" converted the untutored impulses of the child into an exalted patriotism. Much of this was accomplished through the cult of Washington or the pattern of hero-worship, by which simple patriots were converted into exalted objects of patriotic sentiment. Such was the case with Washington, of whom the McGuffey readers said a great deal. It was maintained that:

A true lover of the virtue of patriotism delights to contemplate its purest models; and that love of country may well be suspected which affects to soar so high into the regions of sentiment as to be lost and absorbed in the abstract feeling.[21]

The point is that children find national heroes an appropriate stimulus for their patriotism, and for that reason, if for no other, the cult of Washington was an adequate means of building the patriotic sentiments.[22] A national hero would be more helpful in the West, in the interior, where "the foreign influences which dilute and vitiate this virtue, cannot reach. . . ."[23] It was, then, by the cult of heroes and the claim to a purer Americanism that the West hoped to be unique; while the East had to do the best it could despite its foreign influences. Reverend Gannètt expressed the same thought, declaring that

the arrival of a steamship every fortnight at our doors, freighted with the influences which the Old World is no less eager to send than we to receive, must increase the danger of our losing independence, as well as our neglecting to cultivate originality of character. . . . All that we can do is to form a national character with the help of these influences. . . .[24]

Many would no doubt have agreed that however humble one's circumstances,

the poor man should not feel poor when he thinks that his humble roof and circumstances are sheltered by a canopy of ideas and sentiments, such as never before arched over any palace in the world.[25]

This reverence for the ideas and sentiments on which the nation was founded was another aspect of the cult of heroes, for, we are told in one of the lessons:

When sublime virtues cease to be abstractions, when they become embodied in human character, and exemplified in human conduct, we should be false to our own nature, if we did not indulge in the spontaneous effusions of our gratitude and our patriotism.[26]

These remarks by Webster on the occasion of Washington's birthday were wholly within the pattern of patriotism established by the McGuffey readers. And though they lamented the tendency of some people to find fault with America's past,[27] they increasingly found the heroic basis for their devoted patriotism. The lesson of the "Hero of Haarlem," the familiar story of the little boy who put his finger in the dike and thereby saved his country from ruin, taught, among other things, a devotion to the nation's past.[28] That past was, as Patrick Henry pointed out in one of the lessons, a means of judging the glory of the future.[29] "For my part," said Patrick Henry, "whatever anguish of spirit it may cost, I am willing to know the whole truth; to know the worst, and to provide for it. . . . Give me liberty, or give me death!"[30]

This pattern of patriotism has no where been better summarized than in the words of Gideon Hawley:

In the character of the men, who stood foremost in the contest for independence, the measures of provocation, by which they were roused to resistance, the trials through which they passed, the reverses which they sustained, the triumphs which they achieved, and the great political principles which were vindicated by them, there are lessons of instruction not inferior in value, to any which can be drawn from the history of any age or people; and if the mind of every youth can be made familiar with them, and his feelings imbued with the moral they contain, no better security can be provided against the degeneration of that unconquerable spirit, in which the foundations of our freedom were laid.[31]

Such was apparently the design of the McGuffey readers. We find, for example, many lessons on the character of Washington, one of which declares:

It is the happy combination of rare talents and qualities, the harmonious union of the intellectual and moral powers, rather than the dazzling splendor of any one trait, which constitutes the grandeur of his character.[32]

Another lesson begins with Webster's address at Bunker Hill ceremonies, recognizes America's material exports to Europe, then branches off to the models of politics and morals that America and Americans have given to the world. "But America," argued the lesson, "exercises influences, or holds out examples for the consideration of the Old World, of a much higher type, because they are of a moral and political character."[33] Lest this great lesson be lost on his auditors, Webster gives an example of the type he has in mind: "America has furnished the world the character of Washington. And if our American institutions had done nothing else, that alone would have entitled them to the respect of mankind."[34]

Other lessons described American greatness as the "pillar of divine glory, descending from God,"[35] and characteristically noted of Washington that, "there was no unsound spot, nothing little or mean in his character."[36] Moreover, it was asked, "Washington was the first man of his type: when will there be another?"[37] Still another lesson, attributed to John Quincy Adams, discussed "Washington's Sword and Franklin's Staff," asking, at the same time, "What other two men whose lives belong to the eighteenth century of Christendom have left a deeper impression of themselves upon the age in which they lived, and upon all after time?"[38] Another lesson declared:

I will not sit unconcerned while my liberty is invaded, nor look in silence upon public robbery. I will exert my endeavors at whatever hazard, to repel the aggressor, and drag the thief to justice, whoever may protect him in his villainies, and whoever may partake of his plunder.[39]

As if this determination were not enough, another lesson emphasized how Washington combined the personal virtues of the Greek and English gentlemen. From this premise the lesson concludes that in the same manner America may combine and so supplant the English and Greek empires. London, the lesson argued, will join Athens as a sad relic of the past.[40] "Happy, proud America! The lightnings of heaven yielded to your philosophy! The temptations of earth could not seduce your patriotism."[41] When, in another lesson, Patrick Henry is asking for the admission of Tory fugitives from the Revolution, he argues, "What, sir, shall we, who have laid the proud British lion at our feet, now be afraid of his whelps?"[42] Moreover, argued Henry, "Instead of refusing permission to the refugees to return, it is your true policy to encourage emigration to this country, by every means in your power."[43]

But it is to the cult of Washington that one always must return. For the name of Washington, one of the lessons in the McGuffey readers informs us,

is intimately blended with whatever belongs most essentially to the prosperity, liberty, and the free institutions and the renown of our country. . . . And it will be so, in all time to come, so long as public virtue is itself an object of high regard. The ingenuous youth of America will hold up to themselves the right model of Washington's example, and study to be what they behold; they will contemplate his character, till all its virtues spread out and display themselves to their delighted vision.[44]

Mingled with these fair visions was the conviction expressed in one of the lessons that,

for stolidity of reasoning, force of sagacity and wisdom of conclusion, under such complication of difficult circumstances, no nation or body of men, can stand in preference to the general Congress at Philadelphia.[45]

Nor could the wicked cynics quite destroy the heritage of the Pilgrim fathers. After discussing the difficulties the Pilgrims faced, the author of the lesson inquires:

Is it possible that from a beginning so feeble, so frail, so worthy, not so much of admiration as of pity, there have gone forth a progress so steady, a growth so wonderful, a reality so important, a promise yet to be fulfilled so glorious?[46]

And having gone back as far as the Pilgrim fathers into the stream of history, the compilers of the McGuffey readers did not hesitate to go back as far in America's history as the time of Columbus, noting that Columbus was a man of God and a great inventive genius who blessed our shores.[47]

Professor Curti has admirably explained how:

History textbooks were a supplementary means of presenting the American past in patriotic and nationalistic terms. Weems' biographies of national heroes were augmented by those of other no less patriotic authors and compilers, among whom Samuel Goodrich and William McGuffey take high rank. Other writers of school books in this field spared no pains to create in the minds of the growing generation of Americans dislike of England and a conviction that the Revolution was a heaven-sent revolt against intolerable tyranny, that the American people had been essentially united, not divided, in the struggle for independence, and that in subsequent historical events the nation and its leaders had right on their side.[48]

That is clearly the case of the McGuffey readers, though with some exceptions as we shall subsequently note. "Some writers, it is true," Professor Curti continued, "did occasionally criticize the treatment of the Indians or suggest some grays in the all but universally bright picture of the American past."[49] It is with respect to criticism of the treatment accorded the Indian that the McGuffey readers deviate from the general description Dr. Curti has laid down, and in that respect, must be found superior to other readers that turned no critical gaze on the unfortunate treatment of the once-powerful Indian. Whether treatment of the Indian properly falls within the pattern of nationalism and patriotism may be open to doubt; but at least it seemed to the McGuffey readers as though humanitarian treatment of the Indian was a mark of a patriotic but condescending spirit.[50]

III

The inspiration of America's glorious past, while no doubt potent enough to arouse the patriotic sentiments, was buttressed with a considerable emphasis on America's mission in the future. The doctrine of the American mission may be traced, with more or less precision, from the earliest readers to the latest; but it is clearly in the decades following the Civil War that this pattern becomes purified and sharpened in the McGuffey readers. One may turn to the earlier editions, however, and find some trace of the doctrine of a glorious future.

One aspect of the doctrine of a mission was the advancement of liberty, so gloriously the heritage of America, among other nations and backward peoples. In establishing the pattern, however, recourse was often had to English authors who, like Addison, would declare:

Do thou, great Liberty, inspire our souls, And make our lives in thy possession happy, Or our deaths glorious in thy defence.[51]

Some of the lessons, indeed, draw on historical examples of the defense of liberty in other nations, ending with the note that such liberties were finally accomplished in America, although other peoples had made many ill-fated attempts to rise to the same moral heights.[52] There is, for example, the lesson of the celebrated battle between the Swiss and the Austrians at Lempach. The Swiss were held up at a mountain pass until a patriot hurled his body on Austrian spears and made a breach in the formidable Austrian defense. This heroic act resulted in the rout of the Austrian army. Thus the poem celebrates his deed:

> Make way for Liberty! he cried;
> Make way for Liberty, and died!
>
> Marshaled once more at freedom's call,
> They came to conquer or to fall.[53]

Even the downfall of Poland receives appropriate treatment in a lesson which explains how:

> *Hope, for a season, bade the world farewell,*
> *And freedom shrieked—As Kosciusko fell!*[54]
>
> *Where was thine arm, O Vengeance! Where thy rod,*
> *That smote the foes of Zion and of God.*[55]

The belief that, "Our prejudices will recede, as our proximity to each other shall increase,"[56] while not without foundation in fact, was almost wishful thinking in view of the approaching sectional conflict. Nevertheless, hope is buoyed up by the thought that, "New bonds will be thrown around the Union, which will grow stronger as we pursue our onward march."[57] This onward march was depicted in the McGuffey readers in the manner of Longfellow:

> *Thou, too, sail on. O ship of state.*
> *Sail on, O Union, strong and great.*
> *Humanity, with all its fears,*
> *With all the hopes of future years,*
> *Is hanging breathless on thy fate.*[58]

In all this the watchwords were the flag, the Constitution, and the church. With these three the great mission was to be accomplished.[59] Wherever our flag is planted, declared the McGuffey readers, "there may freedom have a foothold, humanity a brave champion, and religion an altar."[60] Moreover, let us remember that, "The consequences of American independence will soon reach to the extremities of the world."[61] Should our desire to extend the benefits of freedom to foreign lands be opposed by ship or sword, let us remember that God has ordained that the Union should, like the sun, "shed its glorious influence backward on the states of Europe, and forward on the empires of Asia."[62]

The conception one gets from the McGuffey readers, then, is that America has a glorious destiny, a mission, which has been ordained by divine Providence. The flag, the Constitution, the church,—these were the rocks on which the lusty patriots of the nineteenth century built their arguments. For those who opposed the arguments of the expansionist, "We feel no emotion but pity for those whose philanthropy, or patriotism, or religion, have led them to believe that they can prescribe a better course of duty than that of the God who made us all."[63] God was on the side of those who saw America's manifest destiny; and in seeing that destiny and the greatness of the Union whose beneficence the heavens had ordained should be spread to all the world, the McGuffey readers were apt to believe that it was all "part of the divine scheme for the moral government of the world."[64] And this same divine scheme, as Professor Curti points out, was not without its value to the business community.

The needs and values of business enterprise were intimately associated with patriotic and nationalistic ideas and sentiments. The Constitution was increasingly regarded as an incarnation of that law and order so essential to the countinghouse, the factory, and the mercantile establishment. Choate, Hillard, Webster, and other legal spokesmen for business regarded the Constitution as a sacred document on which the entire economic, political, and social fabric rested. It was the instrument that tied the states together into the national whole so essential to a national market and to the foreign and domestic policies through which business alone could expand. Protecting property rights as the Constitution clearly did, its provisions, once clarified by the Supreme Court, must be obeyed even if, as in the Dred Scott decision, humanitarian sentiments were outraged. Thus the Constitution became a symbol of an order secure against revolutionary change and congenial to all the values dear to business enterprise.[65]

The expansion of America's commerce overseas entailed, among other things, a strong Union capable of protecting and encouraging American fleets. The romantic era of American overseas commerce had begun, and many like George F. Train dreamed of an American commercial empire overseas.[66] Even an English observer could not avoid commenting on the beauty and romance of the tall-masted sailing vessels of the American fleet in contrast to "the round-sterned, lumpish billyboys and nondescripts of the eastern coast of our isle!"[67] The expression of gratitude to the sailors who manned these tautly-rigged sailing vessels of the fleet is reflected in many of the lessons of the McGuffey readers. One, for example, explains that, "Our young friends owe a debt of gratitude to those whose home is upon the great waters, and who bring them the luxuries of other countries."[68]

Despite this appreciative attitude, the McGuffey readers are willing to admit that a sailor's life is a hard one, although those who sail the seven seas are looked upon as brave and adventurous lads.[69] One lesson explains how we should be kind and generous to sailors because they face many dangers and undergo many hardships for the good of our country and our people.[70] Another expresses the seafarers' depreciation of the timid landsman,[71] and a third offers a bit of verse in tribute to a sailor-boy lost at sea:

> Oh! sailor boy! Sailor boy! never again
>   Shall home, love, or kindred, thy wishes
>   repay;
> Unblessed and unhonored, down deep in the main
>   Full many a score fathom, thy frame shall
>   decay.[72]

It would be difficult to determine whether these lessons had the effect of detering boys from entering upon so dangerous a mission, or whether, on the contrary, the very adventure and danger of the sea would attract many a youthful lad to roam the green waters. Perhaps, in Tennyson's description of freedom, many found the light they would follow, whether on sea or on land.[73] Or, perhaps, with the model of Napoleon or Washington constantly before him in the lessons and stories of the McGuffey readers, the lad would decide to be, like Napoleon, "the man without a model, and without a shadow."[74]

The cult of the hero seemed related both to America's past and America's future. Of the foreign "patriots," Napoleon commands an amount of attention inappropriate for his *democratic* achievements. The lesson on Napoleon runs from the earliest editions throughout the whole series; but the explanation of this popularity remains, for us, a closely guarded secret. Such a devotion to the cult of Napoleon and other national heroes deserves proportionate emphasis here, so let us note in detail what was said of the Little Corporal. It was claimed of Napoleon that:

He was a medley of contradictions, and at the same time such an individual consistency were never united in the same character. A royalist . . . a republican . . . an emperor . . . a subaltern and a sovereign . . . a traitor and a tyrant . . . a Christian and an infidel . . . a Catholic and a patron of the synagogue . . . he was, through all his vicissitudes, the same stern, impatient, inflexible original . . . the same mysterious, incomprehensible self . . . the man without a model, and without a shadow.[75]

Moreover, "Nature had no obstacle that he did not surmount."[76] Perhaps it was this last characteristic that endeared Napoleon to the vigorous patriots of the nineteenth century. Whatever the cause for the continuity of the lesson in the McGuffey series,[77] it is interesting to note that the first lesson on Napoleon appeared in the earliest editions, only a little more than two decades after the Congress of Vienna, and was apparently the choice of Dr. McGuffey in compiling selections for the first editions.[78]

However much Napoleon may have prospered in the hands of the compilers of the McGuffey readers, Byron and Alexander came in for worse fates. Byron is denounced, though covered with titles and fattened with fame, because of his evil; and his evil consisted in a flagrant violation of all human and Christian convention.[79] On the other hand, Alexander is praised for his greatness, his military prowess, his indomitable will; but it is lamented that

his glory was of short duration, for he had one very great fault, that of being excessively fond of eating and drinking. He wanted to make the world think that he was a God, and could do whatever he chose. . . . How shocking it is to think, that the man who had subdued so many nations, should suffer himself to be conquered by the sin of intemperance.[80]

Despite Alexander's intemperance, however, it is not denied that his greatness consisted in conquest; and though Byron is denounced for his evil in one lesson, his words on "Rome," whose "Imperial Mount" eventually falls, are carefully preserved in another.[81] Another lesson finds Pitt august, overbearing, majestic, but praises him because he was right and lived a clean and uncorrupted domestic life. At the same time, it is said of Pitt that "His object was England; his ambition was fame."[82] On the other hand, the Swiss hero, Arnold Winkelried, is praised because, as we have seen, his charge of the Austrian phalanx "made way for Liberty."[83] The American heroes are Washington, Hamilton, Marshall, and Franklin, and each, in his own way, comes in for appropriate responses in the McGuffey readers. The cult of Washington, was pronounced, as we have already noted in an earlier portion of the present chapter; but it may be well to recall here that Washington was, to the compilers of the McGuffey readers, the best example of the virtues of patriotism and godliness.[84] Lafayette, though of course not American, was praised for his aid in the American Revolution, and becomes, in the hands of Everett, somewhat of an obscure and legendary figure, hardly as clearly defined as Washington or Franklin.[85] Franklin, next to Washington, was, as we have already seen, the most frequently noted American hero, while John-Marshall is recognized as the preserver of the Constitution.[86] Hamilton, while a man of many excellent traits, is brought into question because of his unfortunate dueling.[87] William Penn is noted for his kindness to the Indians.[88] While foreign heroes are praised for their bravery, magnanimity, or justice, American heroes are treated almost with an air of sacredness, and a divine light shines gloriously over their heads.

IV

One must not imagine, however, that this expansionist policy and the unvarnished patriotism of the McGuffey readers would lead them to any hasty approval of war. On the contrary, the numerous stories and lessons condemning war and its miseries are abundant testimony that the compilers of the McGuffey readers were unalterably opposed to war. "War is the work, the element, or rather the sport and triumph of death," the readers declare.[89] "It is remarked by the most ancient poets, that in peace, children bury their parents; in war, parents bury their children; or is the difference small."[90] And another lesson declares that it is well nobody sees the battle, "for a battle is one of those jobs which men do, without daring to look upon."[91]

These outspoken condemnations continue almost to the outbreak of the Civil War; and while one may find one or two traces of the same anti-war spirit, it is clear that condemnation of war is primarily the product of pre-Civil War sentiment. But these sentiments are wholly in line with pacifist and socialist denunciations of war. Though some would go so far as to condemn the American Revolution, the McGuffey readers would not follow.[92] The religious sentiments and convictions of the McGuffey readers, though they may have buttressed the conservative cause in politics, certainly did not condone militarism or war. When pacifists called upon the word of God in their denunciations of the human losses and miseries of war, the McGuffey readers supported them with numerous stories and lessons. "The lot of those who perish instantly may be considered, apart from religious prospects, as comparatively happy," declared the McGuffey readers, "since they are exempt from those lingering diseases and slow torments to which others are so liable."[93]

Even the Mexican War came in for a great deal of criticism, though in indirect ways, to be sure. There is, for example, an ironic demand that politicians "pause" in the midst of war to examine the miseries they have brought upon innocent people. "O! that you would put yourselves on the field of battles, and learn to judge of the sort of horrors you excite."[94] Considering that this quotation bears the publishing date of 1844, it appears quite liberal. Other lessons following the Mexican War, but preceding the Civil War, are likewise adequate in their condemnation of war. While the McGuffey readers would not have gone so far in the condemnation of war as the socialist journals, the position of the latter is interesting in the light of the opposition of the readers to all wars.

You talk about the connection of religion and patriotism, vainglorious Pharisee; yet when the homes of the defenceless and innocent are dripping with warm blood of those who have bared their breasts to the sword of the invader, when the gaunt and haggard emigrant, fleeing from the intolerable agonies of famine in an oppressed land, finds no cheerful welcome in this abode of the free, when the cry of unrequited labor is ringing in the ear of Christian benevolence, from the cotton fields of Carolina and cotton mills of New England, when the Gold calf is enshrined as the supreme object of worship in the seats of our money changers and the halls of our merchants—no thrill of indignation convulses your heart, no words of fiery rebuke fall from your lips, no hope of victory of the true God over the demons of hell kindles your eye. Your love of country and your love of religion are both equally a pretense.[95]

The McGuffey readers dared not and could not go so far; but their condemnation of war is no less articulate. There is a touching story of the brothers who kill each other in battle, unknowingly, and so were buried together.[96] Another lesson paints a grim picture of the slain, the wounded, the sorrowing, and the inactive behind the lines, noting that nations under battle are all "mingled in promiscuous massacre and ruin."[97] And Byron's description of the Battle of Talavera, in one of the lessons, brings no comfort to the war mongers:

> *There shall they rot, Ambition's honored fools!*
> *Yes, honor decks the turf that wraps their clay!*
> *Vain sophistry. In these, behold the tools,*
> *The broken tools by tyrants cast away.*[98]

In view of the approach of the irrepressible conflict, it is interesting to note one of the lessons which appeared in an edition of 1857. The lesson tells the story, appropriately enough, of a New Hampshire man and a Georgia man who were wounded in a terrible battle. In a moment of remembrance they recall their childhood together and forgive each other in the agony of death.

> *Forgive each other while we may;*
> *Life's but a weary game,*
> *And, right or wrong, the morning sun*
> *Will find us dead, the same.*[99]

In a similar vein, a charming lesson tells how some children ask their father to tell a story about "a bloody murder." In response to this request the father tells the story of hundreds of men who march along and coldly set themselves to murdering hundreds of other men in battle. "I do not know of any murders half so bloody," the father tells them.[100] A somewhat later lesson explains that it is better to be a warrior of Truth in the ranks of the free than a soldier of blood and gore.[101]

Of course there are the lessons, just noted, which glorify the vigorous man of action and the military hero. But one indeed, quite counteracts this tendency. Perhaps it will be recalled that one of the lessons told of Alexander's greatness and lamented only the fact that his intemperance caused him to loose his empire. Despite this fault of intemperance, however, the lesson made it clear that Alexander was a great conqueror. Somewhat later, however, appeared a lesson that contained a child's inquiry concerning Alexander's greatness:

> *How big was Alexander, Pa*
> *That people called him Great?*
>
> *Did killing people make him great?*
> *Then why was Abdel Young,*
> *Who killed his neighbor, training day,*
> *Put into jail and hung?*
> *I never heard them call him great.*

Then they that kill and they that praise,
The Gospel do not mind.
You know, my child, the Bible says
That you must always do
To other people, as you wish
To have them do to you.

But, Pa, did Alexander wish
That some strong man would come
And burn his house, and kill him, too,
And do as he had done?[102]

Not only did the McGuffey readers denounce the horrors and blood-shed of war, however, they proposed that the Christian sentiment was the only force strong enough to prevail over those who make and desire war. "I can look to nothing but the progress of Christian sentiment upon earth," one lesson notes, "to arrest the strong current of its popular and prevailing partiality for war."[103] In this connection, of course, the Mc-Guffey readers cannot be praised too highly. For their denunciation of war, injustice, crime, and inhumanity, and for their magnificent sponsor-ship of the brotherhood of man under the fatherhood of God, the Mc-Guffey readers must stand among the great textbooks of America.

V

However much the McGuffey readers denounced war, they were in-creasingly responsive to the arguments of Webster and Story in defense of nationalism and the Union. The editions of 1844 and 1853 are con-veniently sprinkled with nationalist arguments, though the lessons which seemed sympathetic to the antislavery crusade were withdrawn after the first editions. Though the McGuffey readers clearly support the nation-alist arguments of Webster and Story in the conflict between North and South, it is equally clear that they go out of their way to avoid offending their Southern readers. The Webster-Hayne debate, for example, is pre-sented with an apparent attempt at disinterested neutrality,[104] but subse-quent lessons contain numerous patriotic and nationalistic disquisitions from the pen of Daniel Webster.

The slavery controversy receives scant attention, even in the early edi-tions of the thirties when the antislavery crusade had not yet risen to the heights of violence and war. One lesson on the "Character of Mr. Wilber-force," though it was included, no doubt, because of other considerations, may be taken as a denunciation of the slave trade.

And the man whose labors abolished the Slave Trade, at one blow struck away the barbarism of a hundred nations, and elevated myriads of beings, degraded to the brute, into all the dignified capacities of civilized man. To have done this is the most noble, as it is the most useful work, which any individual could accomplish.[105]

However satisfactory this outspoken approval of Mr. Wilberforce's labors in the British parliament, it was further noted that, "The speeches of Mr. Wilberforce are among the very few good things now remaining in the British parliament."[106] Moreover, it is worth noting that this serene character was above the party squabbles that caused so much distress in the West. Mr. Wilberforce, the McGuffey readers explain, "maintains great respectability of character, by disdaining to mix in the daily paltry squabbles of party: he is no hunter after place."[107]

Nevertheless, Daniel Webster, a hunter after place and a mixer in the daily paltry squabbles of party, finds generous amounts of space devoted to his nationalistic and patriotic utterances. His reply to the advocates of particularism and states' rights is marked by its legal arguments.

How can any man get over the words of the Constitution itself?—"We, the People of the United States do ordain and establish this Constitution." These words must cease to be a part of the Constitution, they must be obliterated from the parchment on which they are written, before any human ingenuity or human agreement can remove the popular basis on which the Constitution rests, and turn the instrument into a mere compact between sovereign states.[108]

To this argument the thorough historians of the South replied that not the people of the United States, but rather the people of the several states had ordained and establishd the Constitution.[109] Thus in its original form the Constitution specifically enumerated each of the thirteen states. But the provision for ratification by only nine of the states made the drafters of the Constitution substitute, "We, the people of the United States," for they did not know which states would ratify the Constitution.[110] As a consequence of this, argued Calhoun and Davis, the Constitution created a new government but not a new people. The original sovereignty of the states was not meant to be impaired, "for sovereignty in an American republic can belong only to a people, never to a government."[111]

Webster argued that indeed the Constitution had been established in the name of the people, but that the people were to be considered in the aggregate, not as the people of the several states:

So far from saying that it is established by the governments of the several States, it does not even say that it is established by *the people of the several States*. But it pronounces that it is established by the people of the United States in the aggregate. Doubtless the people of the several States, taken collectively,

constitute the people of the United States. But it is in this their collective ca-
pacity, it is as all the people of the United States, that they established the Constitution.[112]

These arguments were based primarily on the preamble to the Constitution; but they could be supported by the contention of an able jurist
that such a foundation for nationalist arguments was wholly justified.

It is an admitted maxim in the ordinary course of the administration of justice, that the preamble of a statute is a key to open the mind of the makers, as
to the mischiefs which are to be remedied and the objects which are to be accomplished by the provisions of the statute.[113]

One bit of strategy which may have been unnoticed in political circles
was the reprint of a lesson by Grimke from one of the early editions of
the readers for the edition of 1853. Now Grimke was a Southern gentleman who participated in the lectures of the Western Literary Institute
meeting at Cincinnati. His views, however patriotic, were evidently not
made in the heat of the sectionalist controversy; but by reprinting the
lesson, which originally appeared in the thirties, in an edition of the
fifties, the nationalist argument won the advocacy of a Southern gentleman who was speaking in behalf of cementing loyalty to the union. "Be
it then the noblest office of American eloquence," declared Grimke, to
cultivate, in the people of every state, a deep and fervent attachment to
the union,"[114] for the orator is responsible for the "cause of Christianity,
patriotism, and literature."[115]

However wise the strategy of the North, the historical and legal minds
of the South were not to be outdone. To Webster's argument of the col-
lectivity of the community that had established the Constitution, Calhoun was apt to argue that:

The limited reason and facilities of man, the great diversity of language, customs, pursuits, situation and complexion, and the difficulty of intercourse, with
various other causes, have, by their operation, formed a great many separate
communities, acting independently of each other. Between these there is the
same tendency to conflict,—and from the same constitution of our nature,—as between men individually.[116]

If, then, there was no national community, but rather a number of
separate communities, state sovereignty could not have been surrendered
when the Constitution was adopted. The proof that there is no national
community lies in the Constitution itself, for were men's interests identical, and were the action of government so to affect equally the interests
of each and every portion of the community, the laws which would impoverish one section would impoverish all others, and the right of suf-

frage would of itself form a perfect constitutional government. On the contrary, however, argued Calhoun,

nothing is more difficult than to equalize the action of the government in reference to the various and diversified interests of the community; and nothing more easy than to pervert its powers into instruments to aggrandize and enrich one or more interests by oppressing and impoverishing the others; and this too, under the operation of laws, couched in general terms;—and which, on their face, appear fair and equal. . . . The more extensive and populous the country, the more diversified the condition and pursuits of its population, and the richer, more luxurious, and dissimilar the people, the more difficult it is to equalize the action of the government,—and the more easy for one portion of the community to pervert its powers to oppress and plunder the other.[117]

To Justice Story this argument was of no weight against the fact that the fundamental law of the land had been established and had become obligatory upon all. Whether it was formed by different and diverse peoples, states, or communities does not alter the fact that upon ratification it becomes obligatory as the fundamental law. A constitution, therefore, is the rule of action prescribed by the supreme power of the state, and as such, it regulates the rights and duties of all communities and peoples upon whom it has become obligatory and fundamental.[118] "It is a *rule,* as contradistinguished from a temporary or sudden order," argued Story. "Like the ordinary municipal laws, it may be founded upon our consent or that of our representatives; but it derives its ultimate obligatory force as a law, and not as a compact."[119] Moreover, argued Story, "If it is the supreme law, how can the people of any State, either by any form of its own constitution or laws or other proceedings, repeal or abrogate or suspend it?"[120]

This line of argument is important in considering the strategy of Webster and the McGuffey readers in the legal and historical arguments involved in the approaching irrepressible conflict. Calhoun's approach to the problem is historical and philosophical, as we have seen. But Webster strikes out in the direction of legality and constitutionalism, insisting that the Constitution is organic and irrevocable law rather than a mere compact among states. This approach met equally with the approval of Story and the McGuffey readers.[121] To Calhoun's reasoned demonstration that if the Union really embodied an identity of interests there would be no partisan and sectional plundering, and that fundamental law should prove as beneficial to one state as to another, the McGuffey readers and Daniel Webster replied with a eulogy of the benefits enjoyed under the Constitution and the argument that states' rights were protected, not endangered, under the Constitution and the fundamental law of the land.[122]

In his attack on Calhoun's doctrines of nullification and secession,

Webster pointed out that the compact which had resulted in the Constitution, if indeed it was a compact, was now irrevocable organic law:

The Constitution, Sir, is not a contract, but the result of a contract; meaning by contract no more than assent. Founded on consent, it is government proper. Adopted by agreement of the people of the United States, when adopted it has become a Constitution. The people have agreed to make it a Constitution; but when made, that Constitution becomes what its name imports. It is no longer a mere agreement. . . . When the people agree to erect a government, and actually erect it, the thing is done; and the agreement is at an end. The compact is executed, and the end designed by it attained. Henceforth, the fruit of the agreement exists, but the agreement itself is merged in its own accomplishment; since there can be no longer a subsisting agreement or compact to form a constitution or government, after that constitution or government has been actually formed and established.[123]

And those who met at Philadelphia to frame this remarkable instrument, the McGuffey readers argued, were "for stolidity of reasoning, force of sagacity, and wisdom of conclusion" superior of all groups of assembled legislators throughout the whole course of history.[124] These eulogies, in the face of the arguments among the proponents of nationalism and sectionalism, were more than mere patriotic effusions; they were, by implication at least, settled arguments for nationalism, patriotism, and the Constitution. Whoever would upset the benefits these gentlemen of the congress at Philadelphia have conferred upon our nation would indeed be open to the charge of treason;[125] for "under such complication of difficult circumstances, no nation or body of men, can stand in preference to the general Congress at Philadelphia."[126]

The elaborate arguments of Calhoun for a conception of the concurrent majority found no place in the McGuffey readers, but they proved themselves theoretically sound in the great struggle against the nationalism and constitutionalism of Webster. Since the diversity of interests in men and in the different communities of the nation make it well-nigh impossible that law can support one section or group without injuring the interests of another, Calhoun was ready to propose a new concept, the concept of "concurrent consent."

It results, from what has been said, that there are two different modes in which the sense of the community may be taken: one, simply, by the right of suffrage, unaided; the other, by the right through a proper organism. Each collects the sense of the majority. But one regards numbers only, and considers the whole community as a unit, having but one common interest throughout; and collects the sense of the greater number of the whole, as that of the community. The other regards interests as well as number;—considering the community as made up of different and conflicting interests, as far as the action of government is concerned; and takes the sense of each, through its majority or appropriate organ, and the united sense of all, as the sense of the entire community. The former of these I shall call the numerical, or absolute majority; and the latter, the concurrent, or constitutional majority.[127]

The nationalists were quick to realize the cogency of these arguments in behalf of the will of the people, taken in Calhoun's sense of a constitutional majority as opposed to the numerical or absolute majority. To combat this doctrine Webster declared that, "This government, Sir, is the independent offspring of the popular will."[128] It follows, therefore, that it is superior to the states which compose the architecture of the Union. The government, argued Webster,

is not the creature of State legislatures; nay, more, if the whole truth must be told, the people brought it into existence, established it, and have hitherto supported it, for the very purpose amongst others, of imposing certain salutary restraints on State sovereignties. The States cannot make war; they cannot contract alliances; they cannot make, each for itself, separate regulations of commerce; they cannot lay imposts; they cannot coin money. If this Constitution, Sir, be the creature of State legislatures, it must be admitted that it has obtained a strange control over the volition of its creators.[129]

Then Webster went on to admit the economic foundations of constitutionalism and nationalism in the period when the Constitution was established:

The leading object in establishing this government, an object forced on the country by the condition of the times and the absolute necessity of the law, was to give Congress power to lay and collect imposts *without the consent of particular States.* The Revolutionary debt remained unpaid; the national treasury was bankrupt; the country was destitute of credit; Congress issued its requisitions on the States, and the States neglected them; there was no power of coercion but war; Congress could not lay imposts, or other taxes, by its own authority; the whole general government, therefore, was little more than a name.[130]

Thus the Constitution was necessary to establish a government superior in authority and power to the individual state sovereignties which composed it. The object, argued Story, was to substitute a government of the whole people for a mere confederacy of states.[131] The economic motives for the foundation of the Union were thus frankly admitted both by Webster and the McGuffey readers. Both declare that the Union had its origin in the necessities of commerce, finance, and credit.[132] The noble sentiments of the Declaration of Independence which declared the natural equality of men were necessary merely to "strengthen our position abroad" and to "encourage our forces in their endeavor."[133] Under the Constitution, argued the McGuffey readers, the commercial groups were strengthened, the house of finance was set in order, and the credit was established.[134] To preserve these great interests we must follow Washington's model and greatly fear God.[135]

The mobilization of the moral and patriotic resources of the nation through textbooks like the McGuffey readers undoubtedly aided the arguments of nationalists and preservers of the Union, though the publishers of the McGuffey readers were astute enough to remove all lessons *obviously* unsympathetic toward the Southern cause. The elaborate arguments of Calhoun for a concurrent majority, while no doubt theoretically sound as sectional arguments, could not have aroused the sentiments of those whose patriotism was identified with the flag, the church, and the Constitution; and it was through these symbols that the McGuffey readers worked. The arguments for the preservation of the Union, always in the words of Webster, center on the far-reaching benefits that our national union has brought us, and ask innocuously whether dismemberment of the union does not strike at the very heart of security, liberty, and happiness, which each man enjoys.[136] No state, no individual, no group has the right to destroy what the wise men at Philadelphia have given us, the wise laws and perpetual union of a glorious Constitution.[137]

Calhoun's elaborate argument which conceived of the community as the concurrent majority could strike no responsive chord in Northern breasts.

The necessary consequence of taking the sense of the community by the concurrent majority is . . . to give to each interest or portion of the community a negative on the others. It is this mutual negative among its various and conflicting interests, which invests each with the power of protecting itself;—and places the rights and safety of each, where only they can be securely placed, under its own guardianship. Without this there can be no systematic, peaceful, or effective resistance to the natural tendency of each to come into conflict with the others, and without this there can be no constitution. It is this negative,—the power of preventing or arresting action of the government,—be it called by what term it may, veto, interposition, nullification, check, or balance of power,—which, in fact, forms the constitution. . . .[138]

But Calhoun's logic could not meet the test of Webster's legal arguments. To Webster it seemed that what Calhoun was proposing was no less than revolution, since no state had the authority to dissolve the Union.

Therefore, Sir, since any State, before she can prove her right to dissolve the Union, must show her authority to undo what has been done, no State is at liberty to *secede,* on the ground that she and other States have done nothing but *accede.* She must show that she has a right to *reverse* what has been *ordained,* to *unsettle* and overthrow what has been *established,* to *reject* what the people have *adopted,* and to *break up* what they have *ratified;* because these are the terms which express the transactions which have actually taken place.[139]

This view the McGuffey readers accepted without reservation, pointing out that all misfortunes can be borne while we have the Constitution and the Union. Dismemberment strikes at the Constitutional liberties and safeguards of all the people. "We have, while it lasts," argued the McGuffey readers,

a political life capable of beneficial exertion, with power to resist or overcome misfortunes, to sustain us against the ordinary accidents of human affairs, and to promote, by active efforts, every public interest. . . . But dismemberment strikes at the very being which preserves these faculties. . . . Other misfortunes may be borne, or their effects overcome. . . . But who shall reconstruct the fabric of demolished government? Who shall rear again the well-proportioned columns of constitutional liberty? Who shall frame together the skillful architecture which unites national sovereignty with state-rights, individual security, and public prosperity.[140]

By extracting from the Webster-Hayne debates those portions which stressed nationalism and patriotism, the McGuffey readers could do no harm to the nationalist cause. "If there be *one state* in the Union . . . that may challenge comparison with any other, for a uniform, zealous, ardent and uncalculating devotion to the Union, *that State* is *South Carolina*," argued Hayne in the McGuffey readers.[141] Answering Hayne's speech in praise of South Carolina during the Revolution, Webster stresses the fact that he is above regional pride, looking on the heroes of Massachusetts as American patriots. American freedom and liberty owe their existence to the heroes of Massachusetts, Webster insists in the McGuffey readers.[142] On the other hand, counters Hayne in one of the lessons of the McGuffey readers:

Sir, I honor New England for her conduct in that glorious struggle. . . . But great as is the praise which belongs to her, I think at least equal honor is due to the South. Never were there exhibited in the history of the world, higher examples of noble daring, dreadful suffering, and heroic endurance, than by the whigs of Carolina during the Revolution.[143]

And there the debate ends, though by gradual degrees it spreads and inflames the whole nation, and in the Civil War men set about to settle in blood and arms what they could not settle with all the logic and rhetoric of their vitriolic debate.

VI

We have taken some pains to point out that the McGuffey readers, like other readers and textbooks, displayed broad patterns of nationalism and patriotism. Within these broad patterns, however, the early editions found space for a sectional outlook that prided the West for its institutions and ideals. In a plea for institutions comparable to those of the East, Lyman Beecher expressed the conservative fear that without religious and moral culture, culture to be made secure by the school and the church, the West, indeed, might fall into the depths of despairing ignorance, and the wildmen of the Ohio and the Mississippi might upset established institutions. Other Western gentlemen were pleading for the support of Western citizens in the enterprises of publishing and culture that were just being felt in the Middle Border. In all this, it was clear that Western apologists hoped to make of the Middle Western frontier a paradise of culture rivaling the East, its sharpest critic.

But this early sectionalism passed into a broader patriotism and nationalism, and in one phase of this passage it was noted that pure Americanism was found only in the West, which, it was averred, was fortunately freed from the foreign influences of the East. However that may be, it is clear that the McGuffey readers did not neglect either patriotism or nationalism. The first was founded on the cult of Washington, buttressed with numerous examples of foreign patriots whose deeds secured the liberties and freedoms of their countries. In this latter tendency, however, the McGuffey readers seemed carried very far from the original patriotic purpose. Napoleon, Alexander, Louis the Fourteenth of France,[144] and Lafayette, among others, come in for praise. In the case of Alexander, however, reservations were made because of his intemperance, while Louis the Fourteenth, "though he constantly exposed himself to the public gaze, in situations in which it is scarcely possible for any man to preserve much personal dignity, he, to the last, impressed those who surrounded him, with the deepest awe and reverence."[145]

Though these heroes may be questionable in view of their military conquests and lack of reverence for the rights of the people, the American heroes are, in a similar manner, surrounded with the deepest awe and reverence. The cult of Washington is so pronounced as to be almost a pious worship, and the interesting notes on Washington's piety, truthfulness, Christianity, and honesty are numerous enough to raise him to the heights of patriotic devotion. Other Americans who found their way into the cult of heroes were Marshall, Franklin, Hamilton, though the latter was unfortunately driven by the imperious desire of convention to participate in a duel. This barbarous custom deprived America of one of her great men. Nevertheless, it is pointed out that Washington's sword and Franklin's staff have won for America heroes of the highest calibre.

As the cult of heroes inspired reverence for America's past, however, it also inspired hope for the mission on which America was embarked. According to some of the lessons in the McGuffey readers, this mission was ordained as of God. His ordinance for the moral government of the world made the American union the property of the world, whose glorious mission was to spread backward on the states of Europe, and forward on the empires of Asia. Other lessons gave the impression that the men assembled to frame the Constitution of the United States were far superior to any other assembled body of legislators, and in consequence of that fact, America has been blest with ideals, sentiments, and laws which no nation has yet equalled. All this, of course, was under the hand and zeal of a heavenly sovereign who looked down benignly on the nation whose mission was but the carrying out of His ordinance.

But we must not imagine that the imperious needs of this mission would lead the McGuffey readers to condone an expansionist and unjust war. On the contrary, the McGuffey readers contain very strong denunciations of war and militarism, though this tendency contrasts somewhat with the emphasis on the military accomplishments of some of the heroes, domestic and foreign, singled out for study. However that may be, it is overwhelmingly evident that the McGuffey readers stood with the pacifists and socialists in their violent denunciation of wars, and even went so far as to question politicians who resort to war without regard to the human costs involved. It is very significant that a lesson appearing just three years before the outbreak of the irresistible conflict should stress the common bonds and ties of a soldier from New Hampshire and another from Georgia, who, mortally wounded in combat, realize that their common heritage really requires that they be friends. It is lessons of this latter type that moved us to maintain that the McGuffey readers, perhaps more than any other readers of the same period, were most outspoken in their denunciations of war, and, in view of the imperious demands of war mongers, militarists, and expansionists, must, for that reason, be commended for their magnificent sponsorship of the brotherhood of man under the fatherhood of God.

In the conflict between the nationalists and sectionalists, however, the McGuffey readers were increasingly responsive to the nationalist note in the writings of Story and Webster. Webster is given considerable space in the readers, and his arguments are, at times, identical with those of the McGuffey readers. In sponsoring the cause of patriotism, nationalism, and the Constitution, an attempt was made to avoid offending Southern gentlemen who were arguing for states' rights. But it is clear that the strong emphasis on nationalism and the Constitution nullified these attempts at disinterested neutrality. One must conclude, then, that the patterns of nationalism, patriotism, and constitutionalism were strongly established in the McGuffey readers; and as a consequence of that fact, it is clear that they played a part in strengthening the cause of those who would preserve the Union.

3

Religion and the Conservative Tradition

THE CONSERVATIVE TRADITION in politics found its purest expression in terms of religious and moral ideas. With the assistance of the clergy, the cohorts of conservatism and established institutions worked out a great clerical and legal synthesis which identified the law of courts and the interpretations of Marshall, Kent, and Story with the moral order imposed by the omnipotent will of a sovereign God. In this great conservative synthesis, the McGuffey readers played an important, but probably unconscious, part. The foundation of this synthesis was the recognition that religion was the most important basis of society; and its public appeal lay in the fact that Jeffersonian and Jacksonian radicalism had carried with it the hint of atheism and scepticism. Even mighty Jefferson professed strong anticlericalism and a hatred of the priestcraft. It is with this orientation that many of the ideas of the McGuffey readers are clothed with meaning.

I

The current of anticlericalism in the social philosophy of Jefferson broke like a monstrous wave on the turbulent political sea. In the election of 1800 Jefferson's "atheism" was a violent issue of the campaign, and the Federalists seized upon it as an opening wedge in the conservative attack on the citadel of democracy. When the election went against the conservative party, Hamilton sought desperately to rejuvenate Federalist politics by promoting Christianity and the Constitution. In support of the former, he proposed the formation of a Christian Constitutional Society whose purpose was to hedge the law with divinity. In support of the latter, Hamilton sought refuge in the courts, and John Marshall proved not unhelpful in securing the law from the inroads of those who had no respect for judicial interpretation.[1] But Jefferson failed to live up to the fears of the clergy who had predicted that his election would be the end of religious institutions. As the powerful forces of political necessity drove Jefferson in a steady retreat from his theoretical position, the religious issue faded for a time from the political scene.

When, in 1815, Lyman Beecher, progenitor of the Beecher brood and friend of Dr. McGuffey, proposed that a qualified religious instructor be established for every thousand citizens, Jefferson was stirred beyond measure, and the latent anticlerical sentiments burst forth. "You judge truly that I am not afraid of priests," he wrote to Spafford.

They have tried upon me all their various batteries, of pious whining, hypocritical canting, lying and slandering, without being able to give me one moment of pain. I have contemplated their order from the Magi of the East to the Saints of the West and I have found no difference of character, but of more or less caution, in proportion to their information or ignorance of those on whom their interested duperies were to be plaid off. . . .[2]

But religion, as we have seen, took a firmer hold on the Middle Border, where, not long after Beecher's proposal, lessons which strengthened the great conservative and religious synthesis were being selected for the early editions of the McGuffey readers. "Religion is a social concern," maintained Channing in one of the McGuffey readers, "for it operates powerfully on society, contributing, in various ways, to its stability and prosperity." No man is aware how much "moral and social sentiments are fed from this fountain." Without religion, "how powerless conscience would become," and without conscience and "the belief of God," how "palsied would be human benevolence."[3]

And, let men thoroughly believe . . . that human existence has no purpose, and human virtue no unfailing friend; that this brief life is everything to us, and death is total, everlasting extinction; once let them *thoroughly* abandon religion; and who can conceive or describe the extent of the desolation which would follow.[4]

The point was well taken, for it was the desolation which would follow abandonment of religious belief, rather than matters of conscience, which wrinkled the brows of conservatives. The nineteenth century gentlemen who discreetly followed the enlightened course of deism or scepticism in religion were nevertheless concerned that revealed religion should restrain the lower orders of society. Such was the view of Calvin Colton, preacher and Whig pamphleteer, who declared that:

Christian morality and piety, in connexion with the intelligence of the common people are the last hope of the American Republic, and the only adequate means of bridling and holding in salutary check that rampant freedom, which is so characteristic of the American people.[5]

Well might he advocate an alliance between religion and conservatism as the Jacksonian hordes marched triumphantly to political power, the Eastern proletariat and the Western farmer dogging their heels.

Significant in the proposed alliance was the great synthesis of judicial interpretation and the moral order of a sovereign God. In one of the stories we find an old gentleman listening with seeming indifference to an argument on religion, but when the contestants reach a certain point he comes over and answers the arguments in order as they have been made. This gentleman, we learn, is Chief Justice John Marshall of the United States. "So perfect was his recollection," the reader tells us, "that every argument urged against the Christian religion was met in the order in which it was advanced."[6] Other aspects of this great synthesis we shall return to later, but let us note here that the identification of legal interpretation and the moral order gave to official decree the sanction of moral law.

The basis of this great synthesis, as we have noted, was the religious foundation of society. Without religion, argued the clergy and the courts, the benevolence of established institutions would be dissipated and human society would be brutalized. The charges of atheism hurled at Jacksonians and Jeffersonians served only to discredit political liberalism, and the Sabbatarian controversy and the incident of the Sunday mails seemed to confirm conservative suspicions that radical democrats had forgotten God. The sanctity of the Sabbath seemed threatened by political democracy, and conservatives made all haste to point to democratic laxity in matters of Sunday observance.

The battle is reflected in a lesson entitled "Observance of the Sabbath," in which a good gentleman proposes that the Sabbath must be maintained as a day of rest, as there is great danger to the whole structure of society when one of the mainstays is taken away. One sees immediately that the important thing to the conservative is not that the Sabbath should be forgotten, but rather that in being forgotten, atheism and scepticism might arise to threaten the whole structure of society. The community must never be permitted to doubt the sacredness of the Sabbath, argued the author of the lesson, and children of the age of Jackson read the inescapable conclusion in their McGuffey readers:

If you can induce a community to doubt the genuineness and authenticity of the Scriptures; to question the reality and obligations of religion; to hesitate, undeciding, whether there be any such thing as virtue or vice; whether there be an external state of retribution beyond the grave; or whether there exists any such being as God, you have broken down the barriers of moral virtue, and hoisted the flood-gates of immorality and crime.[7]

The alliance between religion and conservatism could hardly prosper, however, without some rationalization of the glaring inequalities in wealth which disturbed conservative and liberal alike. In working out the great conservative synthesis and defense, the clergy proved of inestimable help. Even as early as 1835 a skilled clergyman could assure the Massachusetts legislature that religion "recognizes and sanctions the principle of inequality in the distribution of wealth amongst men . . . to be acquiesced in as a permanent condition of society."[8] And the Reverend Hubbard Winslow pointed out, "That there should be inequality in the conditions of men, as there is in all the other works of providence, is clearly a wise and benevolent ordinance of heaven. . . ."[9] Moreover, he continued, "it was the levelling disposition, that cast down the shining angels from their starry heights."[10] When the clergymen had thus worked their marvelous powers on the assembled legislators, one Whig member of the assembly insisted on a literal interpretation of their remarks, declaring, "I'm in favor of all Corporations, and those who would oppose them would also oppose the Christian Religion."[11]

Nor was this type of exegesis confined to the clergy. "All that live get life from God," declared the *Eclectic First Reader*. "He made the poor man, as well as the rich man."[12] The conclusion is inescapable: inequalities in the possession of worldly goods are to be acquiesced in, for God "made the poor man, as well as the rich man." Even the German version of the same cosmic scheme admonished children of the Heavenly Father who has made all things:

> *Kind! Gott thut, was er will.*
> *Er ist der Herr der Welt.*
> *Wenn er spricht, steht es da!*
> *Er ruft die Sonn, sie kommt, . . .*[13]

"Who is it that gives us food to eat, and clothes to make us warm?" inquires a child in one of the stories of the *Eclectic First Reader*. "It is God, my child. . . ."[14] If it is God who gives us these good things, surely we must know and love God. "We should love God," for "God sees and knows all things," and "God is everywhere." Let us not, then, utter words of revolution or impiety; let us not, then, speak bad words, for "if I do, God will not love me."[15] Thus was the hand of the Lord heavy in those days, and under the minister's tutelage or that of a pious teacher, the child grew to piety and learned from the Father the ways of men upon the earth.

It was this same Father of all men who pressed Beecher forward in his plans for a religious society which would insure the piety and morals of American citizens. The West was wild enough, but Robert Owen's *New*

Harmony Gazette and the utopian settlements in the wilderness brought a new current of anticlericalism into the troubled seas of American life. When Reverend Ezra Ely of the Presbyterian church proposed, once more, a Christian party in politics, the suspicions of the anticlericalists and Jeffersonians were confirmed. It is doubtful if Ely was directly associated with conservative interests, yet so charged was public sentiment that his proposal met with a storm of protest. "I propose, fellow-citizens," declared Ely,

a new sort of union, or, if you please, a Christian party in politics. If the Presbyterians, Baptists, Methodists, Congregationalists and Episcopalians would only unite on voting day, they could govern every public election in our country.[16]

This move the friends of liberalism and democracy, perhaps over-sensitive concerning the priestcraft, denounced as an attempt to unite State and Church. The subsequent controversy over the Sunday mails drew from Frances Wright the claim that "the whole soul of the priestcraft" was betrayed.[17] George Evans cursed the "Church and State" party in the liberal press,[18] and Orestes A. Brownson used the opportunity to foist ponderous Universalist epithets on the politically-minded Presbyterians.[19] Another Universalist charged that there existed "among the leaders of a proud and aspiring priesthood, a determination to establish an *Ecclesiastical Hierarchy,* and to reduce us to a worse than Egyptian bondage."[20] Meantime the flow of petitions to Congress had become overwhelming, and Johnson was among the incumbents returned to the House; his sentiments apparently expressed the official opinion of the Jacksonian regime. "It is not the legitimate province of the Legislature to determine what religion is true, or what false," Johnson had declared in his first report. "Our Government is a civil, and not a religious institution."[21]

II

Despite this official pronouncement, there were good reasons for believing otherwise. The Federalists had made good their threat to hedge the Constitution with divinity, and Jefferson's success in 1800 only confirmed the sanctity of their refuge in divinity and the courts. There was, indeed, a moral foundation for conservative government. "There are great principles of abstract justice which the Creator of all things had impressed on the mind of his creature man," declared John Marshall in one of his impressive decisions from the bench, "and which are admitted to regulate, in a great degree, the rights of civilized nations."[22] Thus it became clear that those of Federalist persuasions intended to seek strength in clergy and judiciary. To establish the moral and supernatural sanction for the rights of property, and to throw between those who possessed property and those who did not the double protection of church and court,—these were the great tasks which conservatives set for themselves in the days that followed the debacle of 1800.[23]

"In ascending to the great principles upon which all society rests," maintained Joseph Story,

it must be admitted that there are some which are of eternal obligation, and arise from our common dependence upon Our Creator. Among these are the duty to do justice, to love mercy, and to walk humbly before God.[24]

This moral foundation for government many might be willing to accept; but it is, after all, merely the prologue. The problem of government, said this pillar of judicial conservatism, is "how the property-holding part of the community may be sustained against the inroads of poverty and vice."[25] This frank confession of principle makes it clear that the "property-holding part of the community" must seek the supernatural and moral sanction which only the clergy could provide.

The support of law and religion strengthened Federalism incalculably by identifying the deepest desires of man—toward social stability and religious salvation—with a particular social order. It guaranteed Federalism, moreover, the loyalty of the only groups in the population with an authority not dependent on property. It meant that whatever there was of an aristocracy of status would surely be on the side of the aristocracy of wealth. The combination of judges, clergymen and men of property seemed invincible.[26]

If this alliance of the judiciary, the clergy, and the conservative party was in fact an alliance designed to protect the status and property of those who identified themselves in each age with the interests of reaction, conservatism, neo-Federalism and Whiggery, then the social and moral ideas in the McGuffey readers subtracted nothing from their arguments. Here we find the story of the sceptical lawyer who at last convinces himself of the necessity of the moral law which lies behind the world. "I have been looking into the nature of that law," he tells us. "I have been trying to see whether I can add anything to it, or take anything from it, so as to make it better. Sir, I cannot: it is perfect."[27] The same conception of a moral world lying beyond the world of nature, and sometimes identified with it, is the rock on which the authors of the McGuffey readers built their church. "Admirable as the natural world is for its sublimity and beauty," questions one of the authors, "who would compare it, even for an instant, with the sublimity and beauty of the moral world?"[28] Moreover:

The same God is the author of the invisible and visible world. The moral grandeur and beauty of the world of man, are equally the productions of his wisdom and goodness, with the fair, the sublime, the wonderful in the physical creation.[29]

Thus was developed the moral foundation of the world of nature and of man; thus was it written that, "The Design of the Bible is evidently to give us correct information concerning the creation of all things by the omnipotent word of God. . . ."[30] Moreover, we are assured, "We have the most ample and satisfactory proofs that the books of the Bible are *Authentic and Genuine*."[31]

The search for a moral and supernatural basis for Constitutionalism and conservatism provoked the thought that there was a higher moral law which, while it was not of man's creation, was designed to regulate his conduct. While some, like good Justice Story, preserved the distinction between the natural religion of the *philosophes* and the revealed religion of the ignorant orders of society, they left wide the door of polite scepticism through which enlightened gentlemen could enter. "The rights of conscience," wrote Justice Story,

are, indeed, beyond the just reach of human power. They are given by God, and cannot be encroached upon by human authority, without criminal disobedience of the precepts of natural as well as revealed religion.[32]

This same gentleman spoke unkindly of democracy and sought the affection of the mighty, writing to Nicholas Biddle that, if he had attained "a little to your approbation by my labor as a public magistrate," he would be much consoled, for he knew nothing "which ought to gratify one more, than to have a place in the respect of the wise, the good, and the honored of our times."[33] Those of whom he spoke were no doubt the "rich and well born" who, Hamilton said, should inherit the earth.

For the conception of natural law so familiar to the eighteenth-century dreamers of a heavenly city, the good Whigs and neo-Federalists of the nineteenth century substituted the conception of a moral order transcending human power. Such was the foundation of law in the days of Jackson. "The law, as a science," said Chancellor Kent,

is only a collection of general principles, founded on the moral law, and in the common sense of mankind, and applied to particular cases as they arise, by the diligence of the bar and the erudition of the courts.[34]

By such diligence and such erudition, no doubt, did worthy Chancellor Kent arrive at the conclusion that, "The absolute rights of individuals may be resolved into the right to acquire and enjoy property. These rights have been justly considered, and frequently declared, by the people of this country, to be natural, inherent, and unalienable."[35] What a travesty on the natural rights of the Revolution!

If the moral law seems, sometimes, somewhat incomprehensible or contradictory, there is yet the quieting thought of a Supreme Benevolence who, we learn in the McGuffey readers,

pours out his fulness on the whole subordinate domain of nature, and of providence; he bows a pitying regard on the very humblest of his children, and sends his reviving spirit into every heart, and cheers by his presence every home, and provides for the wants of every family, and watches every sick bed, and listens to the complaints of every sufferer; and while, by his wondrous mind, the weight of universal government is borne, oh! is it not more wondrous and more excellent still, that he feels for every sorrow, and has an ear open to every prayer.[36]

And yet so great is the debt of every age to the past that we find the author of one of the readers marshalling his arguments like an Encyclopedist; or, like Voltaire, arguing for the existence of a Supreme Being by design and analogy. We learn in a story of Washington, for example, that when Washington's father planted seeds in his garden he did so in such manner that when they sprouted they spelled out his son's name. Washington was startled; but he guessed correctly that his father had some purpose in mind. "In a thousand things we see design," he told young George. "There must then have been a *designer;* someone who formed these things for a *purpose; for some end.*"[37] It is a good lesson, and well remembered. "All things belong to God. He created them and they are his."[38]

The design was in the nature of things, and the designer "made the poor man, as well as the rich man."[39] But there is the day of final judgment, when even these earthly inequalities will disappear. At the final judgment, we learn in the McGuffey readers,

all the inequalities of the present life shall disappear, and the conqueror and his captive; the monarch and his subject; the lord and his vassal; the statesman and the peasant; the philosopher and the unlettered mind; shall find their distinctions to have been mere illusions.[40]

However unimportant these earthly illusions, it was clear that the earth had passed to the mighty, and that the mighty, chastened by the triumph of Jefferson and his "atheistical" system, had sought refuge in divinity and the courts. Justice Story, for example, insisted on identifying the moral and the natural law, reserving a place of privilege for the judiciary in the interpretation of these laws. "What indeed can tend more to exact and purify the mind," asked Justice Story,

than speculations required of those who profess the law upon the origin and extent of moral obligations; upon great truths and dictates of natural law; and upon immutable principles, that regulate right and wrong. . . ."[41]

Kent's definition of the law as "only a collection of general principles, founded on moral law," did indeed carry the identification of the judiciary and the divinity of a moral order one step further.[42] It is clear that by their close association with the moral order in the administration of justice, the judiciary came to enjoy the same privileged place in the cosmic scheme as that held by the clergy. The divine right of the judiciary to interpret cases in the light of moral and natural law gave to property and conservatism a sanctity which they had not enjoyed in the previous century.

This valuable clerical and judicial synthesis enabled conservatives to identify the malcontent as the foe of both God and the law.[43] In the days of Jackson this synthesis proved particularly valuable, as the Jacksonian hordes of common men spread what must have seemed the most violent radicalism. Many of the most outspoken radicals, like Robert Owen or Fanny Wright, if they were not atheists, were at least sceptical in matters of religion. But the Whig concern reveals itself as a concern not for matters of conscience, not for "atheism" as such, but for matters of property and government. Atheism was not only hostile to established religion, admitted one Whig member of the Massachusetts legislature,

but to all decency and regularity, to the peace of all communities, and the safety of all governments. . . . Atheism is a levelling system. In religion and in politics, it labors to overthrow all ancient customs—all established institutions.[44]

In place of Jefferson's "atheistical system" the Whig conservative could put Jackson's "atheistical system." The goal of this system, charged one Whig conservative, was to "abolish all property. Every thing is to be embodied in one common stock, to which each is to contribute by his daily labor, and from which all are to receive their stated rations of food and clothing."[45] Moreover, atheism, by:

Incorporating itself with national politics, in order to acquire favor among the populace, marches under the banners of political reform. . . . It declares a war of extermination upon the established institutions of religion and government. It denominates all religion priestcraft, all property a monopoly, and all jurisprudence an organized fraud upon the liberties of mankind.[46]

Clearly the cause for alarm was not atheism, but what atheism would do for the great judicial and divine synthesis which conservatives had built up following the debacle of 1800. Now, in the thirties and forties, this great synthesis was again threatened, and threatened by the same "atheistical system" that had furrowed conservative brows in the days of Jefferson.

If the conservative synthesis, the sanctity of property and established institutions, was indeed threatened in the age of Jackson by ungodly radicals, unholy revolutionaries, and assorted types of "atheistical systems," then the children who were fed upon the McGuffey readers were in little danger of falling in with the ungodly. There is, for example, the story of the poor boy who is satisfied with his lot and does not envy the rich. He works diligently at school, and he labors to help his parents, for he appreciates their sacrifices in sending him to school. The moral of the story is revealed as the little boy sums up what he has learned: ". . . the poor, if they are but good, may be very happy: indeed, I think that when I am good, nobody can be happier than I am."[47] Moreover, simple, genuine goodness is the best capital in this world; it is superior even to fame and riches.[48] Such is the lesson we learn from a story entitled "The Best Capital." A pious uncle is explaining to two boys the virtues of a dead relative. "Yes," concludes the uncle to his young auditors, "simple, genuine goodness is the best capital to the business of this life. It lasts when fame and money fail, and is the only riches we can take out of this world with us."[49]

> Oh, my God, let me do no sin.
> Aid me to do as I am bid.
> Our God can see all we do.
> God has an ear to all we say.
> Let me do no bad act.
> Let all I do, be fit for His eye.
> God can see all.
> But who can see God. Not one.
> Do not sin, for God can see you.
> Men may not see you.
> The eye of God is on you.[50]

III

The effect of this great clerical and judicial synthesis, a synthesis which sanctified property, Constitutionalism, and established institutions, was to produce the desired alliance between religion and politics. "Without religion," declared a prominent Whig, "law ceases to be law, for it has no bond, and cannot hold society together."[51] To sanctify the social order and to establish a national religion as well as a national government was the great aim of conservative politics. "The principle of obedience would sit lightly on the people," wrote Daniel D. Barnard, "unless it were enforced by a common sense of religious obligation."[52] The design of the conservatives in their attempt to capture the commonwealth was clear: Even slaves, Barnard insisted, could be more easily governed when "brought under the influence of a common religious faith."[53]

The alliance of religion and politics could thereby effect the proper control of the brute orders of society. "Democracy was said to be a branch of atheism," observed George Bancroft after traveling through Connecticut. Thus, it is "beautifully ordered by Providence," we learn in the Mc-Guffey readers, "that woman, who is the mere dependent and ornament of man in his happier hours, should be his stay and solace when smitten with sudden calamity. . . ."[54] But the women of Shaw and Ibsen would hardly care for this kind of enslavement, whether or not maintained in the guise of an ordinance from heaven. In a similar vein we learn from the same lesson that

. . . a married man, falling into misfortune, is more apt to retrieve his situation in the world than a single one; partly, because he is more stimulated to exertion by the necessities of the helpless and beloved beings who depend upon him for his subsistence; but chiefly, because his spirits are soothed and relieved by finding, that though all abroad is darkness and humiliation, yet there is still a little world of love at home, of which he is the *monarch*.[55]

Thus did the children of the different sexes learn their relative duties and status in the family. But we must not imagine that the monarchy is confined to the home. In the story of the "Remarkable Preservation" Professor Wilson relates his harrowing experience of falling overboard from a ship in midpassage, of drifting about on a wintry sea. But despite these perils, the narrator endured all and was saved by a passing ship. As a consequence of these remarkable adventures, his belief in God was greatly strengthened. "The hand of God was there. . . . I hasten to fall down on my knees before the merciful Being who took pity upon me, and who, at the intercession of our Redeemer, may, I hope, pardon all my sins."[56] A German edition declares:

> Nichts ist, das Gott nicht weiss,
> Er, der dein Aug'Schuf, sieht;
> Und der das Ohr schuf, hört.
> Kind, was du thust, sieht Gott;
> Er weiss wohl, wo du bist.[57]

The conception of God as a heavenly monarch who sees all and knows all, particularly children, who are *natural democrats*, was perfectly created for its purposes. Clearly the heavenly monarch inspires obedience. "We may expect God's protection so long as we live in God's bounds."[58] In a lesson on the Bible we again get the conception of God's sovereignty:

The *Excellency of the Bible* might be proved sufficiently from its sanctifying and transforming influence upon the minds of all who read it with a proper spirit. But this is manifest more especially from the fact of its having God for its author; and that God is its author is evident, from its being the only book which teaches everything that our Creator requires us, either to know, or believe, or do, that we may escape his deserved displeasure, obtain his sovereign favor, and dwell forever in the bliss of his immediate presence.[59]

With God established as a heavenly monarch and the moral law identified with the Constitution and established institutions, the remaining task of conservative politics was to identify the party of Jackson with the atheistical and sceptical associations it had inherited from Jefferson. In the prosecution of this strategy Frelinghuysen prepared a work in which he traced the growth of atheism and scepticism in American government from Jefferson's administration to that of Jackson. "The evil is spreading," wrote the author. Religion is "everywhere *politically* set at nought."[60]

The solution of this problem required that government and religion be united once again, and to accomplish that mission conservative politics mobilized powerful social forces. "Are christian institutions to be administered by unchristian agents?" inquired Frelinghuysen.[61] The evil required that Christian agents administer American government, for, the author condescendingly explained, "Without religion, law ceases to be law, for it has no bond, and cannot hold society together."[62] This view apparently coincided with that of Barnard, who maintained that America was "a national religion, as well as a national government."[63] Then, with a frankness unbecoming Whig politicians, Barnard admitted that, "The principle of obedience would sit lightly on the people unless it were enforced by a common sense of religious obligation."[64] Moreover, added another prominent Whig, "religion—revealed religion, Christianity— should regulate legislation. . . ."[65] But this line of argument could be extended to a defense of the principle of religious persecution, and apparently the author would be willing to see suitable sedition acts passed against those who refused to conform.[66] He added that he expected to be set down "as the enemy of free institutions, of the rights of man," by radicals on the "extreme left of democracy."[67]

In this great struggle between the Christian front and the "extreme left of democracy," it must have been comforting to discover that Washington himself, the father of the republic, was a devout Christian. In the story of "Washington in the Camp," the inconsistency between the Christian and the warrior is explained to the untutored. Isaac, a friend of Washington, while walking in the woods near Valley Forge, was amazed to see the great general kneeling in humble prayer. "I have seen this day what I never expected," we are told in the McGuffey readers. "Thee knows that I always thought the sword and the gospel inconsistent; and that no man could be a soldier and a Christian at the same time; but George Washington had this day convinced me of my mistake."[68] Moreover, added the raconteur with the wisdom of retrospect, "If George Washington be not a man of God, I am greatly deceived; and still more shall I be deceived if God do not, through him, work out a great salvation for America."[69] It is clear that the salvation of America lay in the labor of good Christian men like General Washington, our most distinguished patriot.

Nor were the clergy unavailing in the strategy of identifying Jackson and the "extreme left of democracy" with their inheritance of deism, scepticism, and atheism. An eminent Whig preacher in New York employed the authority of his pulpit to denounce those who believe "the pompous doctrine that 'all men are born free and equal' " when confronted with the unimpeachable evidence "of all the providence of God, in whose unsearchable wisdom, one is born in a manger and another on a throne."[70] Moreover, concluded this Christian disciple, "The axiom of 'equal rights,' is infidel, not christian, and strikes at all that is beautiful in civil, or sacred in divine institutions."[71] The observant George Bancroft, who was himself identified at times with the "extreme left of democracy," noted that in every election the party of Jackson was faced with the charge of atheism. "The community was made to believe," he complained, "that there was danger the Bible would be taken out of their hands."[72] In addition it was claimed that "Democracy was . . . a branch of atheism. . . ."[73]

In combating the unchristian doctrine of natural rights, it was found expedient to employ the natural-rights *philosophes* themselves, whose ungodly doctrines, if carefully selected, could combat the very heresies they represented to the enlightened mind. In the McGuffey readers, for example, we find Rosseau comparing "The Scriptures and the Savior." Here we find Rosseau quoted as saying, "The majesty of the Scriptures strikes me with astonishment, and the sanctity of the gospel addresses itself to my heart. . . . Is it possible, that a book at once so simple and sublime, can be the work of man?" In addition, "if the life and death of Socrates were those of a sage, the life and death of Jesus were those of a God." What is worse than calling the Scriptures mere myth? "Shall we say that the evangelical history is a mere fiction?—it does not bear the stamp of fiction, but the contrary."[74]

Nevertheless, the charges of impiety against the democrats of the extreme left was not without an element of truth. Some of the more radical democrats were willing to denounce the priestcraft in the most violent terms. Others, like Samuel Allen, maintained that, "The clergy, as a class, have always been ready to come in for a share in the advantages of the privileged classes, and in return for the ease and convenience accorded to them by these classes, to spread their broad mantle over them."[75] Even on the floor of Congress a democrat was so bold as to declare:

In the earlier stages of society, priestcraft was the universal method resorted to by the sons of luxury and idleness to filch the pocket of industry and labor . . . and perhaps no system ever was, or ever will again be, devised . . . more effectually to retain in bondage the human intellect, and steep in ignorance, debasement, and degradation, the great mass of mankind. . . . I contend that Christ himself was betrayed . . . by priestcraft.[76]

But in the readers we find this betrayal, both of Christ and Paul, implied of quite another type of priestcraft. In "Paul's Defense before King Agrippa," we find the following:

Whereupon, O king Agrippa, I was not disobedient unto the heavenly vision; but showed first unto them of Damascus, and at Jerusalem, and throughout all the coasts of Judaea, and then to the Gentiles, that they should repent and turn to God, and do works meet for repentance. For these causes the Jews caught me in the temple, and went about to kill me.[77]

Without entering into the Biblical or historical accuracy of this presentation, or the part it might play in the struggle for political power, one may well inquire whether this type of exegesis is suitable in a nation composed of so many diverse religious and racial elements. Again, in another reader, we find that, "The Jewish authors were incapable of the diction and strangers to the morality contained in the gospel, the marks of whose truth are so striking, so perfectly inimitable, that the inventor would be be a more astonishing man than the hero."[78] In the story of "The Good Son" we find a jeweler's son who refuses to sell diamonds to a group of Jewish elders because it meant that he would have to awaken his father who had the key to the diamond chest. In explanation the young lad says: "At his age, a short hour of sleep does him a great deal of good; and for all the *gold* in the world, I would not be wanting in respect to my father, or take from him a single comfort."[79] Truly these words have double edges.

While this type of Biblical exegesis may have proved profitable to some members of society, others were busy turning the liberal democrats of the Revolutionary period into atheists and social radicals. Tom Paine, once the hero of all Americans, became, in the hands of the Whigs, a filthy little atheist.[80] But it was hardly necessary to reach into the past to find those fit to be charged with atheism and witchcraft. Robert Owen, Fanny Wright, Gilbert Vale, and Abner Kneeland, to mention a few, were rabid Jacksonians whose liberal religious views could easily be fitted into the charge of impiety.[81] One cannot but wonder, if patriotism and love of liberty be one of the virtues a school reader might laudably cultivate, why men like Tom Paine and Jefferson were excluded from a series of readers so universal in scope.

Apparently a more important virtue to the compilers of the readers was the silent bearing of distress and agony, economic, social, or spiritual. In a story from one of the readers we learn that Hugh, a little boy who has had one of his legs amputated, is greatly dejected because he cannot hope to be a soldier or sailor. His mother, with pious wisdom, tells him the story of many great men who have borne heavy burdens in the trials of life.

> No doubt their hearts often swelled within them at their disappointments; but I fully believe that they very soon *found God's will to be wiser than their wishes*. They found, if they bore their trial well, that there was work for their hearts to do, far nobler than any the head could do through the eye, or the ear, and they soon felt a new and delicious pleasure, which none but the bitterly disappointed can feel.[82]

This "new and delicious pleasure" we discover to be:

> The pleasure of rousing the soul to bear pain, and of agreeing with God silently, when nobody knows what is in the breast. There is no pleasure like that of exercising one's soul in bearing pain, and of finding one's heart aglow with the hope that one is pleasing God.[83]

Without discounting the value of these virtues in the face of the hardships and discouragements of pioneer life, one may well wonder what its affect was on those who came to maturity while the struggle between the Christian front of conservative politics and those of "the extreme left of democracy" was still raging. To "dirty little atheists" like Tom Paine and to Jefferson's "atheistical system," one could oppose the not unreasonable argument of the natural Christian, as found in one of the readers:

> But I am filled with amazement, when I am told, that, in this enlightened age and in the heart of the Christian world, there are persons who can witness this daily manifestation of the power and wisdom of the Creator, and yet say in their hearts, "There is no God."[84]

That, of course, is about what some democrats did declare, and so the conservative charge was not wholly without foundation. Abner Kneeland, for example, founded the *Boston Investigator,* a weekly journal devoted to assorted forms of scepticism. Formerly a member of the Universalist fellowship, Kneeland thought it proper to propose a political toast to Tom Paine, whom Whigs had denounced as a dirty little atheist. "Andrew Jackson and Abner Kneeland," proposed Kneeland, "Friends of the people but the dread of aristocracy and the priestcraft."[85] As Kneeland's audiences grew, and the *Boston Investigator* found an increasingly large body of subscribers, conservatives viewed the impious old man with alarm.

Conservatism watched his growing audiences with alarm; and early in 1934 he was indicted for publishing in the *Investigator* of December 20, 1833, a "scandalous, impious, obscene, blasphemous and profane libel of and concerning God. Three articles had been found offensive. The first quoted Voltaire's epigram on the Immaculate Conception—a remark held too crude to be repeated in public court, though it could be found in any Boston bookshop which carried the *Philosophical Dictionary*. The second article was considered to hold the Christian doctrine of prayer up to ridicule by comparing the Deity to General Jackson snowed under by various and conflicting petitions. The third, which alone was actually written by Kneeland, stated his disbelief in Christ, in miracles, in immortality, and concluded ambiguously, "Universalists believe in a god which I do not."—a declaration variously interpreted by the prosecution and defense, according to whether the comma was supposed to have been left out by accident or design.[86]

When the case came before Judge Peter Oxenbridge Thacher, it was clear that the political ramifications of the case were more important than the charges of impiety and blasphemy. In his charge to the jury Thacher made it plain that Kneeland's impious and atheistic magazine had circulated "among thousands of the poor and laboring classes of this community."[87] Then Thacher felt called upon to cite the remarks made at the trial of the publisher of Paine's *Age of Reason,*

the poor stand most in need of the consolations of religion, and the country has the deepest stake in their enjoying it . . . because no man can be expected to be faithful to the authority of man, who revolts against the government of God.[88]

The alliance between religion and neo-Federalism was indeed a strengthening of old ties, and the remarks of many of the democrats did indeed give some real foundation for conservative alarm. But it is clear that the alarm arose from political concerns, rather than from a fear that impiety and blasphemy should prevail among the people.[89] If the great concern of neo-Federalism and Whiggery was not impiety but political radicalism, then indeed a revised version of Calvinism and the Salem witchcraft epidemic might be found valuable to the conservative cause. If the strengthening of the religious ties to keep the people from speculating too much about established institutions was the desire of the conservatives, then it is clear that there was nothing in the McGuffey readers which would prove harmful to their cause. On the contrary, it is not difficult to imagine that the McGuffey readers played their part in the great judicial and clerical synthesis which brought success to conservative politics in the years that followed.[90]

IV

If the alliance between religion and property were to prosper, however, other foundations than those of a common hatred and fear of atheism and democracy had to be sought. As industry prospered and commerce expanded, wealth flowed into the hands of the shrewd and enterprising, and the glaring inequalities of condition between rich and poor became more obvious than ever. The new foundation for the great alliance between religion and conservatism came as a resuscitation of the Christian doctrine of the stewardship of great wealth. Though tracing its origins back to the Protestant Reformation, the doctrine of stewardship became extremely useful before and after Appomattox. In the hands of Carnegie and the stewards of the Gilded age, the doctrine of stewardship became the gospel of wealth. But even before the Civil War its main lines of argument had been worked out, and the youngest Americans had met with it in the McGuffey readers.

The clearest statement of the doctrine of stewardship we find in a lesson of *McGuffey's Newly Revised Second Reader* bearing the date of 1844. The rich boy of the lesson is a good boy, generous to the poor and kind to his servants, for "he does not think he is better than other boys."[91] In observing the kindness and generosity of the wealthy boy, the poor boy concludes that *"God gives a great deal of money to some persons, in order that they may assist those who are poor."*[92] Moreover, "If I were a man, and had plenty of money," mused the poor boy, "I think no person who lived near me should be very poor."[93] We have already noted how "God made the poor man, as well as the rich man,"[94] and how, "the poor, if they are but good, may be very happy. . . ." But in connection with these statements, the effects of universal benevolence must be noted.

Were the divine principle of benevolence in full operation among the intelligences that people our globe, this world would be transformed into a paradise, the moral desert would be changed into a fruitful field. . . . Fraud, deceit, and artifice, with all their concomitant train of evils, would no longer walk rampant in every land. . . . Nation would not lift up sword against nation, nor would they learn war anymore . . . but the influence of reason and affection, would preserve order and harmony throughout every department of society.[95]

These conclusions, coming in the great age of philanthropy, should not surprise us. As God's stewards on earth, men of great property and wealth were indeed in a position to extend "the divine principle of benevolence." These ideas are paralleled by those in common acceptance in the middle decades of the nineteenth century. A professor at Harvard noted, for example, that, "The most natural and sensible way of deriving personal gratification from newly acquired wealth, and of making a show of it in the eyes of the world, is to give largely to public charities."[96] Moreover, George Hillard reminded the arch-conservatives at the Massachusetts Convention of 1853,

in our great cities, the aggregation of immense wealth at one end of the scale, and the increasing amount of hopeless poverty at the other, did involve an element of peril to wealth itself, and that the moment the rich men forget the duties of property, the moment that they cease to bridge this interval between themselves and the poor by the perpetual exercise of sympathy, and by the constant recognition of a common humanity and a common brotherhood, their wealth would be in danger of falling upon the mercy of the merciless. And it is only in this—it is only in the moral element, flowing from Christianity and humanity, that a corrective is to be found to the danger which always threatens a country in which, while the rich are growing richer, the poor are growing poorer.[97]

This frank confession of faith the McGuffey readers apparently accepted. But if the tenor of ideas in the McGuffey readers accepted the Christian doctrine of the stewardship of great wealth, it also stressed the necessity of divine benevolence and the exercise of responsibility by the men of wealth. In the story of "The Poor Old Man," for example, we are informed that we should "be kind to the poor."[98] The reason for this kindness to the poor is that all benefits, including wealth or poverty, flow from the hand of sovereign God. "Who is it that gives us food to eat, and clothes to make us warm?" inquires a child. "It is God, my child."[99]

Although the McGuffey readers insist on the charitable activities of the stewards of wealth, reminding them that all benefits flow from God, they would agree with the statement of Francis Bowen, that when man meddled in the social and economic order established by God he only brought down upon himself the curses of a deity whose principle is *laissez faire* in matters of business. Bowen, like many of his contemporaries, believed that free competition and free enterprise would "tend slowly but irresistibly to the equalization of wealth. . . ."[100] Characteristic of the lessons is the conclusion of "Little William" in a story in the *New Third Eclectic Reader*. When "Little William" questioned his father why God had made a thorn bush, the father showed him that the thorns held wool from the sheep's back and the birds came and got it for their nests. "God is wise and good," concluded William, "and has made *everything* for the best."[101] In a similar vein, a lesson in a later edition tells the story of the small child who pricked her finger on the nettle and questioned her father as to the necessity of its existence. After showing her the process of pollenation, he told her that from the nettle may come blisters, food, and a substitute for flax. "Thus you see that even the despised nettle is not made in vain; and this lesson may serve to teach you that we only need to understand the works of God to see that in goodness and wisdom he had made them all."[102]

Despite this unquestioning obedience to God's will and unalloyed promotion of the Christian doctrine of stewardship, the McGuffey readers clearly take upon themselves the responsibility of prodding the rich stewards to action in behalf of the poor. In one of the lessons Job gives an account of his behavior in the days of his prosperity. "Did not I weep for him that was in trouble? Was not my soul grieved for the poor?"[103]

If I have witheld the poor from their desire, or have caused the eyes of the widow to fail, or have eaten my morsel myself alone, and the fatherless have not eaten thereof; if I have seen any perish for want of clothing, or any poor without covering; if his loins have not blessed me, and if he were not warmed with the fleece of my sheep; if I have lifted up my hand against the faithless, when I saw my help in the fate; then let mine arms fall from my shoulder-blade and mine arm be broken from the bone.[104]

In a similar manner, a story of a beautiful infant whose soul was peaceful and gentle grew into manhood as an honored and respected citizen. He had fields and rich grain, much gold and silver, and stately mansions, but he said in secret that these things had come to him by virtue of his own shrewdness and labor, and he returned no thanks to the Lord, neither fearing nor serving Him. "The laborers complained who had reaped down his fields, and the poor cried whose coverings he had taken away." But the wealthy man did not consider that, "the cries of the oppressed were continually entering the ears of the Most High."[105]

But we must not take this prodding of the wealthy too seriously, as the overwhelming number of stories which contain the idea of placing one's trust in God brings to nought this measured criticism of unrestrained wealth. Indeed, the lesson just cited may be taken either as a warning to the wealthy or as a quieting of the poor whose cries were continually entering the ears of the sovereign God. An interesting story in the *Newly Revised Eclectic Fourth Reader* apprises us that rich men need not be too concerned about posterity, for the inheritors of poverty are compensated by the wealth and beauty of nature.[106] In a comparison of the characters of Henry Martyn and Lord Byron by Catherine Beecher in the *Eclectic Fourth Reader*, we find that "the law of God is the true path of happiness."[107] Byron's was a worldly mind, complains Miss Beecher, while that of Martyn was "Christian." Moreover,

if we look only at his years of self-denying trial, where were accumulated all the sufferings he was ever to feel, we can find more evidence of true happiness, than is to be found in the records of the youthful poet, who was gifted with every susceptibility of happiness, who spent his days in search of selfish enjoyment, who had every source of earthly bliss laid open, and drank to the very dregs.[108]

Years of self-denying trial, thrift, industry, labor, and trust in God—
these are the qualifications of the good Christian; and in the bearing of
pain, in humility, in obedience to God's will;—this is the road to eternal
happiness.

> The law of the Lord is perfect, converting the soul:
> The testimony of the Lord is sure, making the wise simple,
> The statutes of the Lord are right, rejoicing the heart.
> The Commandment of the Lord is pure, enlightening the eyes.
> The fear of the Lord is clean, enduring forever:
> The judgments of the Lord are true and righteous altogether.
> More to be desired are they than gold; yea than much fine gold. . . .[109]
> Then shall I be upright,
> And I shall be innocent from the great transgression.
> Let the words of my mouth, and the meditation of my heart,
> Be acceptable in thy sight,
> O Lord, my strength, and my redeemer![110]

With these injunctions before them, the children who read the Mc-
Guffey readers were prepared to admire much in the character of the Puritan. One of the lessons examines the Puritan community and the Puritan
character. As for the Puritan, "He prostrated himself in the dust before
his Maker, but he set his foot on the neck of his king."[111] Though the
Puritans posssesed some extravagant ideas, they can be praised especially
for their love of Liberty and their love of God. But the most admirable
characteristic of the Puritan community lay in the fact that, "there was
not a single community of men to be compared with them, in the respects
of deep religious impressions, and an exact performance of moral
duty."[112]

The characteristics of piety, simplicity, and obedience to a moral duty
laid down as the edict of a sovereign God on the word of the clergy were
indeed characteristics not without benefit to the great conservative and
religious synthesis. The benefits of obedience to God's will often come in
the form of increased wealth. In one of the stories of the McGuffey readers, for example, William Reed, a poor barber, is distressed by his conscience because he keeps shop on the Sabbath in order to increase his
earnings. Finally he is driven to the clergyman who tells him to respect
the Sabbath and trust Providence for his well being. Following the clergyman's advice, the barber is reduced to penury and is forced to seek
cheaper rentals in a poorer district. One night a stranger, a pious attorney, comes for a shave; but the barber is so poor that he cannot afford
the candlelight with which to shave the stranger. The stranger inquires
as to his circumstances and name, and finding the barber to be a man he
has long sought, transfers to him property to which he is the rightful heir.

Such are the rewards of obedience, for the poor barber had "discontinued his Sabbath work, went constantly and early to public services of religion, and soon enjoyed that satisfaction of mind which is one of the rewards of doing our duty. . . ."[113] Moreover, in this situation man's extremity was God's opportunity. "Had the poor barber possessed one half-penny, or even credit for a candle, he might have remained unknown for many years; but he trusted God. . . ."[114]

If you wish to serve God and obey his omnipotent moral law, "Accustom yourself to conceive of God, as a merciful and gracious parent, continually looking down upon you, with the tenderest concern, and inviting you to be good, only that you may become everlastingly happy."[115] The key to this happiness is obedience to one's superiors and content with the station which God's laws has assigned. This idea is cleverly taught in the allegory of "The Little Brook and the Star." In this lesson the brook yearns to be free of the trees that protect it from the sun. It wants to get out into the wide world of the plain. When it does, it is burned up by the sun. "A certain little brook,"

that might have been the happiest creature in the world, if it had but known when it was well-off, and been content with the station assigned to it by an unerring Providence. . . . But in that knowledge and that content, consists the true secret of happiness; and the silly little brook never found out the mystery until it was too late to profit by it.[116]

This acceptance of the established order, so pronounced in the McGuffey readers, and justified as the will of God, led to humility and obedience and a corresponding avoidance, for all who took clerical injunctions seriously, of all social reform. This attitude of acceptance of established institutions and obedience to the moral injunctions laid upon man as the iron fiats of an omnipotent God, an attitude strengthened by the McGuffey readers, led many to object to the growing alliance between religion and property. "To the Conservative," wrote Greeley,

Religion would seem often a part of the subordinate machinery of Police, having for its main object the instilling of proper humility into the abject, or contentment into the breasts of the down-trodden, and of enduring with a sacred reverence for Property those who have no personal reason to think well of the sharp distinction between Mine and Thine.[117]

But Greeley was not alone in his protests, as the alliance between religion and wealth grew in strength and consolidated its forces, sometimes, as we have seen, securing the unconscious aid of textbooks like the McGuffey readers. Even the more democratic members of the clergy were watching the supposed neutrality of the church on matters of politics and property dissolve, and in their alarm maintained that the church must "work for the millions rather than the aristocratic cliques."[118] Then, noting the historical conspiracy between religion and aristocracy to dominate the masses, the same observer announced that the time had come for Christianity to break its historic connection with tyranny, aristocracy, and priestcraft, and play the part of "patron of the aspiring, the fortifier of the weak, the deliverer of the oppressed."[119] He even noted the growing alliance between religion and wealth, warning his fellow clergymen against the "alliance offensive and defensive actually formed between the pretended religion and the real wealth of the country, the hierarchy and oligarchy combined," that attempt to "compass dominion over the people."[120]

It is clear that in their fostering of the virtues of meekness, obedience, and subordination to the will of priest and employer, as well as in their forthright pronouncements in favor of the divinity and legality of established institutions of property, the McGuffey readers were an important, though probably not a premeditated, part of this great synthesis of property and divinity. While some, even the more progressive clergymen, were lamenting the inheritance of the older Calvinistic theory of human nature and urging religious people to forget that "men are incurably fallible, that absolution from pain and woe is impossible,"[121] the McGuffey readers were guilty often of an older and more conservative heritage, and fraught with terrible questions:

And do we take so much anxious thought for future days, when the days which have gone by have so strangely and so uniformly deceived us? Can we still so set our hearts on the creatures of God, when we find, by sad experience, that the Creator only is permanent? or shall we not rather lay aside every weight, and every sin which doth most easily beset us, and think ourselves henceforth as wayfaring persons only, who have no abiding inheritance but in the hope of a better world, and to whom even that would be worse than hopeless, if it were not for our Lord Jesus Christ, and the interest we have obtained in his mercies?[122]

But these concerns were hardly those of Alexander Davis, who in direct opposition to the teachings of the McGuffey readers, issued *A Loud Call to the Citizens of this Nation,* defending the constitutional right to manufacture and sell liquor without consulting any

bastardly priest in existence . . . and without worshiping, kneeling, cringing to the army of wicked, aristocratic, kingly, haughty, lounging and dissipated priests who are ever engaging in seducing, gulling and blindfolding the people, that the people can be more easily wheedled to support their humbuggery, blackguardism, scoundrelism and beelzebubism.[123]

With such observations before them, the McGuffey readers might well lament "the poor speaker of the word of God, the minister who is not anxious about his speaking ability."[124] In combating the evil influences of intemperance and vice, as well as in effecting the great conservative synthesis, it was found that:

> Success in every art, whatever may be the natural talent, is always the reward of industry and pains. But the instances are many, of men of the finest genius, whose beginning has promised much, but who have degenerated wretchedly as they advanced, because they trusted to their gifts, and made no efforts to improve.[125]

This stricture is particularly directed at the Lord's representative on earth, upon whom has fallen the egregious task of uplifting the heart of the common man, of protecting him from the evil influences abroad in society, and of shepherding the flock within the conservative fold. However comforting it may have been to discover that Chief Justice Marshall was a true Christian capable of arguing the good cause of conservatism and religion,[126] it was equally comforting to discover the matchless argument of analogy, to see in the apparent craftmanship of the world the hand of a craftsman.

> What workmanship with no apparent workman . . . the grains of corn, packed into cucumber shapes of pale gold, and each of them pressed and flattened against each other, as if some human hand had been doing it in the caverns of the earth. But what Hand? The same hand (for is it not his workmanship also?) that is tracing these marvelous lines; and if it does not tremble to say so, it is because love sustains, and because the heart also is a flower which has a right to be tranquil in the garden of the all-wise.[127]

Thus the injunction to trust God, whose marvelous symmetry is displayed in all things, becomes the recourse of all that is human. One of the stories in the *New Third Eclectic Reader* illustrates this theme in a convincing manner. Walter lost his father at sea, but he and his mother carried on, sharing in their common tasks. One day Walter was carried down to sea on a stray piece of ice. But Walter's mother was not in despair, for she trusted God. Long after, on a terribly lonely night, Walter returned, kept safe by their common trust in God. Walter had "looked to God and trusted Him."[128] His mother was comforted by "the thought that a good and kind Father would take care of the widow and orphan, if they trust in Him."[129] Walter could justly conclude, then, that, "He knew God would not forsake those who put their trust in Him, and he tried to trust Him."[130]

The effect of this kind of exegesis was to place trust in the ministry, the synod, the pastorate, and the priestcraft, as God's representatives on earth, and to transfer the trust in God, who could not be located definitely in space and time, to an earthly representative who spoke in the name of the

Lord. It was this transfer of trust and obedience from the Lord to the earthly spokesman that radical democrats suspected; and it was the influence and divinity of the clergy that conservative politics actively sought for the alliance between religion and property. The observations of Greeley are worth quoting again in this connection. "To the Conservative," wrote Greeley:

Religion would seem often a part of the subordinate machinery of Police, having for its main object the instilling of proper humility into the abject, or contentment into the breasts of the down-trodden, and of enduring with a sacred reverence for Property those who have no personal reason to think well of the sharp distinction between Mine and Thine.[131]

V

The increasingly dangerous inroads of science upon established conceptions of man's relations with the universe led to appropriate reactions in the McGuffey readers. Though there were many Americans who looked upon the new scientific advances of the nineteenth century as a confirmation of their faith and trust in God, the supernatural deity of the McGuffey readers was indeed in danger from impious scientists. The earlier reactions to the growth of knowledge and science seem directed more at philosophical scepticism than at any particular development in the field of science, but later reactions become more specific and challenge "lying philosophers," those "blaspheming men," whose earlier philosophic scepticisms had drawn "their fellows deep into impiety."[132]

Most of the scientists of the middle decades refused to let their natural framework of inquiry destroy the supernatural basis of their faith.[133] Dr. Thomas Cooper, for example, published a pamphlet entitled, *On the Connection between Geology and the Pentateuch*, in which he deplored efforts to reconcile science and religion.[134] Silliman tried to make his findings accord with the Scripture, contending, despite the wrath of Cooper, that no study of field or laboratory denied the firm truth contained in the Holy Writ. Typical of most scientists, then, was the attitude of Maury, who contended that, "If the two cannot be reconciled (science and religion) the fault is ours because, in our blindness and weakness, we have not been able to interpret aright either one or the other."[135]

This is the burden of the argument in the McGuffey readers. In one of the stories found in an edition of the fifties, the work of coral insects is described. The explanation of how coral insects build up a new continent under the ocean, of how the smallest elements in God's universe are doing something, unknown to man, that fits the demands of the great natural universe, is embellished with the thought that,

vain man . . . pretends to look down on the myriads of beings equally insignificant in appearance, because he has not yet discovered the great offices which they hold, the duties which they fulfill, in the great order of nature.[136]

It is clear, however, that the great order of nature is ruled by a sovereign God whose wisdom and being is beyond the futile gropings of man. A child of six, wondering at the magnitude of God's world, is reminded that, "For the wisdom of the wisest being God has made, ends in wonder; and there is nothing on earth so wonderful as the budding soul of a little child."[137]

DeTocqueville's theory that in Europe, where permanent inequality of condition was in the very structure of society, men confined themselves to "the arrogant and sterile researches of abstract truth, whilst the social conditions and institutions of democracy prepare them to seek immediate and useful practical results of the sciences,"[138] is hardly borne out by the testimony of the McGuffey readers. Here, it is averred, knowledge may be power, but power is dangerous, because, "Knowledge is only an increase of power, and power may be a bad as well as a good thing."[139] Moreover, knowledge must be rectified by the grace of the heavenly Father; for "God's grace in the heart will render the knowledge of the head a blessing; but without this, it may prove to us no better than a curse."[140]

The warning to inquiring philosophers is clear enough when one considers the lesson of "The Philosopher's Scales" in *McGuffey's Rhetorical Guide*. Here we learn that a monk made scales that would weigh strange combinations of things. Voltaire's head weighed less in these scales than the prayer of a penitent thief. Ten chariots weighed less than a plow. Moreover,

> A sword with gilt trappings rose up in the scale
> Though balanced by only a ten-penny nail.
> Last of all, the whole world was bowled in at the grate,
> With the soul of a beggar to serve for a weight.[141]

The moaning winds of winter and the forest filled with frost and crisp snow, frozen leaves, soft rains, muffled brooks, the dull sound of the woodman's ax . . . all these are contrasted with the gay and sparkling sounds of the summer music of nature. The winter is a time of introspection for man, a time when nature is less holy to him, and when he is therefore closer to God.

I believe it is ordered in God's wisdom. We forget ourselves in the enticement of the sweet summer . . . we need a hand to turn us back tenderly, and hide from us the outward idols, in whose worship we are forgetting the high and spiritual altars.[142]

Those who muse on the seasons and those whose rapturous minds are enthralled by the beauties of summer must not inquire too deeply into the nature of things, but in winter must wrest themselves back to the "high and spiritual altars."

The great mathematical synthesis inherited from Newton and the mathematical advances by which American scientists measured and compared, received their appropriate reaction in the McGuffey readers. In one of the lessons devoted to the "Value of Mathematics," the author explains how mathematics has been used in science, bringing us many benefits, comforts, and pleasures.

God has made an unerring law for his whole creation, and made it, too, in respect to the physical system, upon principles, which, as far as we now know, can never be understood, without the aid of mathematics. . . . Do no strong emotions of love and gratitude arise toward that being who thus delights him with the charm of intellectual enjoyment, and blesses him with the multiplied means of happiness?[143]

It is clear that when we inquire deeply into nature we should keep in mind the fact that nature is described particularly well by the Christian writers.[144] In our studies of nature, however much we immerse ourselves in a naturalistic framework, we must remember that:

While the sentiments aroused by admiration of nature seem, however, to spring up unbidden in the mind, they are, in fact, produced by the spirit of religion; and those who imagine that they are not the fit subject of Christian instruction, are ignorant of the secret workings, and finer analogies of the faith which they profess.[145]

The correct attitude toward the mysteries of nature is that exhibited by an observer of the great Niagara Falls. The apotheosis of nature's power, we learn in one of the lessons in the McGuffey readers, controverts all the lies of the philosophers and sages:

God of all truth! in other lands I've seen
Lying philosophers, blaspheming men,
Questioners of thy mysteries, that draw
Their fellows deep into impiety.
And therefore doth my spirit seek thy face
In earth's majestic solitudes. Even here
My heart doth open all itself to thee.
In this immensity of loneliness
I feel thy hand upon me. To my ear
The eternal thunder of the cataract brings
Thy voice, and I am humbled as I hear.

Dread torrent! that with wonder and with fear
Dost overwhelm the soul of him that looks
Upon thee, and dost hear it from itself,
Whence hast thou thy beginning?
Who supplies, age after age, thy unexhausted Springs?[146]

In the year when Asa Gray crossed the Atlantic in search of the herbaria of the Continent with which he hoped to prepare himself for a description of American flora, in the year that saw the increasing hope of the efforts of Silliman and Cooper, the McGuffey readers carried the idea that the best efforts of human science were in vain, that beyond certain limits the human mind, however equipped with methods and tools for its investigations, could not go. Such is the burden of the argument in one of the lessons of the *Eclectic Fourth Reader;* for in that lesson a silver-headed sage, having inquired for many years into the mysteries of nature, having extended a little the boundaries of human knowledge, is forced to conclude:

Alas! . . . how narrow is the utmost extent of human science! how circumscribed the sphere of intellectual exertion! I have spent my life in acquiring knowledge; but how little do I know! The farther I attempt to penetrate the secrets of nature, the more I am bewildered and benighted. Beyond a certain limit, all is but confusion and conjecture; so that the advantage of the learned over the ignorant, consists in greatly having ascertained how little is to be known![147]

Alas! then, what have I gained by my laborious researches, but an humbling conviction of my weakness and ignorance? How little has man at his best estate, of which to boast! What folly in him to glory in his contracted power, or to value himself upon his imperfect acquisitions![148]

The tenor of these arguments coincides with the story of the boy whose ambition to put his name at the very top of those carved on the Natural Bridge in Virginia leads him to climb so high that he can not get down. He is forced to climb up to the top, where, just in time, a rope is lowered to him. "Darkness comes over him, and with the words, God! and mother! whispered on his lips just loud enough to be heard in heaven, the tightening rope lifts him out of his last shallow niche."[149]

Thus it seems that human ambition and human knowledge come to nought, that the farthest extent of human knowledge is not far enough to explain the workings of Providence. The impertinence of man in inquiring into the mysterious workings of nature concerns the McGuffey readers greatly. The theme of the argument runs through most of the readers, in one form or another, and reaches a supernaturalistic conclusion. "I cannot believe that earth is man's abiding place. It cannot be that our life is cast up by the ocean of eternity, to float for a moment on its waves, and sink to nothingness."[150] For the compilers of the McGuffey readers the fear of a life without a future is simply unbearable.

We are born for a higher world than that of earth; there is a realm where rainbows never fade, where the stars will be out before us, like islets that slumber on the ocean, and where the beings that pass before us like shadows, will stay in our presence forever.[151]

In a similar vein the story of a young lawyer and his priest is told. In this story the young man tells the priest of his intention to study the law. The priest asks, "What then?" The young man replies that he will try many cases, become wealthy, and retire to a happy old age. Again the priest asks, "What then?" The young man answers that he will die. To the next query, however, the young man has no answer. But the question repeats itself in his mind, seizes hold of his soul, and he finally abandons the law to enter the ministry where he "spoke and acted in the name of Christ."[152]

When we have done all that we are doing, all that we aim at doing, all that we dream of doing, even supposing that all our dreams are accomplished, that every wish of our heart is fulfilled, still we may ask, what will be then? Whenever we cast our thoughts forward, never let them stop short on this side of the grave; let them not stop short at the grave itself; but when we have followed ourselves thither, and have ourselves lain therein, still ask ourselves the searching question, *And what then?*[153]

Despite this conservatism in matters of speculation, whether in religion or politics, the influence of the McGuffey readers on the Protestant suspicion of Catholicism and the new immigrants from overseas was a noble one. While violent attacks on Catholic churches and Irish immigrants, presumably because of their Catholicism, were frequent occurrences in the middle decades, the McGuffey readers fought a continuing battle for tolerance to all sects and churches and brotherhood to all men. Even distinguished Americans, like Samuel F. B. Morse could maintain that:

The question of Popery and Protestantism, or Absolutism and Republicanism, which in these two opposite categories are convertible terms, is fast becoming and will shortly be the great absorbing question, not only of this country, but of the whole civilized world.[154]

While these attacks raged against Catholic immigrants, the McGuffey readers quietly called attention to the unreasonableness of the attacks. In one of the lessons of *McGuffey's Newly Revised Rhetorical Guide*, for example, the question is asked:

Have the people of England raised a voice against their Catholic fellow-subjects? No; they have the wisdom to see the folly of robbing the empire at such a time, of one-fourth of its strength, on account of speculative doctrines of faith.[155]

VI

The great judicial and clerical synthesis which was worked out during the Jacksonian era maintained itself, with varying degrees of success, throughout practically the whole of the nineteenth century. This synthesis was born of the alliance between religion and politics, an alliance which dated from the days of Jefferson but reached its fullest and strongest expression in the great Whig Counterreformation which followed the administration of Jackson.[156] Out of the alliance of religion and politics had come the great conservative synthesis which identified the rule of courts and established institutions with the moral order of a sovereign God. In the Gilded Age this synthesis found new uses—and new expression—but at its heart it remained an attempt to hedge property with divinity and to protect wealth with the rationalization of stewardship and the cult of success.[157]

Even in the universities the new gospel of wealth found keen expression. Noah Porter, president of Yale University, believed that God had implanted original impulses and rational desire in men which could only be satisfied by the acquisition of property.[158] "The supply of many of the wants of men," he wrote, "implies the existence of property."[159] The great Creator of the Universe has laid upon man the moral duty of acquiring and defending property, and only through the exercise of this noble function can man attain the highest perfection of his nature. Property rights, therefore, come from a law higher than that made by men, though governments were instituted, apparently, to assist man in the accumulation and protection of his property. "Governments exist very largely—in the view of many, they exist solely—for the purpose of rendering this service."[160]

There was nothing in this view with which President McCosh of Princeton could disagree. "God has bestowed upon us certain powers and gifts which no one is at liberty to take from us or to interfere with," wrote good President McCosh; and among these rights bestowed by God is the right to acquire, defend, and use property. "All attempts to deprive us of them is theft. Under the same head may be placed all purposes to deprive us of the right to earn property or to use it as we see fit."[161]

In these views the McGuffey readers would apparently concur. On the principle of entail the earth, its property, and its possessions "God has lent us . . . for our life."[162] Moreover, "it is a great gift of entail";[163] therefore, "when we build, let us think that we build forever."[164]

God has lent us the earth for our life; it is a gift of great entail. It belongs as much to those who are to come after us and whose names are already written in the book of creation, as to us; and we have no right by anything that we do or neglect, to involve them in unnecessary penalties, or deprive them of benefits which it was in our power to bequeath.[165]

To be diligent in one's earthly calling, a moral duty placed upon man by Calvin and Cotton Mather, by the Calvinists and Puritans, by the Protestants and their hundred erring sects, was of the law of the sovereign God. In a similar manner, Benjamin Franklin, though in more secular dress, appealed to his middle-class contemporaries for hard work, thrift, prudence, acquisition. The same theme was caught up by the circuit-riders of the Middle Border whose gospel of hard work and evangelical revival swept through a frontier region laboring to build a new civilization in the wilderness. The theme is carried in the McGuffey readers, and men are warned that while wealth is a worthy ambition, honest service to employers, labor, thrift, prudence, and industry are the real virtues which the acquisition of wealth brings forth. "You are not simply to be kind and helpful to others; but, whatever you do, give honest, earnest purpose to it."[166] Moreover, declare the McGuffey readers, *"By slighting your tasks you hurt yourself more than you wrong your employer. By honest service you benefit yourself more than you help him."*[167]

Wealth, rightly got and rightly used, rational enjoyment, power, fame, these are all worthy objects of ambition; but they are not the highest objects, and you may acquire them all without ever achieving true success. But if, whatever you seek, you put good-will into all your actions, you are sure of the best success at last; for whatever else you gain or miss, you are building up a noble and beautiful character, which is not only the best of possessions in this world, but also is about all you can expect to take with you into the next.[168]

When the cohorts of property and acquisition found new worlds to conquer in the great industrial expansion following Appomattox, the old Puritan code of worldly asceticism and hard labor blossomed with newly acquired importance. And in this new synthesis of religion and wealth the great Moral Governor of the universe, which conservatives had discovered to sanction the judicial interpretations which were to keep radicalism and democracy in check, was discovered anew, as omnipotent and influential as ever. In his new form the Moral Governor sanctions the acquisition of wealth as a means to produce a "noble and beautiful character."[169] In the Gilded Age it was discovered that the Moral Governor "has placed the power of acquisitiveness in man for a good and noble purpose. . . ."[170] To those who were unsuccessful in the race for riches, however, the McGuffey readers had the comforting suggestion that, "for whatever else you gain or miss, you are building up a noble and beautiful character. . . ."[171]

The brotherhood of self-help as expounded in the McGuffey readers found a higher justification in Mark Hopkins' *The Law of Love and Love as Law*. In this book of holiness and love we discover that:

The right to Property reveals itself through an original desire. The affirmation of it is early and universally made, and becomes a controlling element in civil society. . . . Without this society could not exist. With no right to the product of his labor no man would make a tool, or a garment, or build a shelter, or raise a crop. There could be no industry and no progress. It will be found too, historically, that the general well-being and progress of society has been in proportion to the freedom of every man to gain property in all legitimate ways, and to security in its possession. . . . The acquisition of property is required by love, because it is a powerful means of benefiting others.[172]

Even as late as 1900 good Bishop Lawrence of Massachusetts could expound the gospel of wealth as a moral necessity laid upon man by the hand of his Creator. "In the long run," argued the good bishop, "it is only to the man of morality that wealth comes."

We believe in the harmony of God's Universe. We know that it is only along His laws natural and spiritual that we can work with efficiency. Only by working along the lines of right thinking and right living can the secrets of nature be revealed. . . . Godliness is in league with riches. . . . Material prosperity is helping to make the national character sweeter, more joyous, more unselfish, more Christlike.[173]

But the good bishop had not visited the alleyways of *Studs Lonigan*, nor had he looked in upon the private lives of the robber barons or the more staid and letter-perfect thoughts of the merchants of State Street. However that may be, the good bishop was but expanding upon a philosophy acknowledged by the pillars of American society in the nineteenth century, and if, sometimes, his views corresponded with those of the more sober and forthright princes of property, there could be no great harm done. On the other hand, when similar views find their way into sermons, textbooks, and schools, and the gospel of wealth is broadcast as the truth of God, one might conclude with the boy in one of the lessons of the McGuffey readers that indeed God is good to make everybody so rich.[174]

In the great vision of Andrew Carnegie the duties of the man of wealth and the advantages of wealth to the poor are portrayed. The man of wealth should, argued Carnegie, become "the mere agent or trustee for his poorer brethren, bring to their service his superior wisdom, experience, and ability to administer, doing for them better than they would or could do for themselves."[175] By a great and noble stewardship and a magnificent gospel of wealth the problem of inequalities in wealth is to be

solved. "The laws of accumulation will be left free; the laws of distribution free. Individualism will continue, but the millionaire will be but a
trustee for the poor."[176] Such, concluded Carnegie, "is the true Gospel
concerning Wealth, obedience to which is destined some day to solve the
problem of the Rich and the Poor. . . ."[177] The heart of this doctrine
had been preached for almost half a century in the McGuffey readers,
though in diluted and diversified forms. In the editions following Appomattox the doctrine grows in purity and strength, until, in the great edition of 1879, the gospel of wealth, the stewardship of great riches, and the
ethic of thrift, industry, and hard labor attain their clearest expression.
But of all the men of wealth with which America has been blest, those
who were reared on the McGuffey readers seem most likely to remember
their responsibilities and duties to the poor as the great guardians and
trustees of wealth.

However much the McGuffey readers may have justified themselves by
reminding the great stewards of wealth that their stewardship implied
duties as well as rights, in accordance with the Pauline doctrine, it is clear
that in the Gilded Age, as in the age of Jackson, the McGuffey readers
fell quite easily into the basic strategy of the business community. The
conservative cause had been buttressed by both the legal and the divine
orders, who had identified themselves with the natural order. Here we
find all the basic ideas of the old conservative synthesis polished up for
new and more vigorous service in the Gilded Age.

The conservative feared, above all else, the social radical, of whom it
was declared that there was,

no more mischievous person than the man who, in free America seeks to spread
. . . the idea that they (the working class) are wronged and kept down by somebody; that somebody is to blame because they are not better lodged, better
dressed, better educated, and have no easier access to balls, concerts, or dinner
parties.[178]

One justification of the "apparent" differences between the poor and the
great stewards lay in the identification of the divine and natural orders,
an identification that made possible a Christian appeal to the poor and
distressed to be satisfied with their lot and to trust to the hand of Providence for their protection. This theme runs through the entire series of
McGuffey readers. We see, for example, in the case of Little William,
who concluded that, "God is wise and good and has made everything for
the best";[179] and we saw it in the case of the poor boy who discovered that
"the poor, if they are but good, may be very happy. . . ."[180] But the
theme is more pronounced in a story from one of the readers of the 1879
edition. Harry at first felt very poor in comparison with his friend Johnny

who had much spending money and many toys. His uncle, Ben, however, depreciated the value of money in his eyes when he offered the boy large sums for parts of his body and for his dear aunt. When even a larger sum is proposed for the baby of the family, the boy realizes how wealthy he really is. After all, Harry concluded, "isn't God good to make everybody so rich?"[181]

The kind of argument that expresses itself in the theme that God made the poor man as well as the rich man,[182] an idea expressed as early as 1837 in the McGuffey readers and carried, in one form or another, throughout practically all other editions, comes to the surface again in the Gilded Age. Even in the eighties we find Henry Ward Beecher expressing the same idea, declaring that:

God has intended the great to be great and the little to be little. . . . I do not say that a dollar a day is enough to support a working man. But it is enough to support a man! Not enough to support a man and five children if a man insists on smoking and drinking beer. . . . But the man who cannot live on bread and water is not fit to live.[183]

The alliance between religion and property was not dead.

The defense of *laissez faire* and established institutions reached over even into the halls of the universities. Even the great mind of William Graham Sumner believed "that the social order is fixed by laws of nature precisely analogous to those of the physical order. The most that man can do is by his ignorance and conceit to mar the operation of the social laws."[184] And social legislation, any attempt at a collective solution of the problems of society was, he declared, an effort to cure poverty "by making those who have share with those who have not."[185] Even those in the highest university positions, like Paul Elmer More, were willing to argue that "the rights of property are more important than the right to life."[186]

The basic ideas of the older conservative synthesis, then, found new uses in the Gilded Age. The doctrine of stewardship, the ethic of thrift, hard labor, and industry, the identification of the divine and moral orders, and the divine right of property,—the foundations on which the alliance between religion and conservatism had been built—all found their way, in one form or another, into the McGuffey readers. This remarkable correspondence between the basic ideas of the McGuffey readers and the basic ideas of the conservative synthesis can only be explained in terms of what must have been a widespread acceptance of these beliefs. It is the thesis of this inquiry that the widespread acceptance of the basic ideas of the conservative synthesis may be partly attributed to textbooks like the McGuffey readers which strengthened the conservative cause. This cause, as we have seen, was also the cause of judges, clergymen, educators, and men of property. The great alliance between religion and conservatism was indeed a powerful force in making the American mind, for the "combination of judges, clergymen and men of property seemed invincible."[187]

VII

If the religion found a place in alliance with conservative politics, it also played a part in the expansion of the American sphere of commercial and religious influence. The spirit of the missionary movement was caught by Bishop Heber, who found that though in Ceylon "Every prospect pleases and only man is vile," the fault lay with the Christians for not converting the heathen.[188] We must not deny the children of nature the light from heaven, argued Bishop Heber:

> Can we whose souls are lighted,
> With wisdom from on High,
> Can we to men benighted
> The Lamp of Life deny?[189]

In a similar spirit of missionary zeal Bishop Doane had cried:

> Fling out the banner! Heathen lands
> Shall see from far the glorious sight,
> And nations crowding to be born
> Baptize their spirits in its light.[190]

And in the McGuffey readers we find the universal spirit:

> Bow down thy soul in prayer;
> Nor ask for other sign,
> That God is everywhere;
> The viewless spirit, He—immortal, holy, blest—
> Oh, worship him in faith, and find eternal rest.[191]

While religious conferences were sometimes split over the issue of whether or not the unenlightened heathen might be saved after death, or whether if preaching proved unsuccessful the heathen might be led to hell, the general spirit and tone of the denominations was missionary and proselytizing.[192] Missionaries were as far afield as India, China, and the Mediterranean. In the Sandwich Islands (Hawaii) missionaries arrived in time to save the heathen native (and American trade) from going to hell.[193] When the first missionary efforts were crowned with success, many remained on the islands and gained financial and economic control.[194] Even great Mr. Webster recognized the achievements of the devout missionaries by proposing that the islands lay within the American sphere of influence.[195]

Of the Christian blessings of these imperialistic enterprises, young readers and their parents were apprised in the McGuffey readers. A story in one of the early editions relates the activities of the missionaries at the Sandwich Islands (Hawaii), recounting the blessings that have come to the native as the result of the splendid work of the American missionaries. American sailors, the McGuffey readers tell us, docked in a port of the Sandwich Islands on a Sunday, and they are surprised to see throngs of natives attending church. All this is the result of the splendid missionary work of the Americans; for, "it seemed," the reader tells us, "even while I gazed, that the majesty of that Power might be seen rising and erecting to itself a throne, permanent, and as glorious, in the hearts of these but late utterly-benighted and deeply-polluted people."[196]

The Calvinistic conception of the unregenerate who must be saved is clearly implicit in the description of these "late utterly-benighted and deeply-polluted people." The depth of the impression, continued the narrator, "arose from the irresistable conviction that the spirit of God was there: it could have been nothing else."[197] The spiritual advantages of the missionary effort are made clear for the uninformed:

> The simple appearance and yet Christian deportment of that obscure congregation, whom I had once known, and at no remote period, only as a set of rude, licentious, and wild pagans, did more to rivet the conviction of the divine origin of the Bible, and of the holy influences by which it is "accompanied to the hearts of men, than all the arguments, and apologies, and defences of Christianity I ever read.[198]

VIII

In addition to the missionary spirit, the gospel of wealth, the doctrine of stewardship, and the ethic of thrift, industry, and hard labor, one finds a pattern of ideas which seem to have no other purpose than the strengthening of religious conviction. The earliest stories selected for the readers were chosen in the hotbed of evangelical Christianity on the Middle Border, and yet the temper of those stories is that of simple piety and earnest conviction rather than that of rivivalist enthusiasm. The German editions, for example, carried the following bits of pious verse:

> *Gott ist mein Loos und mein Theil.*
> *Er gab mir den Leib und die Seele.*
> *Er zählt mein Haar auf meinen Haupte.*
> *Gott ist die Liebe. Wir lieben den guten Gott.*[199]

O Kind, dein Herz sei stets mit Gott,
Es sei nich falsch, so betest du:
Forsch' in mir, o mein Gott
Und zeige mir mein Herz.[200]

Other lessons taught that the righteous are never forsaken. In the lesson of the widow of Pine Cottage, for example, the lonely widow is described as being hopeful of the return of her long-lost son. He returns, and her trust in God is justified. "God, who sent manna from Heaven," she exclaims, "can provide for us as he did for Israel."[201] Moreover, Catherine Beecher, in a lesson in the *Eclectic Fourth Reader* enjoined children to remember that the rule that "thou shalt love the Lord thy God with all thy heart, and thy neighbor as thyself," is the infallible directory to our highest happiness.

The happiness secured by sympathy in the happiness of others, by being the cause of good to others, and by a course of conscious rectitude, as a matter of course, is best secured by a mind, which is living to fullfil the object of existence, and is employing every energy in promoting happiness.[202]

Miss Beecher's views are represented quite generously in the early editions of the McGuffey readers, and become unusually significant in connection with the religious and social orientations she inherited from her father. In the sweep of democratic forces and the extension of the franchise to the common man in almost every state, both Lyman and Catherine Beecher saw a threat to established institutions.[203] The view that education provides the bulwark and safeguard of republican institutions against the lower orders of society moved Catherine Beecher to write that,

the education of the common people, then, who are to be our legislators, jurymen, and judges, and to whom all our dearest interests are to be entrusted, this is the point around which the wisest heads, the warmest hearts, the most powerful energies should gather, for conservation, for planning, for unity of action, and for persevering enterprise.[204]

These views, taken together, add up to more than a single-minded enthusiasm for either religion or education, and may confirm the judgment of educators of the middle decades who argued for the support of commerce and industry in the cause of the common schools because, as they said, a workman imbued as a child in the common schools with thrift, honest, and obedience could always be counted on to work "more steadily and cheerfully, and, therefore, more productively, than one who, when a child, was left to grovel in ignorance and idleness."[205] Without establishing any direct relationship between the latter statement and the social and moral ideas in the McGuffey readers, one can nevertheless say that the McGuffey readers were indeed capable of imbuing children with the virtues so desirable to industry.

Consider, for example, the conception of God suggested by some of the verses of the German editions:

> Wie glänzt die Sonn so hell!
> So hell glänzt Gottes Aug!
> Er sieht dich, wo du bist.
> Gott hört auch, was du red'st
> Er weiss selbst, was du denkst.
> Er sieht dir im dem Herz.[206]

Or such a conception of death:

> Then for the living be the tomb,
> And for the dead, the smile;
> Engrave oblivion on the tomb
> Of pulseless life and dead bloom;
> Dim is such glare, but bright the gloom
> Around the funeral pile.[207]

In a selection from Dickens, "Death of Little Nell," the schoolmaster reminds his auditors that it is not "in *this* world that Heaven's justice ends." Moreover, think what this world is,

compared with the world to which her young spirit has winged its early flight, and say, if one deliberate wish, expressed in solemn tones above this bed, could call her back to life, which of us would utter it?[208]

As for the character of Christ, "The morality he taught was the purest, the soundest, the sublimest, the most perfect that had ever before entered into the imagination, or proceeded from the lips of man."[209] This is the character boys should hold as their ideal, and each boy is reminded that, "If you have done anything during the day that is wrong, ask forgiveness of God and your parents,"[210] and, "If you have spoken unkind words to a brother or sister, go and ask forgiveness."[211] These are indeed fine qualities, and that which must be avoided if the qualities of a righteous character are not to be soiled is the use of bad words. "The Bible says that you must not use bad words; and you must mind what the Bible says, for it is God's book."[212]

The virtue of temperance and the vice of intemperance we shall note again in another chapter, but it is interesting to observe here the blessings that would flow to all society were intemperance to be stamped out:

What a relief, how delightful it would be, to turn from the awful and horrid past, to the pure, peaceful, and happy future, to see the springs of life, and feeling, and intelligence renewed on every hand; health, industry, and prosperity glowing around us; the altars of domestic peace and love rekindled in every family; and the religion of the Savior presented with a fair field for its celestial action.[213]

In view of these sentiments, one cannot help concluding with the poet, Cowper, in one of the lessons of *McGuffey's Rhetorical Guide*, that:

> The Pulpit
> The Pulpit, . . .
> Must stand acknowledged, while the world shall stand,
> The most important and effectual guard,
> Support, and ornaments of virtue's cause.[214]

It was as the effectual guard, support, and ornament of virtue's cause that the McGuffey readers played their part in the formation of the value system of the average American in the nineteenth century. In promoting the cause of virtue the readers appeal to sceptics and blasphemers not to deny the poor and the outcast the benefits of religious assurance. In a poem entitled the "Consolation of Religion to the Poor," one finds a theme much in evidence throughout practically every edition of the readers.

> There is a mourner, and her heart is broken;
> She is a widow; she is old and poor;
> Her only hope is in the sacred token
> Of peaceful Happiness when life is o'er;
> She asks not wealth, nor pleasure, begs no more
> Of her redeemer. Skeptics! would you pour
> Your blasting vials on her head, and blight
> Sharon's sweet rose, that blooms and charms her being's night.[215]

Though the poetry is hardly convincing as poetry, the tenor of the arguments must have given pause even to the most hardened sceptic. Who, then, would deny the same assurance to a child?

> Fear not, fear not, little ones;
> There is in heaven an eye,
> That looks with tender fondness down
> On all the paths you try.
> A little child who loves to pray,
> And read his Bible too,
> Shall rise above the sky one day,
> And sing as angels do.
> Look up, dear children, see that star,
> Which shines so brightly there;
> But you shall brighter shine by far,
> When in that world so fair;
> A harp of gold you each shall have,
> And sing the power of Christ to save.[216]

And who could deny the little boy at Rugby the courage to do right? One of the stories, an adaptation from Thomas Hughes, tells how a little boy had the courage to do what was right although reviled and laughed at. Albert says his prayers before going to bed. Tom Brown defends him and remembers his own broken promise to do the same. From then on more and more boys are seen to say their prayers every night.

The lesson that he who has conquered his own coward spirit has conquered the whole outward world; and that other one which the old prophet learned in the cave at Mount Horeb, when he hid his face, and the still small voice asked, "What doest thou here Elijah?"—that however we may fancy ourselves alone on the side of good, the King and Lord of Men is nowhere without his witnesses.[217]

In a similar manner, the story of the alarm clock explains how a lady who kept an alarm clock got so used to it that she had to discover other means of getting up on time. The moral of the lesson lies in the analogy between the alarm clock and the human conscience. "But if we allow ourselves to do what we have some fears may not be quite right," explains the author, "we shall grow more and more sleepy, until the voice of conscience has no longer power to wake us."[218] The voice of conscience is, however, the voice of the Moral Governor of the universe, "who sits in the highest heaven, and pours out his fulness on the whole subordinate domain of nature and of providence."[219] It is He who provides "for the wants of every family, and watches every sick bed, and listens to the complaints of every sufferer."[220]

The character of the true Christian is presented in the lesson of George, who resists the temptation to do evil. George was goaded by two older boys to throw a snowball at the schoolroom door. He is too fearful of their censure and of the reputation of a coward which he will receive if he does not throw the snowball. In his fear of public censure George threw the snowball and was whipped for his folly and cowardice. "There will be occasions," the lesson concludes, "in which it will require a severe struggle to preserve your integrity; but ever remember that if you would do any good in the world, you must possess this moral courage." Moreover, "Without possessing this trait of character, to some considerable degree, no one will ever become a Christian."[221] This is the courage required to resist temptation. "It is hard to resist at the time, but it is far better, far nobler, to do what is right, however painful it may be; and in the end it will be far happier for all concerned."[222]

In a lesson on the sparrow and the bee we learn that:

> 'Twas God who taught them all the way,
> And gave them all their skill;
> And teaches children, when they pray,
> To do his holy will.[223]
> Pray ere yet the dark hours be,
> Lift the heart, and bend the knee.[224]

A poem of Christian light and hope tells us:

> If all our hopes and all our fears
> Were prisoned in life's narrow bound;
> If, travelers through this vale of tears,
> We saw no better world beyond;
> Oh, what could check the rising sigh?
> What earthly thing could pleasure give?
> Oh, who would venture then to die?
> Oh, who could then endure to live.[225]

In "A Picture of Human Life" we get a similar lesson:

Remember, my son, that human life is the journey of a day. We rise in the morning of youth, full of vigor and full of expectation. . . . In a short time we remit our fervor. . . . We then relax our vigor, and resolve no longer to be terrified with crimes at a distance, but rely upon our own constancy, and venture to approach what we resolve never to touch . . . temptation succeeds temptation. . . . We entangle ourselves in business, immerse ourselves in luxury, and rove through the labyrinths of inconstancy, till darkness of old age begins to invade us, and disease and anxiety obstruct our way. We then look back upon our lives with horror, with sorrow, and with repentance; and wish, but too often vainly wish, that he had not forsaken the paths of virtue.[226]

These few examples are but a small portion of those that could be cited, but perhaps enough of this pattern has been exposed to suggest the nature of the rest. Of the ideas embodying religious conviction, and seemingly designed for this end, there is an overwhelming number. But the general theme of the majority of ideas which fall within this religious pattern could be summarized in the following verse:

> Remember, child, remember,
> That God is in the sky,
> And that he looks on all we do
> With an ever wakeful eye.[227]

Even the oversoul could be comforted with the thought that, "All infractions of love and equity in our social relations are speedily punished. They are punished by fear."[228] Though fear be the punishment for all infractions of love and equity, it is clear that, "The law of nature is, Do the thing, and you will have the power; but they who do not do the thing have not the power."[229] It could not easily be imagined that the struggle for power might itself be the cause of the infractions of love and equity. This part of the relation between morals and power the compensated oversoul of New England could not understand.

IX

These religious convictions played an important role in the alliance of religion and conservatism. The great clerical and judicial synthesis worked out in the middle decades of the nineteenth century formed the framework on which the apostles of property and conservatism rested the reactionary defense. The alliance of religion and politics to preserve property and established institutions and to build a wall of defense against the inroads of radical democracy drew into its vortex all those who, under the guise of religious conviction, hedged property with divinity and made the acquisition of wealth a moral duty imposed by the decree of a sovereign God. The basic framework of the conservative defense, as we have seen, rested on the doctrine of stewardship, the sanctity of property, the ethic of industry, labor, and thrift, and the divine right of acquisition. In addition, however, the identification of the moral and judicial orders as issuing from a Moral Governor provided both a natural and a supernaturalistic basis for the conservative arguments.

These basic ideas of the great conservative and religious synthesis were uncovered in the McGuffey readers. The strength of the religious conviction and moral enthusiasm in the readers made it inevitable that the influence of the pattern of ideas be thrown into the hands of conservative politics and the guardians of public morals. The compilers of the readers were probably innocent of any political motive in collecting the stories and lessons which went into the readers, and the pattern of ideas contained in those lessons and stories was in widespread acceptance throughout practically the whole of the nineteenth century. It cannot be said, therefore, that the McGuffey readers consciously supported any political cause; but all the basic ideas of the great conservative and religious synthesis were there, and there was nothing else in the readers which could subtract substantially from the conservative cause. The place given to religious sentiments and moral convictions made it somewhat inevitable, that, should any projected alliance between religion and conservatism in politics materialize during the period of the popularity of the readers, the influence exerted by the readers would be thrown on the conservative side.

In the present chapter, therefore, we have examined the pattern of ideas with reference to the alliance between religion and property, and we have noted that the McGuffey readers would, to say the least, take nothing from the conservative cause. In the age of Jackson, as we saw, that alliance was rather clearly drawn, but after Appomattox the ideas basic to the conservative cause were so widely held that it was difficult to draw any precise line between proponents of the right or left. But in the Gilded Age the surge of industrialism brought the differences once more into the open, and the great gospel of wealth which was erected as the conservative defense left little to be desired from the point of view of the older conservative generations. But even in the Gilded Age there was a remarkable correspondence between the basic ideas of the conservative defense and those of the McGuffey readers. In part, this may be attributed to the fact that the American textbook can hardly be expected to make common cause with radicals and progressives. On the other hand, strict neutrality in such basic ideas is well-nigh impossible; and perhaps in their endeavor to be neutral in matters of politics the compilers of the McGuffey readers, with no other thought than that of exercising a healthy moral influence on the younger generations, played into the hands of those who had a sunny room in the social edifice and desired to sing heartily the song of things-as-they-are.

However that may be, it is clear that the morality and religion found in the McGuffey readers were those of the overwhelming majority of Americans in the nineteenth century, and that in exerting their influence in matters of religion and morality the McGuffey readers called many back to that stricter piety and sharper morality known only to the older generations. In the cause of religious toleration, as we saw in the case of the Catholic question, the readers performed nobly, speaking with liberality on the subject of toleration and decency. With respect to matters of religious and racial tolerance, with respect to simple piety and healthy morals, the McGuffey readers were, and are, supreme. That this strong emphasis on religious conviction and moral enthusiasm ultimately played into the hands of conservatism and reaction in politics, and ultimately strengthened the influence of conservative arguments, was hardly the fault of the readers, but was rather inevitable in an age that found the pattern of ideas in the McGuffey readers so widely accepted in the system of values of nineteenth century America.

4

The Morality of the Middle Class

THE RISE of the middle class and the development of middle class ideals has already received the attention of judicious historians. Those who have seen the close connection between the rise of capitalism and the development of the Protestant ethic of thrift, industry, and hard labor have pointed out how the alchemy of history converted many of the ideals of the great Christian heritage into the morality of the middle class. Others have pointed out that the ruling ideas of any age are the ideas of the ruling class. Though these formulae do not work out with precision in the case of American civilization, historians have made it abundantly clear that American civilization, even with its liberalisms and democrats, is interpenetrated with middle class ideals. How the subtle conversion of older Christian ideals into a morality suited to the middle class came about is hardly within our province here; but it is clear to anyone who examines a textbook like the McGuffey readers that the ideals of the middle class are at the very core of our civilization.

I

Poor Richard's philosophy has flourished mightily among us, and the urge to labor in God's vineyard has carried us far on the road to acquisition. An older Christian heritage our Calvinist forebearers converted into the Protestant ethic of thrift and labor, and our middle class predecessors fitted into a convenient morality. The good English Puritan Richard Baxter told us that, "You may labor in that manner as tendeth most to your success and lawful gain, for you are bound to improve all your talents. . . ."[1] There is no excellence without great labor, the McGuffey readers tell us;[2] and we must get a liberal education in the way of chores.[3]

"If God show you a way in which you may lawfully get more than in an-other way, if you refuse this and choose the less gainful way, you cross one of the ends of your calling, and you refuse to be God's steward."[4] Thus was the gospel of acquisition condoned as the chore of God.

It is not surprising, then, to find the McGuffey readers insisting that "God Blesses the Industrious."[5] If we are to carry out the will of God, we must realize that, "Every individual mind he brings into existence, is placed where little can be obtained by ignorance or torpidity, but much by skill and labor."[6] An older edict from heaven admonished us to be "wholly taken up in diligent business of your lawful callings when you are not exercised in the more immediate service of God";[7] for "God has strictly commanded work to all."[8] In the McGuffey readers it was found that:

> We have many pretty descriptions given us of nature and her simple children, sometimes by novelists, but oftener by those falsifying gentry, the poets, who never knew how to keep to plain matters of fact; accordingly, it is very fasci-nating in great rhymes, to have a picture set before us, of nature spontaneously providing for her favorite offspring. . . . Such is, always, and under every cli-mate, the condition of those who do not harken to the voice of the Almighty Benevolence, saying, "Arise and labor."[9]

Not only has the edict to labor been received from the Almighty Be-nevolence, but America is particularly suited for the unleashing of the God-given energies of men. "Neither theoretically or practically, in this country," argued Francis Bowen, is there any obstacle to any individual's becoming rich, if he will, and almost to any amount that he will. . . ."[10] If God has provided such abundant opportunities for the display of en-ergy and talent, "How is it possible, indeed, that the poor should be ar-rayed in hostility against the rich, when . . . the son of an Irish coach-man becomes the governor of a State, and the grandson of a millionaire dies a pauper?"[11]

Moreover, we have the advice of a successful Boston merchant who has risen to the summit and abundantly displays the virtues of the middle class:

> The steps from the foot to the summit are not many, but each has its name which must be distinctly known to all who would seek to climb. The first step is faith, and without this none can safely rise; the second, industry; the third, per-severance; the fourth, temperance; the fifth, probity; and the sixth, indepen-dence.[12]

No wonder the McGuffey readers would insist that the "education, moral and intellectual, of every individual, must be, chiefly, his own work . . . we give their final shape to our own characters, and thus become, emphatically, the architects of our own fortune."[13] There is the story of the boy of whom it was said:

He would gladly do all the work if somebody else would do the chores, he thinks; and yet I doubt if any boy ever amounted to anything in the world, or was of much use as a man, who did not enjoy the advantages of a liberal education in the way of chores.[14]

An interesting story of a farmer who died leaving his sons a "treasure" which they hastily sought illustrates the thoroughness and subtleness with which the ethic of labor was propounded to the young. After searching everywhere for the treasure, the sons tore up the ground, making it easy to grow crops, but they found no "treasure." Finally, one of the sons concluded, "I am sure, at least, that we have found out this, that *industry* is itself a *treasure*."[15] Significant, too, is the following bit of verse:

Work, work, my boy, be not afraid;
Look labor boldly in the face;
Take up the hammer or the spade,
And blush not for your humble place.[16]

These admonitions to the young seem rather to overlook the fact that in the very year they were published the United States census recorded the fact that a million children from ten to fifteen years of age were engaged in gainful work in factories and sweatshops.[17] But evidently they are the continuation of the theme begun in the earliest editions, when most boys and girls labored in the family units of economy of farm and field. However that may be, the theme grows in strength throughout all editions, and the editions corresponding to the Gilded Age, when indeed the problem of child labor was beginning to occupy the attention of humanitarians,[18] is extremely strong on the blessings of hard labor.[19] It must be remembered, however, that the blessings of labor were not the exclusive discovery of the seventies and eighties, but rather stem from an older Protestant and Calvinist heritage.

The view of Mark Hopkins that the instinct of acquisitiveness does most, in the long run, for public institutions was a view that had the whole-hearted support of the McGuffey readers. Hopkins' argument was that:

As men now are, it is far better that they should be employed in accumulating property honestly, to be spent reasonably, if not nobly, than that there should be encouraged any sentimentalism about the worthlessness of property, or any tendency to a merely contemplative or quietistic life, which has so often been either the result or the cause of inefficiency or idleness.[20]

It was the considered view of the McGuffey readers that labor was a virtue and idleness a vice, and that when one slights his tasks "you hurt yourself more than you wrong your employer."[21] It follows, therefore, that by "honest service you benefit yourself more than you help him."[22] The father who told his children that, "it was not *right*, that the *diligent* should give up the fruit of their labor to feed the idle,"[23] was only suggesting the wider implications of rugged individualism which Mark Hopkins had seen so clearly. In its wider implications the morality of the middle class touched at every point the struggle that was going on in the social conscience of nineteenth-century America.

II

The social conscience of the middle class found adequate explanations for the unequal distribution of wealth in the era of Jackson, for the Jacksonian revolution had forced into discard the frank realism of earlier conservatives who had coolly explained, with Hamilton, that the community divides itself into the few and the many, that the "first are rich and well-born, the other the mass of the people. . . ."[24] The Jacksonian revolution in political values had necessitated dropping these frank Hamiltonian premises if the cause of conservative politics were to prosper. Thus came the great Whig counter-reformation in which the forces of religion, property, and the judiciary were mobilized to restrain the radical Jacksonian democrats.[25] This new alignment of power, as we have seen, was in reality the resuscitation of an earlier alliance between religion and conservatism, which had found uses in the election of 1800. But the triumph of Jackson made necessary a revision of the premises of Hamiltonian politics, while the Whigs continued to work toward the old Federalist objectives.[26]

This new conservative synthesis, as we saw in the last chapter, was forged from a renewed alliance of property, religion, and the courts. Part of the conservative strategy required the rationalization of poverty and the great inequalities of wealth. In this scheme the clergy proved invaluable, for men like Bishop Wainwright could declare that religion "recognizes and sanctions the principle of inequality in the distribution of wealth among men . . . to be acquiesced in as a permanent condition of society."[27] And Reverend Hubbard Winslow found himself convinced: "That there should be an inequality in the conditions of men, as there is in all the other works of providence, is clearly wise and benevolent ordinance of heaven."[28] This type of strategy led conservative judges to declare, like Peter Thacher, that:

The diversity of poverty and riches is the order of Providence. . . . Why are not all the flowers of the field equally beautiful and fragrant? Why are not all the fruits of the earth equally rich and wholesome? And why towers the oak in grandeur to heaven, while the shrub at its base is trodden under feet? Will vain regrets, and still vainer discontent change the course of nature?[29]

All this we saw in connection with our examination of religion and the conservative tradition; but there were still other ways in which the conservative cause was fostered and the social conscience quieted through the morality of the middle class. Certainly related to the strategy of neo-federalism, conservatism, and Whiggery in politics was the strategy of identifying the interests of the working and the wealthy classes. Typical of the middle class claims of conservatism was that of Dr. Robert Hare, who declared that:

Never was an error more pernicious, than that of supposing that any separation could be practicable between the interests of the rich and the working classes. However selfish may be the disposition of the wealthy, they cannot benefit themselves without serving the labourer.[30]

Closely related to this strategy was the argument of the McGuffey readers that though one should miss wealth and success in the climb to the top, he could nevertheless count it among his blessings that he had attained a "noble and beautiful character, which is not only the best of possessions in this world, but also is about all you can expect to take with you in the next."[31] It follows from this argument, as we have seen, that, "By slighting your tasks you hurt yourself more than you wrong your employer."[32] Moreover, "a man may be poor in purse, yet proud in spirit."[33] It is clear that not wealth but good will and a noble character are the most desirable worldly goods,

when you have gained millions, you may yet be poorer than when you had nothing; and it is that same reckless ambition which has brought many a bright and capable boy, not to great estate at last, but to a miserable failure and disgrace; not to a palace, but to a prison.[34]

The argument that if you slight your tasks you harm yourself more than your employer was paralleled by the argument of Calvin Colton that, "The blow aimed at the moneyed capitalist strikes over on the head of the laborer, and is sure to hurt the latter more than the former."[35] This is the great theory of mutual dependence which conservatives worked out in the decades of Jacksonian democracy, and from it has come much of the conservative argument even in our own day. And it follows from that argument that while one must be industrious because, as we have seen, God blesses the industrious, one must, nevertheless, stick to one's job; or, as the McGuffey readers have it, "stick to your own bush."[36] In that story a young man sticks to the business he has selected for a life career and is rewarded by being taken into partnership.

When I had a good place and was getting on well, I was not willing to leave it and spend days or weeks in trying to find a better place. When other young men said, "Come with us, and we will find you something better to do," I shook my head, and stuck to my bush. After a while my employers took me into partnership with them in their business.[37]

In addition to this success psychology, the conservative cause seemed aided by the flood of books depicting the lot of the rich as wearisome, tiring, and harassed, in stark contrast to the carefree lot of the workers.[38] Channing buttressed the cause greatly with his argument that the hardships of the working class were exaggerated; indeed, wrote this great preacher, "That some of the indigent among us die of scanty food is undoubtedly true, but vastly more in this community die from eating too much than from eating too little."[39] Such is precisely the point of a story in the McGuffey readers. Duhobret, a student of Albrecht Durer, after much labor and many years of hardship is rewarded by the wealth his paintings bring.

He became the master of a castle, sold it, and resolved to live luxuriously for the rest of his life, and to cultivate painting as a pastime. But, alas, for the vanity of human expectations. He had borne privation and toil; prosperity was too much for him, as was proved soon after, when an indigestion carried him off.[40]

Channing's claim that "many of our daughters are victims of *ennui*, a misery unknown to the poor, and more intolerable than the weariness of excessive toil,"[41] would hardly comfort those who shivered for want of clothes or those who saw the *bourgeois* dressed in their finest, anything but bored, as Channing had suggested. Nevertheless, we are cheered up from the sadness occasioned by these unjust distributions of wealth by the reflection that, as the McGuffey readers tell us, there may be a change in position:

> Lend a hand to one another
> In the daily toil of life;
> When we meet a weaker brother,
> Let us help him in the strife.
> There is none so rich but may,
> In his turn, be forced to borrow;
> And the poor man's lot to-day
> May become our own tomorrow.[42]

Moreover, we discover in story after story, the merchant is a good, kind, man. Such seems to be the point of the story in which a merchant, who was very fond of music, was asked by a poor widow to give her some assistance. She asked for five dollars. In the check the merchant put down fifty and sent her across the street to the bank to cash it. She took the check back to him and showed him the mistake: "I did make a mistake," the merchant told her. "I wrote fifty instead of five hundred. Give the poor widow five hundred dollars, for such honesty is poorly rewarded with even that sum."[43] Here, then, is the recurrent theme that honesty, integrity, truth, industry, thrift, and hard labor are virtues more to be desired than gold; yet the reward of such virtues is, in contradiction, the gold itself. The contradiction is found throughout the conservative arguments as in the McGuffey readers: the reward of virtue is gold, though gold itself is supposedly despised by those who seek to build a noble and beautiful character.

A second means by which the social conscience of the middle class relieved itself from the bludgeonings of obvious inequalities and injustices was the argument of reform from within, or, as Channing called it, "the elevation of the labouring classes." This elevation was, however, not an elevation of material condition. "It is not an outward change of condition," argued Channing. "It is not release from labour. It is not struggling for another rank. It is not political power. I understand something deeper. I know but one elevation of a human being, and that is Elevation of Soul."[44] This doctrine, a recent student has pointed out, "enabled men of good will to indulge an honest compassion for the working classes without facing the economic implications of the problem."[45]

This thesis the McGuffey readers apparently accepted.

There are no principles but those of religion, to be depended on in cases of *real distress;* and these are able to encounter the worst emergencies, and to bear up under all the *changes* and *chances* to which our lives are subject.[46]

Moreover, "a man may be poor in purse, but proud in spirit."[47] Perhaps this was the kind of elevation of soul that Channing sought in relieving the distressed and indigent classes of the population. Moreover, much of the distress of the community, the McGuffey readers say, is caused by irresponsible persons, both workers and business men, who do not know their business and whose souls must be elevated.

There is a class of people who are the pest of every community, workmen who do not know their trade, business men ignorant of the first principles of business. They can never be relied upon to do well anything they undertake. They are always making blunders which other people have to suffer for, and which react upon themselves. They are always getting out of employment, and failing in business. To make up for what they lack in knowledge and thoroughness, they often resort to trick and fraud, and become not merely contemptible but criminal.[48]

Thus the distresses of any community are to be laid at the foot of those few who do not work proficiently, honestly, and with the utmost diligence. "Legislation can do nothing," said one reformer. The fate of the masses must be left to "the justice and mercy of the employer."[49] The futility of listening to the social conscience when the demands of private property are involved is illustrated in a story of young Franklin. Ben made a dock out of some building stones that he knew were going to be used for a building nearby. The use of the stones is discovered and he is reprimanded, almost arrested. His father tells him about the danger of this freedom with other people's property. When young Franklin was asked, "what could induce you to take property which did not belong to you?" he replied:

Why, father . . . if it had been merely for my own benefit, I never should have dreamed of it. But I knew that the wharf would be a public convenience. If the owner of the stones should build a house with them, nobody would enjoy any advantage but himself. Now, I made use of them in a way that was for the advantage of many persons.[50]

But this argument did not meet with the approval of Ben's father. "My son," said Ben's father solemnly,

so far as it was in your power, you have done a greater harm to the public than to the owner of the stones. I do verily believe, Benjamin, that almost all public and private misery of mankind arises from a neglect of the great truth,—evil can produce only evil, that good ends must be wrought out by good means.[51]

The truth is that any attempt to bring convenience to the public by a violation of private property is a breaking of the sanctity of God's law which had provided stewardship of great wealth to some so that they may take care of the poor according to their own conscience.[52] By such strategy did the middle class compound its protective morality; and such a theory, writes a recent student "was most successful in relieving the conscience of the upper middle class."[53] Nothing could be more reassuring than the formula proposed by the McGuffey readers: *"God gives a great deal of money to some persons, in order that they may assist those who are poor."*[54]

III

This point of view was more than the philosophy of a few rich men. It was the moral code of a class which had converted the idealism of

Christianity into the ten commandments of the gospel of wealth, and it was more widely accepted in the nineteenth century than most of us imagine. In answer to those who bemoaned the fact that in 1890 the gathering of wealth in accordance with the Lord's injunction was somewhat more difficult than it had been two or three decades before, Andrew Carnegie replied:

Avenues greater in number, wider in extent, easier of access than ever before existed, stand open to the sober, frugal, energetic and able mechanic, to the scientifically educated youth, to the office boy and to the clerk—avenues through which they can reap greater successes than ever before within the reach of these classes in the history of the world. . . . The millionaires who are in active control started as poor boys, and were trained in that sternest but most efficient of all schools—poverty. . . . Congratulate poor young men upon being born to that ancient and honorable degree which renders it necessary that they should devote themselves to hard labor.[55]

This middle class faith was held by the overwhelming majority of Americans in the last three decades of the nineteenth century. No purer statement of its doctrines could be found than those in the McGuffey readers. A story entitled "Advantages of Industry," for example, tells of Charles Bullard who worked hard and successfully during his days in schools. His idle and careless classmate, George Jones, is amazed at the rewards Charles' industry brings him:

Many situations of usefulness and profit were opened to him, for Charles was now an intelligent man, universally respected. He is still a useful and happy man. He has a cheerful home, and is esteemed by all who know him. Such are the rewards of industry. How strange it is that any person should be willing to live in idleness when it will certainly make him unhappy. The idle boy is almost invariably poor and miserable; the industrious boy is happy and prosperous.[56]

These stories of success and reward for the industrious must have warmed the hearts of thousands of school boys working on farm or in factory. Like the Horatio Alger stories, the stories in the McGuffey readers taught the morality of the middle class, and taught, too, the rewards that come to him who lives up to the Protestant ethic of thrift, industry, honesty, hard labor, and acquisition. Moreover, for those who still were unmoved by the handsome rewards promised to those who followed the great ethic of industry, there was a conclusion similar to that of the "Advantages of Industry."

Does God notice little children in school? He certainly does. And if you are not diligent in improving your time, it is one of the surest evidences that your heart is not right with God.[57]

There was, then, the threat of punishment as well as the hope of reward to urge the young on in modelling their lives after the great stewards who, like Andrew Carnegie, were willing to promise, even as late as the nineties, that the avenues to wealth were still open to any who acquired the virtues of the middle class.

When the theme is taken up by the McGuffey readers, the impact of the lessons becomes overwhelming. Even a lesson entitled "The Intemperate Husband," which, one is ready to conclude, is a lesson condemning vice, is a thinly disguised lesson on the virtues of industry. "Habits of industry, which had begun to spring up in him, proved themselves to be without root."[58] The great danger of intemperance is that it destroys industry and diligence and is therefore in the catalogue of sins against the middle class. "Intemperance," the story concludes, "like the strong man armed, took possession of a soul that lifted no cry to God, and girded on no weapon to resist the destroyer."[59] Well might the Lord enter the struggle against evil and sin, the great destroyers of the virtues so dear to the great stewards of the middle class.

For those who weary of excessive toil and hardship there were stories like "The Discontended Pendulum," which stops out of boredom with its unending and unnoticed toil. The other parts of the clock convince it that it has only one swing to make at a time. "Thus," the story concludes,

in looking forward to future life, let us recollect that we have not to sustain all its toil, to endure all its sufferings, or encounter all its crosses at once. One moment comes laden with its own little burdens, then flies, and is succeeded by another no heavier than the last; if *one* could be borne, so can another and another.[60]

"Two men I honor, and no third," wrote Carlyle in one of the stories in the McGuffey readers. "First, the toil-worn craftsman, that with earth-made implements laboriously conquers the earth and makes her man's. . . . A second man I honor, and still more highly; him who is seen toiling for the spiritually indispensable; not daily bread, but the bread of life."[61] Well might man celebrate the powers of the stream:

> *Hurrah! Hurrah! the waters o'er*
> *The mountain's steep decline,*
> *Time, space, have yielded to my power,*
> *The world, the world is mine.*[62]

And Henry Bond, in one of the stories in the McGuffey readers, seemed to have been the boy who took the admonitions of Carnegie seriously. He was born to poverty, a fitting condition to develop true character in the eyes of Carnegie; but what was more, Henry was only ten years old when his father died, and found himself too poor to have the

books that he needed in school, so he went to bed wondering where he
could get the money. In the morning he found that it had snowed. By
shoveling the sidewalks for a few homes, he had the needed money. "Ah,"
said he, "it is an ill wind that blows nobody good."[63] From that time,
"Henry was always the first in all his classes. He knew no such word as
fail, but always succeeded in all he attempted. Having the 'will,' he always found the 'way.' "[64]

A similar story tells how "Poor Davy" was sad because the children
were laughing at his ragged clothes. The teacher gave him a plan to get
better ones. His family could not help him because his mother was a
widow and very poor. So poor Davy gathered beautiful flowers in the
woods and fields and sold them in the nearby city, making enough to
buy clothes. "He soon earned enough money to buy new clothes. Now
the sunshine and the bird's songs make him glad."[65] The stories of these
plucky lads were not only welcomed by the younger generation, but were,
in some cases, actually true. The theme that runs through many of these
stories of perserverance and industry is symbolized in the following bit
of doggrel:

> *Once or twice though you should fail,*
> > *Try, Try Again;*
> *If you would, at last, prevail,*
> > *Try, Try Again;*
> *If we strive, 'tis no disgrace,*
> *Though we may not win the race;*
> *What should you do in that case?*
> > *Try, Try Again.*
> *If you find your task is hard,*
> > *Try, Try Again;*
> *Time will bring you your reward,*
> > *Try, Try Again;*
> *All that other folks can do,*
> *Why, with patience, should not you:*
> *Only keep this rule in view;*
> > *Try, Try Again.*[66]

Not only persistence but punctuality is a virtue much esteemed in the
catalogue of the middle class. In one of the lessons we are given examples
of disasters that occurred when someone was behind time. Napoleon lost
at Waterloo because of Grouchy; a bank failed because the remittances
from the West came one boat too late. "It is continually so in life."

The best laid plans, the most important affairs, the fortunes of individuals, the
weal of nations, honor, happiness, and life itself are daily sacrificed, because
somebody is "behind time." There are men who always fail in whatever they undertake, simply because they are "behind time." There are others who put off

reformation year after year, till death seizes them, and they perish unrepentant, because forever "behind time."[67]

One cannot avoid noticing that by this time the Christian moralism and the ideals of the middle class have become so interpenetrated that they can hardly be separated. Appeals for a moral reformation are linked with dire threats of those who have not developed the virtue of punctuality. On the whole, the resulting synthesis of Christian and middle class virtues was a new growth; it seemed a reconstruction of the body of the Christian tradition to fit the altered conditions brought about by industrial society. In the McGuffey readers this new synthesis of Christian and middle class ideals, however long ago it may have emerged, persists through all editions and all revisions.

How the new synthesis might assign a status for woman busy about her kitchen labors is apparently the point of the story of the little girl, Margery, who likes to look at nature, pure and serene outside the kitchen door. "O, mother, do let me live on the door-step! I don't like houses to stay in. What makes everything so pretty and so glad? Don't you like to wonder?"[68] But this kind of inquiring and wondering mind was apparently not approved in the catalogue of duties, for,

Margery's mother was a good woman. But then there was all the housework to do, and, if she had thoughts, she did not let them wander outside the kitchen door. . . . So she pinned the shawl around the child's neck again, and left her on the door-step, saying to herself, as she returned to her work, "Queer child! I wonder what kind of woman she will be!"[69]

On the other hand, the story of "John Carpenter" explains that John Carpenter did not like to buy toys that somebody else had made. He preferred the fun of making his own toys, and the "thought that they were his own work delighted him."[70] Contrasted with John was Tom Austin, who never thought "a toy worth anything unless it cost a great deal of money."[71] The conclusion to the story is significant:

Do you know what became of John? Well, I will tell you. He studied hard in school, and was called the best scholar in his class. When he left school, he went to work in a machine shop. He is now a master workman, and will soon have a shop of his own.[72]

In a similar manner, the story of the illiterate boy who was employed by a merchant illustrates how deeply the psychology of work and success had taken root. "It is well for us all to have work to do," the employer told his young apprentice. "It is bad for us not to work."[73] Then, interpenetrated with this advice on the virtue of hard labor is the advice that,

John, you must bear in mind that it was God who made you, and who gave you all that you have, and all that you hope for. . . . He sent His son, to show you his will, and to die for your sake. . . . He can tell all that you do, and all that you say, and all that is in your mind . . . ever seek this God, pray to him. . . . Keep his day, hear his word, and do his will. . . .[74]

The foundation of the American faith in individualism and independent enterprise unhampered by restraints from the state lies in this widespread acceptance of the middle class ideals of industry, thrift, and hard labor. The morality of the middle class, which Dr. Gabriel prefers to call the gospel of wealth, must not be thought of as the philosophy of a few wealthy individuals. Indeed, Dr. Gabriel insists:

Had the gospel of wealth been nothing but hypocrisy . . . it could scarcely have outlasted the century. It was, in fact, not merely the philosophy of a few rich men but a faith which determined the thinking of millions of citizens engaged in small enterprises. Its basic emphasis was upon the responsibility of the individual, confronting the hard uncertainty of life. The gospel of wealth explained the meaning of life with a metaphor that called life a testing period in which those selected for distinction must unite character with ability, and magnanimity with power. It was the philosophy which lay behind the private charity for which Americans of the Gilded Age became justly famous. It was an effort to carry the idealism and the moral code of Christianity and of the democratic faith into a rapidly developing capitalism.[75]

Most famous of all the stories stressing the virtue of hard labor is that of Hugh Idle and Mr. Toil, a story that has persisted from the earliest editions right up to the most recent.[76] Hugh ran away from school and met a kind fellow who shows him several taskmasters who all seem better at first than the tyrannical schoolmaster, Mr. Toil, but who later turn out to look like him and, indeed, to be his brothers. One is a farmer; one is a carpenter; and another is a soldier. Finally the man with whom he has toured the country brings him back home and, in his turn, appears to be another Mr. Toil. The description of Mr. Toil, the schoolmaster, by Nathaniel Hawthorne, is tolerably well written:

Those who knew him best affirmed that Mr. Toil was a very worthy character, and that he had done more good, both to children and grown people, than anybody else in the world. He had, however, a severe and ugly countenance; his voice was harsh, and all his ways and customs were disagreeable to our young friend, Hugh Idle.[77]

And so it was said of little Hugh Idle that he "had learned a good lesson, and from that time forward, was diligent at his task, because he now knew that diligence is not a whit more toilsome than sport or idleness."[78] One can only regret that the story of Hugh Idle and Mr. Toil is not in modern readers, for our modern Hugh Idle could well ponder the meaning of that story. Paralleling the story of Hugh Idle, however, is the story of an idle school boy who, later, when he had grown to manhood, had a fortune left to him.

> But he was too lazy to take care of it, and now he goes about the streets, begging his bread. He often wishes that he had been more attentive to his books, when young. But he can not live over again the time he has spent so badly, and he must be a poor ignorant fellow for the rest of his life.[79]

In a similar vein, one of the stories in the McGuffey readers repeats part of the tale about George Jones, who was expelled from his academy for not learning anything. Sometimes, it was said of him,

> he would make such ludicrous blunders, that the whole class would burst into a laugh. Such are the applauses an idler gets. He was wretched, of course. He had been idle so long, that he hardly knew how to apply his mind to study. All the good scholars avoided him; they were ashamed to be seen in his company. He became discouraged, and gradually grew dissipated. . . . This story of George Jones, which is a true one, shows how sinful and ruinous it is to be idle. Every child, who would be a Christian and have a home in heaven, must guard against this sin.[80]

Thus to the sanctity of judicial interpretation, to the theology of property, to the great synthesis of Christian and worldly interests was added the morality of the middle class. "Every child, who would be a Christian and have a home in heaven, must guard against this sin of idleness."[81] It is clear that God blesses the industrious, and that those who labor perform the noblest calling of man. Thayer expressed the same idea as late as 1880:

> It is quite evident . . . that religion requires the following very reasonable things of every young man, namely; that he should make the most of himself possible; that he should watch and improve his opportunities; that he should be industrious, upright, faithful, and prompt; that he should task his talents, whether one or ten, to the utmost; that he should waste neither time nor money; that *duty,* and not pleasure or ease, should be his watchword. And all this is precisely what we have seen demanded of all young men in reliable shops and stores. Religion uses all the just motives of worldly wisdom, and adds thereto those higher motives that immortality creates. Indeed, we might say that religion demands success.[82]

This code was far more than a mere cult of success; it was nothing less than the conversion of the Christian doctrine into a moral code befitting the growing power of capitalist economy. Beginning with *Poor Richard's Almanac,* joining with Emerson and the transcendentalists, and flowing out in the Gilded Age in a torrent of books, magazines, and newspapers, the doctrine of success by individual effort became so interpenetrated with the great Christian heritage that to be idle, or to sit on the door step observing the world of nature, was indeed to be questioned as a sin against God. That part of the synthesis of the Christian heritage and middle class ideals which we have called the morality of the middle class was abundantly in evidence in so universal a textbook as the McGuffey readers; and by the time of the Glided Age these readers were selling millions of copies. It was during the post-civil war decades, the seventies, eighties, and nineties, that the philosophy of the middle class was universalized. It was, perhaps, in expressing the hopes, the sentiments, and the convictions of nineteenth-century America that the McGuffey readers proved their inestimable worth.

However that may be, it is clear that a story like Henry, the boot-black, is direct from the pages of Horatio Alger and just as exciting to read. Henry was a good boy who was polite to his customers and took home his money to his poor parents. "He was so polite that gentlemen began to notice him, and to let him black their boots. The first day he brought home fifty cents, which he gave to his mother to buy food with."[83] Another story advises early rising, in the manner of Franklin:

> For God gives us daylight, dear sister, that we,
> May rejoice like the lark, and work like the bee.[84]

Still another lesson concerns "Frank and the Hour Glass." Frank is a very obedient young fellow, and very inquisitive, but not when he is told that he should stop asking questions. He learns of the hour glass, that it never stops, never hurries, never complains; it just goes on doing its little task of telling the time, and doing it accurately. The sands never hurry, never tire, "because they keep at work every minute. They do not stop to think how much they have yet to do and how long it will take them to do it."[85] In a similar manner, the story of the four MacNicols tells of four lads in a fishing village in the north of Scotland who, being left orphans by the drowning of their father, learned the "great lesson of self-help."[86] By hard labor and the scrupulous observances of the Lord's commandments the four boys built up a fishing business, their hauls growing from a basket to a boat-load.[87] Another story seems to follow the tradition of Aesop, though its argument cuts two ways in application. A fox sent several branches floating down the river past a flock of feeding ducks. After they became accustomed to the branches, he climbed on one himself and floated near enough to grab two for his dinner. "Right among the flock drifted the sly old fox, and, making quick snaps to right and left, he seized two fine young ducks, and floated off with them."[88] The fox, the lesson concludes, "must have had a fine dinner to pay him for his cunning and patient work."[89] It is difficult to decide whether the lesson is intended to warn the student of those who cunningly contrive plans to catch others, or whether, on the other hand, it is designed to encourage the child to "cunning and patient work." In any case, the sword is double-edged and cuts both ways.

IV

Page after page, lesson after lesson, the conviction grows that the virtues of the McGuffey readers are the virtues of the middle class, and that the McGuffey readers have so thoroughly integrated Christian and middle class ideals that they can hardly be distinguished. It is clear, for example, that we should not be wasteful, for wastefulness is almost as bad as unholiness. In one of the stories Ben saves the string from his package, while John cuts his. Later Ben uses his on a top and saves the day in an archery contest when his string breaks. "Ben's last arrow won the prize; and when the bow and arrows were handed to him, John said, 'How valuable that whipcord has been to you, Ben, I'll take care how I waste anything, hereafter.' "[90] Another story teaches the virtue of perserverance. A little boy becomes disgusted when he repeatedly fails to get his kite aloft, although aided by his sister and aunt. His aunt, however, succeeds in making him try again until finally the kite is kept up. "Yes, my dear children, I wish to teach you the value of PERSEVERANCE. . . . Whenever you fail in your attempts to do a good thing, let your motto be, TRY AGAIN."[91]

Labor is a great virtue as a means to happiness. Happiness consists in keeping busy. Such is the moral of a story of Mrs. Lord and her two girls. They have a quiet evening by the fireside, but they find that they have all been happier than the previous night when all had a livelier time of playing. The secret is that the work kept them busy and therefore happy. When one of the girls is unable to explain the secret of this happiness, the other, Katie, shouts: "I know! I know! It is because we have all been doing something useful tonight. We feel happy because we have been busy."[92] A lesson on Franklin reveals that the secret of his success has been his industry and temperance:

His youth had not been wasted in idleness, nor overcast by intemperance. He had been, all his life, a close and deep reader, as well as thinker; and by the force of his own powers, had wrought up the raw materials which he had gathered from books, with such exquisite skill and felicity, that he had added a hundred-fold to their original value, and justly made them his own.[93]

Moreover, honesty is the best policy. One of the lessons advises young men to be honest, not only in financial affairs but also in the sense of being honorable men. According to this lesson, if you seek the road to success, you should:

Let your first step, then, in that discipline which is to give you decision of character, be the heroic determination to be honest men, and to preserve this character through every vicissitude of fortune, and in every relation which connects you with society.[94]

However, circumstances do alter cases, as one lesson explains. For farmer Derby tells Scrapewell that he would like to borrow his horse and gets the most complete set of excuses on record why the horse is unobtainable. The fact that Derby was going to find out about a deal that would have netted Scrapewell fifty dollars changes the whole situation, and there follows the complete explanation of all the excuses. On the other hand, another story warns us to keep out of the reach of our enemies. It is the story of the fox who tries to convince the cock that he is now his friend. The cock replies that the same thing may not be true of the dogs running down the road in the fox's direction. The fox agrees that perhaps not all the animals have heard about the friendship among former enemies and hurries off to security in the woods. "This story shows us," the lesson concludes, "that when a known enemy wishes to seem a friend, there is most cause for us to keep out of his reach"; and, adds the author, hoping to convert a mere warning into a virtue, "that shame is likely to follow falsehood."[95] One is tempted to conclude that the leaders of the world who are now concerned about the atom bomb have read the story of the cock and the fox and agree with the fox that perhaps not all the animals have heard about the friendship among former enemies.

The contrast between Charlie and Rob illustrates a theme that occurs many times in the lessons. While both boys are splitting wood, Rob tells of his plans to become a bank clerk, starting out by keeping the books for his father's small business. Charlie, however, is skeptical of the value of such a small beginning, and prefers to dream of the time when he may get rich. "I'd like to sleep over the next ten years, and wake up to find myself a young man with a splendid education and plenty of money," Charlie tells Rob. But Rob has other ideas. "I don't care how I get rich, you know," he tells Charlie, "so that it's in an honest and useful way."[96] In concluding the lesson, the author asks, "Now, which of these boys, do you think, grew up to be a rich and useful man, and which of them joined a party of tramps before he was thirty years old?"[97]

Another lesson illustrates the dangers of truancy from school. James Brown became truant and told his mother that he had gone to school. One day some "bad boys" took him on the water in a boat, and they all nearly drowned. That taught him to go to school as he should, and to obey his parents. The situation in which James found himself is worthy of the attention of every prospective truant:

> Think of James Brown, the truant, at this time! He was far from home, known by no one. His parents were ignorant of his danger. He was struggling in the water, on the point of being drowned. Some men, however, saw the boys, and went out to them in a boat. They reached them just in time to save them from a watery grave. . . . James was very sorry for his conduct, and he was never known to be guilty of the same thing again. He became regular at school, learned to attend to his books, and, above all, to obey his parents perfectly.[98]

The importance of a well spent youth is a theme that recurs frequently enough to be noted. One of the lessons on this theme warns of the dangers that befall those who forget the ways of God and spend their early days in idleness and sin. In the dictionary of the middle class idleness and sin are synonymous, and a life of toil is a life that is holy.

> As spring is the most important part of the year, so is youth the most important period of life. Surely, God has a claim to our first and principal attention, and religion demands the morning of our days, and the first season, the spring of our lives: before we are encumbered by cares, distressed by afflictions, or engaged in business, it becomes us to resign our souls to God.[99]

Let us, then, take an example from the industrious bee:

> *Oh! we may get weary,*
> *And think work dreary;*
> *'Tis harder by far*
> *To have nothing to do.*[100]

Typical of the success stories is the lesson of Robert, who is forced to go to the store for a job when another boy who stole their last five cents made his mother cry. The owner of the store is touched, offers Robert a bit of money, but it is refused because the boy's mother would not like to have Robert beg. Then Robert is hired as a cash boy, and runs home with an advance on his salary. By such virtues are the poor rewarded. But for all those who are to become cash boys and workers in the counting houses there stands the lesson of "The Maniac" as a terrible and solemn warning to those who make mistakes in counting revenues. Conrad Lange, a collector of revenues in Berlin, made a mistake in his accounts. He said, "Once one is two." During the investigation he was imprisoned for two days; released, he went insane, repeating always, "once one is two." Accuracy is indeed a virtue prized by the counting houses and the collectors of great revenues.

This affecting story, whether true or untrue, obviously abounds with lessons of instruction. Alas! how easily is the human mind thrown off its "balance"; especially when it is stayed on *this world* only—and has no experimental knowledge of the meaning of the injunction of Scripture, to cast all our cares upon Him who careth for us, and who heareth the young ravens when they cry.[101]

An interesting story on peaches tells how a father gave his four sons each a peach. He then asked what they had done with them. The first had planted the seed of his. The second had eaten his and also some of his mother's peach. The third had taken the pit of his brothers peach and had eaten the kernel of it, then he sold his own peach. The fourth son had given his peach to a sick friend. To the first the father said, "Provide for the *future* by taking care of the *present*."[102] To the second the father said, "You have acted in a natural and childlike manner, as might be expected. There is still room enough in your life to learn wisdom."[103] To the third the father said, "It was prudent, but it was by no means natural act for children. I pray God, that you may not be a miser."[104] Concerning the fourth? "Charles was silent, but his mother embraced him with a tear in her eye."[105]

In another lesson, which is primarily a dialogue between Mary and Sarah, we learn the virtues of "keeping everything in its place."[106] While little Amy, in another lesson, was figuring out how much she would earn by picking berries for Mr. Thornton at 13 cents a quart, a group of enterprising boys set about the work, so that by the time Amy was ready with her decision the berries had all been picked. "Amy was a dear little girl," the lesson tells us, "but she was too apt to waste time in getting ready to do her tasks, instead of doing them at once as she ought."[107] Still another little girl was careless about her studies and would rather play than learn. When her father learned that she was doing poorly in the business of acquiring knowledge," instead of smiling at her, he turned away his head with a frown, and put her hand out of his, and turned from her, and went into another part of the garden."[108] Finally, however, Mary learned her lessons; "She was so pleased with the knowledge which she had thus gained, that she loved her father more than she had ever done, for having made her do what had given her, and might still give her so much pleasure."[109] Evidently there are lessons for parents as well as for children.

But many of the lessons turn on the theme of the proper conduct in the acquisition of wealth. One lesson, for example, warns that love of popularity generally leads men to do wrong as easily as right. We are told that we should do right, even if not immediately rewarded. Sudden riches generally leads to sudden ruin. "If it be admitted, then, that strict integrity is not always the shortest way to success; is it not the surest, happiest, and best?"[110] A bit of verse strengthens the virtue of hard labor:

> *Little child, now learn of me.*
> *Let thy youth the seed-time be. And,*
> *When wintry age shall come, richly*
> *Bear thy harvest home.*[111]

Not only hard work, however, but sticking to one's task is also an ingredient of success:

> *So little child, your duty do*
> *In cheerfullness all day;*
> *And you, like me, shall soon be blest*
> *With flowers upon your way.*[112]

The story of Casabianca, a boy of thirteen who stood on a burning deck rather than disobey his father, illustrates the virtue of obedience which good Christian children should display. The story is in the form of a poem, but is followed by this prose explanation of its moral: "But no voice of permission could come from the mangled body of his lifeless father; and the boy, not knowing that he was dead, would rather die than disobey."[113] It might be added, in passing that in refusing to disobey and remaining on the deck of the ship the boy was condemned to death in a watery grave. A closely related lesson tells how Mr. Rose took Edgar and Thomas Read out on the lake in a boat, and how, in violation of Mr. Rose's injunction to sit quietly, the children began to play, upsetting the boat. The lesson concludes: "Children should always be careful and quiet when they are in a boat on the water, and should obey what older people tell them."[114]

Even the lessons on intemperance return to the theme of virtuous industry. A lesson entitled "The Whiskey Boy," for example, relates how John's father taught him to drink whisky mixed with water and sugar. Soon he drank it "straight" and would not stop. He grew ugly and sore and was disliked by other boys. He ended up by dying in the poorhouse. "Oh, that there were no such thing as whisky," for whisky is the bringer of evil and destroys the virtue of industry, thrift, and hard labor.[115] Another lesson on intemperance entitled "Don't Take Strong Drink," explains that, "No little boy or girl should ever drink rum or whiskey, unless they want to become drunkards."[116] Moreover, the "Bible says that no drunkard shall inherit the kingdom of heaven."[117] But most important, "Whisky makes the happy miserable and it causes the rich to become poor."[118]

But the theme of idleness and its sinfulness is clearly the most recurrent in the whole series. There is, for example, the story of the idle school boy who, after a badly spent youth in school, "often wishes that he had been more attentive to his books, when young," for "he cannot live over again the time he has spent so badly, and he must be a poor ignorant fellow for the rest of his life."[119] Another lesson tells how John, a little idler, didn't like school or books and had no friends. On one very lonesome day John couldn't even get the animals to play with him because they all had something to do. This made him resolve to change his ways. "I see that all have something to do," concluded the little idler, "while I am idle and good for nothing. I am not fit company even for the animals."[120] And a poem about lazy Ned explains:

> Thus he would never take the pains
> To seek the prize that labor gains,
>   Until the time had passed;
> For, all his life, he dreaded still
> The silly bug-bear of up hill,
>   And died a dunce at last.[121]

Even the flight of an eagle to its young teaches the lesson of the determined spirit that will brook no obstacles to its path. Joseph, the boy in the lesson, watches an eagle carrying fish to its young. When some cruel men stone the bird to make it drop its catch, the bird returns to the sea to search for more food for its young. "Glorious bird!" shouts Joseph,

I will learn a lesson from thee today. I will never forget hereafter, that when the spirit is determined, it can do almost anything. Others would have dropped, and hung the head, and mourned over the cruelty of man, and sighed over the wants of the nestlings; but thou, by at once recovering the loss, hast forgotten all.[122]

But none of the tenderer virtues are in contradiction with the vigor, perseverance, and industry with which one pursues one's private goals. This theme is illustrated in the story of Fred, who cooly rescued a young girl from a blazing house. "It was no time for words," the lesson tells us, "but for instant, vigorous action."[123] Moreover, Fred "trusted in an arm stronger than his own, and silently sought help and guidance."[124] This brave deed, carried out with vigor and concern for others illustrates that "true manliness is in harmony with gentleness, kindness, and self-denial."[125] The same theme is illustrated in the case of George, the son of a poor, sick woman, who went to collect firewood for his mother. At dinner time he chanced to find ripe strawberries growing in the woods. He would have eaten them immediately, but he thought of his mother and decided to save them for her. Her gratitude and tears were infinitely more pleasing to him than the whole heap of strawberries.[126] The moral synthesis, then, does not deny the virtues of kindness, tenderness, and love.

The good Christian virtues of kindness, tenderness, and love are displayed by an unusual number of merchants and wealthy men in the stories of the McGuffey readers. Whether this attempt to present the merchant and the man of wealth as a good steward who is kind to the poor was an attempt to form such a picture of the merchant and man of wealth in the child's mind, or whether it was, on the other hand, an attempt to spur the wealthy with a reminder of the duties to the poor that God has laid upon His stewards, are questions which seem impossible to answer. But in the stories and lessons of the McGuffey readers the merchants and men of wealth perform their duties as stewards in the most rmarkable and sympathetic manner.

One story, for example, explains how Henry is forced to go into the streets of Philadelphia to beg for some money for his poor sick mother. Washington, as it later turns out, notices him, sends him for the doctor for his mother, and goes himself to the poor hovel and comforts the mother, leaving her a draft on his money for a considerable sum. We are given a picture of Henry, "The tears running fast down his cheeks, but nobody seemed to care; for although clean, Henry looked poor and miserable, and it is common for the poor and miserable to cry."[127] In explaining his miserable state to Washington, Henry says, "My father was a rich merchant of this city; but he became a bondsman for a friend, who soon after failed, and he was entirely ruined."[128] Let the children who read this story, concludes the lesson, "when they think of the great and good Washington, that he was not above entering the dwellings of poverty, carrying joy and gladness to the hearts of its inmates."[129]

In another story Mr. Lawrence, traveling by coach, discovers a poor little girl riding on the top of the coach, even though it is a cold and stormy night. He is touched further by her sad story, and finally decides to adopt her. In answer to the objections that, "she is a poor child, in charge of the master of a workhouse, and one does not know what she may have about her," Mr. Lawrence nobly replies: "Let her come in, at any rate, for poor or rich, she is equally sensible to cold, and no one, I am sure, who has a child of his own, can bear the idea of her being so exposed."[130]

Still another lesson tells how Julian lived in abject poverty with his father. His only possession was a rabbit which he loved dearly. The poor and wretched life Julian led made him very ill and his condition soon became grave. A rich man who lived in the negihborhood was greatly moved by Julian's plight and had the boy removed to his house where he restored him to health in a short time. He also clothed him and helped the father rise from his impoverished condition. Julian was so grateful that he felt he ought to repay the kind man in some way. Yet the only possession he could offer was his beloved rabbit. The gentleman was so touched by this gesture that he took Julian under his complete care, sending him to school, and buying his clothes and his books. To Julian's offer of the rabbit, the rich man replies, "We ought to be grateful to those who do us a kindness. But I do not wish to take from you your rabbit. Besides, I will do more for you than I have done."[131]

The theme of these lessons on stewardship was well stated by another lesson which made the point that one should, "Be thus ever ready to help the poor, and wretched, and distressed, and every year of your life will be to you a happy New Year."[132] The Christian duty of giving money to the poor was abundantly illustrated in the McGuffey readers, and perhaps they played a role in the great gifts of charity of the last three decades of the nineteenth century. However that may be, it is clear that the buying of books, particularly McGuffey readers, was likewise a duty laid upon rich and poor alike. The final lesson of one of the first readers contains a farewell note to the children, stressing their progress so far, and emphasizing the point that they are ready now for the second reader of the McGuffey series:

There are many children whose parents are too poor to send them to school. Do you not pity them? They can not have nice books, and learn to read them, as you do. Are not your parents kind to send you to school, and buy new books for you? Should you not try to please them? You must not waste time in school. Try always to know your lessons. If you are good, and try to learn, your teacher will love you, and you will please your parents. When you go home, you must ask for a New Second Reader.[133]

V

The morality of the middle class, then, was erected on the theory that the Lord had commanded that all good Christians should labor in the Lord's vineyard. It follows from that theory that those who refuse to labor and to acquire in accordance with the commandments of the middle class refuse the right to stewardship. In attempting to account for those who labored thriftily in the Lord's vineyard but who were unable to attain to God's holy stewardship, it was necessary to have recourse to the older Calvinist notion of the elect. Those who were the elect of God

were chosen for stewardship, the Calvinists had warned. It was not difficult to pass from this premise to Peter Oxenbridge Thacher's conviction
that, "The diversity of poverty and riches is the order of Providence."[134]
Nor, accepting this premise, could one deny Bishop Lawrence's conviction that, "Godliness is in league with riches. . . ."[135]

Moreover, one could believe that God had elected some for the responsibilities of holy stewardship, for while many failed, some climbed from
the lowest and humblest ranks of society to the highest pinnacle of financial success. John D. Rockefeller climbed from the heartless poverty of
the waif to the leadership of a great oil combination. James Farrell forged
for himself the virtues which carried him from humble labor to the presidency of the United States Steel Company. Henry Ford climbed from a
humble position paying two and a half dollars a week to leadership in
the automobile industry; and Julius Rosenwald lifted himself from ped-
dling small wares to the highest position in the mail-order business. Truly
God was on the side of the elect, and surely the Christian virtues formed
the character which resulted in these amazing successes.

The McGuffey readers accepted the premise that the Christian virtues
of thrift, labor, industry, honesty, punctuality, and good-will carried men
to the successes which daily could be witnessed by the humblest man. One
must keep these premises in mind in evaluating the amazing bulk of success literature which flooded America in the last three decades of the
nineteenth century, and they can not be overlooked in any explanation
of the McGuffey readers. All the virtues of success were taught in the Mc-
Guffey readers; the stories of success in many of the lessons rivaled those
of Horatio Alger; and the middle class virtues stressed in the McGuffey
readers were those stressed by many of the authors of succss literature.
The nature of these virtues has been admirably summarized by Professor
Curti who, writing of William Thayer, tells how Thayer, author of numerous books on success, in his life of James A. Garfield, *From the Log
Cabin to the White House,*

reminded his readers that Garfield, like Lincoln, had worked hard and improved
every moment of leisure by reading, and that he had become known for his industry, tact, perseverance, integrity, courage, economy, thoroughness, punctuality, decision, benevolence, and geniality. Such traits were indispensable for the
success which, Thayer never forgot to remind his readers, could be won only
through strict regard for morality and religion.[136]

This description of middle class virtues would be as accurate for the
McGuffey readers, with the additional note, perhaps, that the McGuffey
readers completed the middle class and Christian synthesis so thoroughly
that the Christian virtues can hardly be separated from those of the

middle class. Indeed, this great moral synthesis, though enjoined by the Puritans and Protestants, was the work of generations of Americans who achieved so striking an integration of Christian and middle class virtues as to put the Puritan fathers in the shade. The great achievement of the McGuffey readers is the complete integration of Christian and middle class ideals; and in that respect, the McGuffey readers are the great textbook product of American middle class culture. ·

5

The Social Virtues

THE DUTIES of the good Christian citizen required the development of virtues which, though they generally came in the guise of morality and religion, were, in fact, virtues of a more secular nature. The origins of these virtues one may seek in the great Hebrew-Christian tradition, and perhaps the force of that tradition in American civilization made the inclusion of such virtues imperative to the compilers of the McGuffey readers. But it is more probable that the lessons and stories which taught the social virtues were included in the McGuffey series in reaction to patterns of behavior not wholly acceptable in the eyes of good Christians. But whether the ideals represented in the McGuffey readers are Christian or social ideals is a question which we cannot undertake to answer here; for it is clear, as we saw in the last chapter, that social and moral ideals so interpenetrate one another as to defy distinctions.

I

However that may be, it is clear that the compilers of the McGuffey readers fought intemperance throughout the whole history of the McGuffey readers. Even in so early an edition as that of the original compilations by Dr. McGuffey, the readers carried lessons and stories vitriolic in their denunciations of the vice of intemperance, and the reasons for these strong denunciations of the vice of intemperance, as we shall see, were both Christian and social. A lesson in one of the early fourth readers, for example, tells the story of Jane Harwood, who had borne a child who was sickly from birth and had to be attended to constantly. The mother, always kind and indulgent, was keenly aware of the child's affliction, and made every effort to overcome its initial defects. The father, on the other hand, was unkind and intemperate. He didn't want the boy coddled and treated him roughly. Slowly the youth wasted away and died. His mother was moved to tears by this terrible event, and even the father seemed visibly afflicted. It was the hope of the mother that this terrible experience would cause the father to repent his unkindness and his vicious taste for whisky. But the calamity, unfortunately, was only temporary for the father. He soon forgot his son's death and returned to his old habits, drinking more than ever. "Intemperance," concludes the lesson, "had destroyed his respect for man and his fear of God."[1]

The connection of a lesson of this type with the contemporary opinion of the more stable elements of American society seems clear. Even by 1830 a temperance movement had begun to get under way; and in the Middle Border evangelical Christianity took up the cry for temperance, as indeed there was need for such a cry among the riotous of the New West. Most of the reform movement, however, was concentrated in the area east of the Hudson, where the state of New York could boast of seven hundred societies devoted to the cause of temperance.[2] Even at so early a date as 1833, however, a national convention was held at Philadelphia "with more than four hundred representatives from twenty-one states in attendance."[3] More interesting in this connection were the hundreds of children's clubs formed for this purpose, participating in temperance parades as youthful combatants against a prevalent vice. In the late thirties the movement for total abstinence split some of the intemperance societies, but we have the reassuring word of Governor Trimble of Ohio that:

The societies that have adopted the total abstinence pledge are active and increasing their numbers. Those societies that go upon the principle that distilled spirits alone should be excluded, are dragging heavily, and I think retrograding, rather than advancing.[4]

The same year that Governor Trimble issued his encouraging statement on the condition of the temperance movement, the newly-published McGuffey readers were carrying abundant illustrations of the horrors of the vice. "Wine is a mocker," one of the lessons informs us, "and strong drink is raging. Who hath woe? who hath sorrow? who hath contentions? who hath babbling? who hath wounds without a cause? who hath redness of eyes? They that tarry long at wine."[5] To buttress this strong argument, the authority of Seneca was marshalled, and it was recalled that he had spoken of those who "let in a thief at the mouth to steal away the brains."[6] The example of the reformed drunkards must have seemed convincing enough; for when men of great personal power and eloquence, like John B. Gough, whom Dr. McGuffey had invited to temperance meetings at the University of Virginia, carried the evangelical call for temperance, many were moved to renounce their sinful ways.[7]

The increasing amount of temperance literature from writers like Holmes, Whittier, Lydia G. Sigourney, Horace Greeley, Bayard Taylor, Fanny Forrester, and many others was not overlooked by the hungry compilers of the McGuffey readers. Lucius M. Sargent, whose six volumes of *Temperance Tales* won great popularity, challenged only by Timothy Shay Arthur's *Ten Nights in a Bar-Room,* is generously represented between the covers of the McGuffey readers; while Mrs. Sigourney's unnumbered sentimental temperance stories were likewise generously represented. The story of the intemperate husband whose son died because of cruelty and neglect, and who, without feeling sufficient remorse for his sins, returned to his evil ways, is typical of Mrs. Sigourney's sentimental tales. "Intemperance," wrote Mrs. Sigourney in the story just referred to, "like the strong man armed, took possession of a soul that lifted no cry to God, and girded on no weapon to resist the destroyer."[8]

One of the lessons in the McGuffey readers makes the direct connection between the stories in the readers and the cause of temperance. After explaining the evils of drink, the lesson insists that,

the progress of the temperance cause will be so great, at the period when the child, which is now an infant, shall come upon the theater of life, as to render all use of ardent spirit as a drink disreputable, can scarce be questioned.[9]

While the desired millennium did not arrive, "the results of this moral reform were not to be despised; in fact, they more nearly justified the hopes of its advocates than the slurs of its foes."[10]

Those who doubted the justification of the moral reform proposed by temperance advocates had not reckoned with the McGuffey readers. "How often does the hand of the intoxicated man," inquired one of the lessons,

lifted perhaps against his dearest friend, perhaps the wife of his bosom,—in one rash hour, perform a deed that haunts him to the grave?[11]

Those who were still not convinced were confronted with the story of Alexander the Great who lost his life and his empire through the rashness of his vice.

How shocking it is to the mind, that a man who had subdued so many nations, should suffer himself to be conquered by the sin of intemperance. It is a lamentable truth, that intemperance kills more than the sword.[12]

Moreover, though the worm in the garden of Eden was eventually the cause of the downfall of man,

there is a species of worm, found in various parts of this state, which conveys a poison of a nature so deadly, that, compared with it, even the venom of the rattlesnake is harmless. . . . Youths of America, would you know the name of this reptile? It is called the *Worm of the Still.*[13]

The same lesson appears in the edition of 1853, a powerful warning to those who let the bitterness of the slavery controversy lead them into the ways of temptation. But, aided by textbooks like the McGuffey readers, the apostles of temperance kept up the good fight. In New York the temperance demons took up the fight on the public squares, speaking on Sunday to avert further the calamities of the vice.[14] By this time, however, the movement had spread west and south, and in North Carolina applications for charters for temperance societies were granted over the protests of southern gurglers who "quoted from the Bible, Shakespeare, and Hudibras."[15] Even Hawthorne entered a plea for temperance in one of the stories of the McGuffey readers. To those who come to drink at a town pump, the pump asks, "Fill again, and tell me, on the word of an honest toper, did you ever, in cellar, tavern, or any other kind of dramshop, spend the price of your children's food, for a swig half so delicious?"[16]

The crushing arguments of temperance forces and the power of moral persuasion on a subject so closely linked to the great Christian tradition eventually forced several states to record their legal disapproval of the disgusting vice. Maine passed the first great prohibition law in 1851, and this step was hailed as a landmark in the temperance crusade.[17] Mobilizing their forces, which, as we have seen, included textbooks as well as pamphlets and lectures, the crusading forces invaded the legislative sanctity of other states. Vermont, Rhode Island, and Massachusetts were quickly forced to follow in the footsteps of Maine. "By 1855 every Northern state legislature except New Jersey had approved some form of prohibition."[18]

The opposition of some of the Democratic journals and politicians to the temperance movement, and the drinking proclivities of several Democratic politicians, whose abilities and tastes had been exposed by the Whig press, threw the temperance movement into alliance with conservative politics at many points. Though perhaps a numerous body of the Democratic party might oppose the temperance movement on one ground or another, an equally numerous group within the party would favor the temperance cause. Despite this fact, the Whig press succeeded in branding the Democratic group as the "whisky party."[19] This strategy fitted in perfectly with the plans of the great alliance between religion and property, as we have already seen, and drew those who had no other cause than temperance to promote into the conservative fold. The pillars of the church and the protectors of the public morals found other reasons than those of religion and morality for their support of the temperance crusade.[20]

Perhaps there were reasons equally as good for the generous representation of the views of Lyman Beecher and other conservatives between the covers of the McGuffey readers. With respect to the moral and social necessity for temperance, Beecher could only point out, in one of the lessons of the McGuffey readers:

Look at the generation who have just preceded you. The morning of their life was cloudless, and it dawned as brightly as your own. But behold it, now, smitten, enfeebled, inflamed, debauched, idle, poor, irreligious, and vicious, with halting steps dragging onward to meet an early grave. . . .[21]

"My child will not be a drunkard!" Cheering thought! How it swells the heart with emotions too big for utterance! What animating prospects does it open to the mind! Almshouses, and jails, and penitentiaries, and state-prisons, will then stand only as so many monuments of the vices of an age gone by.[22]

These are excellent arguments, not only against intemperance and the vice of drinking, but also against the notion that moral reform necessarily requires a reformation of government or society. It is the argument of Channing: the soul must be elevated and the individual reformed from within; and such an argument was an effective weapon against radical democrats who seemed bent on social legislation. In the face of arguments like those of Lyman Beecher, Harriet Beecher Stowe did the temperance cause no harm when she accepted, on the eve of a voyage to Europe, an invitation to dine at the Atlantic Club on the specific condition that no wine be served.[23] Nor was the cause done any harm by the sentimental anecdote of William Wirt found in one of the lessons of the McGuffey readers.

According to this lesson, William Wirt, shortly after his marriage, began drinking. This so affected his wife that it caused her death. Wirt moved to Richmond and became well-known. However, he again began drinking heavily, his business began to fail, and he seemed headed for ruin. Hoping to enlist the charm of a good woman in the cause of temperance, Wirt's friends advised him to marry again. Following this advice, the story tells us, Wirt approached Miss Gamble with an offer of marriage. She was fond of Wirt, but refused to marry him unless he stopped drinking. He refused, created a scene, and stormed out of the house. A week later he returned with the same proposal, but Miss Gamble was ada-

mant and the conditions remained the same. Again Wirt stormed from her
house, and, running to the grog shop, got drunker than ever. In the midst
of one of his stupors, while Wirt lay dead drunk in the gutter, a woman
passed by, placing her handkerchief over his face. When Wirt arose from
his drunken stupor and found the handkerchief on his face, it had a
powerful effect over him; he determined to reform, sought the hand of
Miss Gamble, married her, and lived a happy and successful life. "How
many noble minds might the young ladies save, if they would follow the
example of the heroine-hearted Miss Gamble, the friend of humanity, of
her country, and the relation of Lafayette."[24]

The coming of the Civil War was a serious reverse for the cause of temperance. When the post-war temperance forces took stock about them, they
found that only Massachusetts and Maine were still prohibiting the sale
of liquor, though the former sought to renew the licensing system following the war. The temperance forces were somewhat strengthened, however,
when a prohibition party began to be formed in the East and Middle
West.[25] The first state political organization of the new party was formed
in Ohio as early as 1869, and later a national convention of delegates met
at Chicago. The platform insisted on statuatory prohibition of the liquor,
but note, significantly, that the best means of bringing about the desired
result was the support of the woman suffrage movement. Though disap-
pointing in its gathering of votes for the cause in national elections, the
success of the party in renewing the dying spirit of the temperance crusaders was impressive.[26]

At the same time, the Women's Christian Temperance Union began a
significant movement in the temperance crusade. At the invitation of a
health reformer greatly addicted to the lecturing platform, women were
urged to begin a praying crusade in behalf of the temperance and health
of the nation.[27] When the nation awoke to the movement, women were
already organized into temperance squads, singing hymns before saloon
doors and entering those houses of horrors to pray before the befuddled
spectators.[28] These zealous beginnings eventually led to the formation of
the Women's Christian Temperance Union in 1874, an organization with
which tapsters have had to cope for some time. However that may be, it
seems clear that women, like Miss Gamble in the McGuffey readers, could
do much to fight the evil of rum and the demon of whisky.[29]

These more formal organizations of the temperance crusade undoubtedly played a great part in the increasing strength of the temperance
movement in the Gilded Age. The increasing strength of the whisky crusade is reflected in the McGuffey readers, though the emphasis is not quite

so strong as in the pre-Civil War editions. Authors like Whittier, who appeared in some of the earlier editions, are carried through to the Gilded Age, but whether on the basis of their literary reputation or the temperance lessons of their stories are questions which it seems impossible to answer. However that may be, we find a story by Whittier in which the narrator is walking along a beautiful seashore as the sun dips slowly into the darkening waters. Suddenly the narrator comes across a dissipated figure who grovels in the sand, eating the dirt. When a child asks the disgusting figure what he is doing, the drunkard answers that he is taking comfort. The full revelation of the figure groveling in the dirt is evidently intended to repel the most hardened imbiber: "The prostrate groveler struggled half-way up, exhibiting the bloated and filthy countenance of a drunkard."[30]

Melville's story of Israel Potter's visit to Dr. Franklin likewise buttressed the cause of temperance. Among the bits of advice which Dr. Franklin offered was the statement that, "if you are poor, avoid wine as a costly luxury; if you are rich, shun it as a fatal indulgence. Stick to plain water."[31] Closely related to intemperance, both in the eyes of Dr. Franklin and in the eyes of the compilers of the McGuffey readers, was the vice of gambling. This vice was, indeed, but another form of intemperance, even in the eyes of the whisky crusaders. The basic strategy of the temperance forces seemd to be to link the sin of intemperance with other evils with which society suffered, so that good citizens outraged by the lawlessness, corruption, crime, and gambling which accompanied the saloon would join forces with the crusading knights and ladies of the temperance movement.[32]

The same evident relationship between intemperance, on the one hand, and corruption, crime, gambling, and vice, on the other, is shown in the stories and lessons of the McGuffey readers. One story, for example, warns us to "Beware of the first drink";[33] for the first drink leads inevitably to assorted forms of vice and corruption. Thus in one of the stories Uncle Philip tells his young nephews about Tom Smith, the town drunkard, Tom, once a fine man, went to the city and fell in with "bad companions." He learned to gamble, drink, "go to theaters," and to do other things which "bad companions" are likely to teach. When he came home to repent, he tried to give up these evil ways, under the influence and guidance of his wife; but soon he began drinking again, and there was no escape. His mother and wife died, and not long afterwards Tom was sent to prison for stealing. "Instead of spending his evenings in reading," the lesson warns us, "he would go to the theater, to balls, and to suppers."[34] As though this were not bad enough, however, Tom "soon learned to play cards, and of course he played for money."[35] Thus the first drink leads "to the theater, to balls, and to suppers," and eventually to playing cards for money. Tom, of course, should have been "spending his evenings in reading" the McGuffey readers.

The reaction to gambling seems rather naturally the product of a Western heritage. One of the earlier editions of the McGuffey readers carries the warnings of no less an observer of Western morals and manners than venerable Timothy Flint. In a lesson entitled "Effects of Gambling," good Mr. Flint feels called upon to explain that, "Another appalling view of gambling is, that it is the *prolific stem,* the fruitful parent, of all other vices."[36] His own view was that the "love of gambling" steals upon its intended victim, "more than any other sin," with an "imperceptible influence on its victim."[37] Moreover, Mr. Flint continues, "Blasphemy, falsehood, cheating, drunkenness, quarreling, and murder, are all naturally connected with gambling. . . ."[38]

Well might Timothy Flint hurl his words at the demon of gambling, for that vice and many others, as we noted in our first chapter, was well advanced on the frontier of the New West. The lessons against gambling and its related forms of vice were, however, not without great need in other portions of the nation. A recent historian, surveying the situation during the period in which most of the lessons on gambling appeared in the readers, noted that:

Gambling was in the blood of the time. When such a proportion of the population was taking its future into its hands by venturing forth to seek new homes, when those with little capital were risking it in such precarious new enterprises as railroads and gas companies, it is not surprising that men bet on horse races, and that lotteries were a feature of the day.[39]

Closely related to intemperance and gambling in the catalogue of sins prohibited in the McGuffey readers were the vices of greed and unrestrained ambition. The former receives adequate treatment in a story entitled, "The Greedy Girl." Indeed, there are many lessons to be drawn from this story. We learn, among other things, that animals know better than to eat too much.[40] "If the squirrel lived in a house made of acorns, he would not need a doctor. He would not eat an acorn too much."[41] Moreover, the story of Laura English is illuminating. "Laura English is a greedy little girl. Indeed she is quite a glutton. Do you know what a glutton is? A glutton is one who eats too much, because the food tastes well."[42] The author of this story baldly declares that, "I do not love little girls who eat to much. Do you, my little readers? I do not think they have rosy cheeks, or such bright eyes, or such sweet, happy tempers as those who eat less."[43]

Not only those who are gluttons, but those whose ambitions outrun their strength come in for treatment at the moral surgery of the McGuffey readers. In one story a painter tortures a slave in order to get the right model for a picture of Prometheus. After relating the story the author apparently decided to enforce the moral by appending a little verse beginning:

> How like a mountain devil in the heart
> Rules this unreigned ambition![44]

In a similar mood, one of the lessons inquires, "What is ambition"; and answers, "It is a glorious cheat."[45] Enforcing the lesson with bits of verse, the author concludes:

> The bright, fiery boy,
> That it was a daily blessing but to see,
> His spirit was so birdlike and so pure,
> Is frozen in the very flush of youth,
> Into a cold, care-fretted, heartless man.[46]

Still another lesson compares ambition to chasing the butterfly, concluding:

> Boy! in thee the Poet's eye
> Man's true emblem may decry,
> Like thee, through the viewless air
> He doth follow visions fair!
> Hopes as vain, pursuits as wild,
> Occupy the full-grown child![47]

II

Lessons and stories designed to teach kindness were strongly emphasized from the earliest editions to the latest; and while no direct cultural connection can be singled out to parallel this emphasis, it is clear that the Christian ethic and the code of the Golden Rule occupied the minds, if not the practices, of many Americans. Perhaps there were many phenomena of American society which justified this emphasis on human kindness; but whatever the cause, the compilers of the McGuffey readers apparently agreed in all revisions and changes to reserve a large portion of the available space for lessons of kindness and of love.

One of the early lessons, for example, praises the school girl who "does what she is bid, and is kind to all."[48] Another lesson combines the admonition to be "kind and good to the blind,"[49] and the generalization that "none but a bad girl will tear or soil a book."[50] In the story of the kind boy, James Bland found a bird, cold and wet. He took it home and dried and warmed it; then, instead of caging the bird, he let it fly away. This kind act brings forth the thought that "James was a good boy and would not be cruel, even to a bird,"[51] and the hope that "no boy who reads this book will ever rob a bird's nest," for it is "very cruel and wicked."[52] Another lesson tells us that we "must feel for the lame and do all we can to help them."[53] On the other hand, a cruel boy drowned a kitten, pulled the wings and legs off flies, and scared a dog and cat. A more considerate friend told him that his acts were wrong, so the cruel boy learned the lesson that "everything that could move, could feel; and that it was wrong in anyone to hurt or kill them."[54] The story of Mr. Post who took a foundling and guided her growth to maturity, although he could not afford to do so, teaches that such kindness will be reciprocated when the kind man gets too old to take care of himself. "How kind Mr. Post was," the lesson tells us. "He did not know what to do with the innocent little babe, but he could not let it die."[55]

Despite the fact that there seems no specific cause to which one can assign these lessons, it seems clear that the emphasis parallels the humanitarian movements of the thirties and forties.[56] Men like Grant and Lincoln, whose later fame gave such stories political interest, are said to have disdained the killing of animals in the hunt. Less reasonable individuals, however extended this tenderness to trees, birds, and fish.[57] Moreover, the rough practices of cock fighting, animal baiting, and wrestling, so prevalent, as we have seen, on the Middle Western frontier, could hardly have met with the approval of Dr. McGuffey and some of the earlier compilers of the McGuffey readers. The scenes described by a famous British traveler, while exciting enough to read, are not such as would induce kindness in the wildmen of the Ohio and Mississippi regions.

Stories like that of the cruel boy who is punished for his inhuman tricks and hoaxes must have had rough parallels in frontier life. The boy in this lesson called a dog to him as if to offer it a piece of bread and butter. As the dog came up to the boy, the boy hit it on the nose with a stick. The dog ran away, howling, and the boy laughed loudly at his cleverness. A man who had witnessed the scene from across the street called the boy and asked him if he would like a half-dollar. When he extended his hand, however, the boy received a sharp rap on the knuckles.[58] A much clearer example of the humanitarianism which worked its way into the readers are the numerous stories about robbing bird's nests. One, for example, tells of a little boy who stole a bird's nest, but who was convinced of his error by his sisters, who spoke very tenderly of the wasted efforts of the mother bird and how she would feel when she discovered that her nest had been pilfered. The boy's "heart was touched—he yielded to the sweet impulse of humanity."[59] Moreover, he enjoyed "more satisfaction from this act of humanity, than any amusement could bestow."[60] Another lesson, capsuled in a bit of verse, appears rather to require obedience without questioning, though there can be little doubt of its tender purposes.

> Let the cat be; she has a kit.
> Do not go to her now.
> Why may I not go to her now:
> Do not ask why. Do as you are bid.
> I will do as I am bid.[61]

The changed emphasis in preaching and the insistence upon good works of a highly elevated and humanitarian character, as found in lectures and sermons like those of Emerson and Channing, perhaps had much to do with the continued humanitarian emphasis of the forties and fifties.[62] However that may be, it is clear that the taking of revenge, however justified, is not among the good works man can perform. One of the lessons of this period carries the story of Philip who wanted to take revenge on farmer Robinson's son. He was stopped by Stephen, however, who pointed out that the boy was already punished by the ill-will he had generally created. The farmer's son had himself tried to get revenge on a bee by sticking a pole into the hive and knocking it around. The stings had sent him to bed for several days. Philip later helps farmer boy with a load he was carrying, and thereby shames the boy into remorse for his meanness. "Young Robinson," the lesson remarks, "was quite ashamed at the thought of this unmerited kindness, and heartily repented of his behavior."[63]

Another lesson tells how Harry has to stay in bed while other boys and girls are playing outside his window, picking fruit from the trees. Even though Harry had refused to share his breakfast with his faithful dog, Frisk brings Harry one of the fallen fruit from outside.

Is not Frisk a fine, grateful fellow? And does he not deserve a share of Harry's breakfast, whether he begs for it or not? And little Harry will remember that kindness will always be rewarded, and that ill-nature and bad temper are connected with nothing but pain and disgrace.[64]

But kindness is far from being reserved for animals. The story of Sam and Harry explains how Sam had just spent all his money for a book.

When he met a poor, blind man, therefore, he had no money to give and felt rather sad. Harry and his mother drove up in a fine carriage and the mother gave Harry some coins to give to the blind. Instead of doing this, Harry threw the coins into the bushes. Sam saw all this, turned back, spent a long time looking for the coins, and gave them to the blind man. "Which, do you think was most truly *kind* to the poor man?" the lesson asks. "I know which he thanked most in his heart," the lesson concludes.[65] Another lesson tells of Lucy and her fondness for apples. Despite the fact that she has but two apples left, she gives them to Fred and Charlotte. They are so grateful that they give her an apple a day and a doll. Then, in a poetic summary, the author concludes,

> *The good and the kind*
> *Find flowers in their path ever springing,*
> *And angels around ever singing.*[66]

Many are the lessons which teach that, "Good children are careful not to hurt any animal," and "Good children do not hurt each other."[67] Moreover, "Good children are kind to everyone." In this they are like God. He is kind not only to the good, but to the unthankful, and to the evil."[68] Though this point of view was not strictly that of the older generations, it perhaps explains Bryce's opinion that no other country equalled America in the sums spent for beneficence.[69] At the same time, William Graham Sumner noted that there was "an unlimited supply of reformers, philanthropists, humanitarians, and would-be-managers-in-general of society."[70] Though the lessons in the McGuffey readers did not, according to Sumner's structure, teach children to be managers of society, they did implant the virtue of humanitarianism in numerous ways.

One of the lessons attempts to combine instruction in gratitude with that of kindness. A child's mother is sick in bed, asking for a glass of water. The child refused the mother her final request, though he had only meant the gesture as a bit of sport. The next morning the poor old lady was dead, leaving the child to lament the unkindness of his ways. As old as I am now, lamented the bereaved man in later years,

I would give worlds, were they mine to give, could my mother but have lived to tell me she forgave my childish ingratitude. But I can not call her back; and when I stand by her grave, and whenever I think of her manifold kindness, the memory of that reproachful look she gave me, will bite me like a serpent, and sting like an adder.[71]

However horrible the prospects of remorse, however, it is more likely that lessons stressing the practicality of kindness were more effective. One lesson, entitled "The Little Lord and the Farmer," utilizes its space to teach a number of virtues in one story. A boy, identified only as "the little lord," threw his ball across a brook. When he saw that it would be difficult to retrieve the ball, he ordered a passing farmer boy to get it for him. When the farmer boy refused, the little lord attempted to cross the brook, but was rewarded for his efforts by a cold dash in the brook. He ordered the farmer boy to pull him out, but again the farmer boy refused. Gradually, however, the little lord's tone becomes more restrained and he politely asks for aid. With this, however, the farmer boy is willing to comply.

> *Be kind to all you chance to meet,*
> *In field, or lane, or crowded street;*
> *Anger and pride are both unwise;*
> *Vinegar never catches flies.*
> *There are few things I would not dare,*
> *For gentlemen who speak me fair;*
> *But for rude words, I do not choose*
> *To wet my feet, and soil my shoes.*[72]

The famous story of the contest between the wind and the sun to make a man remove his coat is included, and the compilers think it well to note that, "This fable teaches us, that gentle means will often succeed, where force will fail."[73] Another story explains how Sam and Rob find a turtle. Sam turns it over on its back and Rob urges him to turn it back because he is sure that turtles feel as we do, and that, therefore, it is cruel to leave turtles helpless on their backs. "I think," the author reminds us, "we should remember the Golden Rule, 'Do unto others as you wish them to do unto you,' in our treatment of animals, as well as in our treatment of men."[74]

In a similar manner, the story of the good-natured boy has many instructive lessons. Henry, setting out for a walk through the woods, meets a dog that is hungry, a horse that is starving, a blind man walking in a marsh, and a sailor who is hobbling along on crutches. These unfortunates Henry is kind enough to aid in several ways. On his way back from the woods, however, the situation is reversed: the dog brings him food; the horse gives him a ride; the blind man and the sailor combine to warn him of robbers. "A good action is never thrown away," the lesson tells us, "though done on a dog."[75] With this lesson in mind, the little boy, Henry, "took care of his dog as long as he lived, and never forgot that we must do good to others, if we wish them to do good to us."[76]

While we hope to do good, however, we must remember that one argument against evil is that it will be imitated by others. Such a theme is brought out in the story of the monkey who observes how one man mistreats another and, in imitation, proceeds to do likewise to a dog.[77] Still another story seems to imitate the black-beauty theme. Jenny Templar, age twelve, was able to manage a rough horse that even stablemen could not manage. The secret of this control lay in her habitual kindness toward the animal.

"Fanny! O Fanny!" called Jenny, and the beautiful creature turned her head. That gentle tone she well knew, and, glad to see her friend, she came directly to the fence, and rubbed her head on the girl's shoulder. As soon as the gate was opened, she followed Jenny to the barn. The men had treated her roughly, and she remembered it. But she knew and loved the voice that was always kind, and the hand that often fed and caressed her. She gave love for love, and willing service for kindness.[78]

On another occasion, a group of boys went sleigh-riding. During the ride they scared an old man by exciting his horse to run faster. They eventually told their adventures to their teacher. With a simple wisdom, the teacher reversed the story, telling how some rude boys had frightened his father's horse, causing both the teacher and the father considerable distress.

When the boys perceived how rude and unkind their conduct appeared from another point of view, they were very much ashamed of their thoughtlessness and most of them had the manliness to apologize to their teacher for what they had done.[79]

Another story demonstrates that, "Kindness, even though shown to a dog, will always be rewarded; and that ill-nature and bad-temper are connected with nothing but pain and disgrace."[80] And, as if this kind of testimony were not enough, the case of Susie Sunbeam indicates that Susie "never used an unkind word, but tried to do whatever would please her playmates best."[81] But her kindness was apparently not limited to playmates and friends, for when she met a poor little girl with a ragged dress, "she cheered her up with kind words, and gave her a nice dress and a pair of shoes."[82] Perhaps, another lesson informs us apropos of other kindnesses, "some may say that these are *little* things. We must begin with little labors of love."[83]

In the face of this kind of evidence, it is difficult to see how anyone would knowingly be unkind. As Susie advised us, we must begin with "little labors of love." And this appropriate beginning is apparently the stay and support to the lessons on kindness; for, in addition to those, there were unnumbered lessons and stories that taught brotherly, sisterly, and parental love on the part of the child. The lessons on love and sympathy seem, indeed, to be closely related to those on kindness, and, taken together, make up a great part of the lessons. There is, for example, the lesson that advises:

My little reader, have you brothers and sisters? Then love them with all your heart. Do all you can for them. Help them when in need; and wait not to be asked. Add to their mirth. Share their grief. Vex them not. Use no cross words. . . . So shall you make the hearts of your parents rejoice. So shall you have the blessing of the great God who made you.[84]

As if this prescription for a happy family life were not enough, we are given a picture of the ideal home life for the McGuffey students. Both children, Harry and Kate Brown, have done well in school. After supper the whole family gathers around the table, reading and doing the little domestic chores that make home life so comfortable. "Harry and Kate read a story in a new book, the father reads his newspaper, and the mother mends Harry's stockings." Accompanying this picture of domestic bliss is the question, "Do you not wish that every boy and girl could have a home like this?"[85] In a similar vein, another picture of home life explains how three children, "By their conduct . . . secured their own bliss, and gained the love and esteem of all around them."[86] We are afforded, in addition, the following poetic prescription for domestic peace and tranquillity:

> Whatever brawls disturb the street,
> There should be peace at home;
> Hard names at first, and angry words,
> That are but noisy breath,
> May grow to clubs and naked swords,
> To murder and to death.[87]

Following this, however, we find out how to win friends and influence people. "No person can be happy without friends," we are told; and "You cannot find others to love unless you will also love them."[88] From these premises it follows that, "There is but one way to make friends and that is, by being friendly to others."[89] Thus,

if it is seen that you have a noble spirit, that you are above selfishness, that you are willing to make sacrifices to promote the happiness of others, you will never be in want of friends. . . . Your heart must glow with kindness, if you would attract to yourself the esteem and affection of those around you.[90]

Moreover, this prescription for winning friends and influencing people has one exception:

If your companions do not love you, it is your own fault. They can not help loving you, if you will be kind and friendly. If you are not loved, it is a good evidence that you do not deserve to be loved. It is true, that a sense of duty, may, at times, render it necessary for you to do that which will be displeasing to your companions.[91]

Though most of us have found it convenient to follow the exception rather than the rule, it is clear that the practise of the Golden Rule will render society worthy of human ideals. For the little girl who inquires about the meaning of the Golden Rule, a mother, in one of the lessons, replies:

It implies, in the first place, a total destruction of all selfishness: for a man who loves himself better than his neighbors, can never do to others as he would have others do to him. We are bound not only to do, but to feel, toward others as we would have others feel toward us.[92]

Another lesson suggests that it is better to speak gently and to "rule by love than fear,"[93] implying at the same time the lesson a little girl learned, in one of the Spanish editions, from her grandmother: "Siempre es tan bondadosa, y tiene tan buen cuidado de mi que siempre me gusta hacer lo que elle me manda."[94] Kindness and human love are not enough, however, unless one strengthens them with the virtues of gratefulness and human sympathy. In developing these virtues, however, courage is sometimes necessary. So it seemed to Henry when Robert called him a coward because he would not fight; but when Robert fell in the water and was about to drown, Henry displayed true courage in saving his life. "Henry had learned," the lesson informs us, "that true courage was shown most in bearing reproach, when not deserved, and that he ought to be afraid of nothing but doing wrong."[95]

It is clear, however, that if we wish to do good we should "Make people happy, and there will not be half the quarreling or a tenth part of the wickedness there is."[96] Even the laughter and derision of the world should not deter us from doing good. A lesson of three boys who discuss throwing a snowball at the schoolhouse door illustrates this point. Henry, the oldest of the boys, is the leader of the plot; while James, the second brother, is ready to dare his younger brother, he will not himself throw the snowball. George, the youngest brother, refuses the urging of his companions for some time, but finally succumbs to temptation and throws the snowball. As a result of this action, George is thoroughly whipped; but he is rewarded by discovering the rule which is to govern his future action: "I will not do that which I think to be *wrong*, if the whole town should join with you in laughing."[97]

Another type of thoughtfulness is illustrated by a bit of verse beginning:

We must not talk, but whisper low,
Mother wants to work we know,
That, when father comes to tea,
All may neat and cheerful be.[98]

However, lest these designs on our play and fun be taken too seriously, we learn that one cannot be doing wrong if one is ignorant that it is wrong.[99] For that reason, however, it is necessary to make it abundantly clear through the lessons of the McGuffey readers what is wrong and what is right. One story, for example, reminds boys that, "I do not like to see boys cling to carriages that pass along."[100] These warnings, buttressed with numerous stories and examples, may indeed beseech boys and girls to do the right and avoid the wrong. But as a final reminder, let us remember that,

when we are puzzling our brains with plans to help ourselves out of trouble, let us always stop a moment in our planning, and try to think if there is not some simple way out of the difficulty which shall be in every respect perfectly *right*. If we do this, we shall probably find a way more easy and satisfactory than any which we can devise.[101]

III

In addition to the primary virtues of kindness, tenderness, and love, modesty comes in for specific treatment in the McGuffey readers. A fable of the clock and the sundial tells how the clock lorded it over a sundial, saying that it had to depend on the sun which the clock went around all the time and even struck the hours. Just then the sun came out, showing that the clock was one half hour slow. The moral of this story, the Mc-Guffey readers tell us, is that, "Humble modesty is more often right than a proud and boasting spirit."[102] In a similar manner, Gray's "Elegy Written in a Country Churchyard," explains that, "The paths of glory lead but to the grave."[103] For the wildmen of the Middle Border these sentiments were indeed most discomforting.

But the strongest argument against the vanity of human desires lay in the story of Charlotte Jones who was found dead at her dressing table. The death was caused by heart disease, and it came at the moment Charlotte was curling her hair and rouging her cheeks. "The ghastly visage of death was leering through the tinselry of fashion. The 'vain show' of artificial joy was a horrible mockery of the fooleries of life."[104] As if this point were not strong enough, the author added the point that the young woman's death was "a satire upon human vanity, so repulsive, unsightly, and loathsome a spectacle, as a corpse dressed for a ball."[105] Thus, vanity and immodesty are horrible in the sight of man's fellow creatures, and the world awakens to the death of all that is vain and intolerable.

Another lesson from one of the early editions gives considerable attention to the virtues desired for the youth, noting that, "The virtue of youth is modesty; and when a young person has lost his modesty, possess what he will, he is an object of horror."[106] The same lesson is not above suggesting other virtues, insisting, in characteristic fashion, that, "Innocence is better than repentance"; that, "He that is extravagant will quickly become poor"; that "To say little and perform much, is the characteristic of a great mind."[107] In the midst of these warnings, we learn that, "The transient day of sinful pleasure is followed by a dark and tempestuous night of sorrow."[108] Moreover, "A good man shines amiably through all the obscurity of his low position; and a wicked man is a poor degraded wretch in the midst of all his grandeur."[109] In summarizing the course of the wise, one must advise that,

If you are wise, study virtue, and condemn everything that can come in competition with it. Remember that nothing else deserves one anxious thought or wish. Remember that this alone is honor, glory, wealth, and happiness. Secure this and you secure everything. Lose this and all is lost.[110]

One of the most striking and popular of the lessons teaching modesty, however, is Whittier's story, "The Fish I Didn't Catch." A young lad goes fishing and finds that there is a great deal to do after the fish is on the line before he can be called caught. The first haul is of weeds; the first real fish escapes before he can be hauled ashore.

How often since have I been reminded of the fish that I did not catch. When I hear people boasting of a work as yet undone, and trying to anticipate the credit which belongs only to actual achievement, I call to mind that scene by the brookside, and the wise caution of my uncle in that particular instance takes the form of a proverb of universal application: Never brag of your fish before you catch him.[111]

In the forest, one of the stories tells us, the trees are bragging of their particular distinctions. Finally, however, a forester cuts them all down regardless of distinctions. "Thus you see how foolish it is to be proud of any qualifications we possess, as like these boastful trees, we have no power to insure their continuance."[112] Still another lesson tells of the pride of the moon: how it grew as she approached the full, then the waning that taught her humility, and finally hiding behind the clouds she learned the humility necessary for a heavenly body. Since this first trial, the lesson tells us, the heavenly bodies have lived in harmony, for the stars now find no reason to envy the large moon.[113] It is interesting to note, as a sidelight, that the story of the moon and the stars is told from a naive point of view, stressing the point that the moon looks to man larger than the stars.

From the stars to the pebbles is quite a trip, but one we must pursue if we are to follow the pattern of modesty. The pebble talks about the shy acorn that falls near it. The acorn in shame at its ugliness goes under ground. When the oak shoots up the pebble realizes he has nothing to do but wait there until he is worn into nothingness.

> *Useless and vain, a cumberer here,*
> *I have been idling from year to year.*
> *But never, from this, shall a vaunting word*
> *From the humble Pebble again be heard,*
> *Till something, without me or within,*
> *Shall show the purpose for which I have been.*[114]

The spider spins a beautiful web, of course, but we must remember that she gets her dinner by killing flies.

> *My child, who reads this simple lay,*
> *   With eyes down-dropped and tender,*
> *Remember the old proverb says*
> *   That pretty is what pretty does,*
> *And that worth does not go nor stay*
> *   For poverty nor splendor.*
> *'Tis not the house, and not the dress,*
> *   That makes the saint or sinner.*
> *To see the spider sit and spin,*
> *   Shut with her walls of silver in,*
> *You would never, never, never guess*
> *   The way she gets her dinner.*[115]

In the "Race of the Winds," Zephyr and Breeze have a race, the latter roaring across the countryside bothering the whole populace, the former softly cooling and delighting everyone. "Do you not think that Zephyr with his quiet manners was more lovable than Breeze with his bluster and noise?"[116] Then there is the usual story of the spider and the fly, with the admonition that, "To idle, silly, flattering words, I pray you, ne'er give heed."[117] And a note about the violet teaches the pleasantries of humility and modesty:

> *Then let me to the valley go,*
> *   This pretty flower to see;*
> *That I may also learn to grow*
> *   In sweet humility.*[118]

Thus, the pattern of ideas teaching the virtues of modesty, humility, and simplicity in thought, word, and action were designed to bring about these desired effects in the conduct of children. The whole pattern could be suggested by the moral of one of the lessons that, "The virtue of youth is modesty; and when a young person has lost his modesty, possess what he will, he is an object of horror."[119] Just as much an object of horror, however, was the disobedient youth, and the obedience pattern runs throughout the McGuffey series. Though parts of this pattern fit in better with the preceding chapter, as we have seen, most of it seems to be of genuine social utility.

Take, for example, the case of Frank. Frank was a polite little boy who did whatever he was told. When he crawled under the tea table and was told to come out without touching the table leg, he did so. Then he found out why he was told to come out. But he did not quarrel when asked to come out; he obeyed without asking why.[120] It is clear that the kind of obedience desired is complete and unquestioning obedience of an older variety than any we are familiar with. Harry and Annie, for example, go upon the ice in direct violation of what their mother had told them.

Harry managed to get to the shore without any help, but poor Annie was nearly drowned before a man could reach her. Harry went home almost frozen, and told his mother how disobedient he had been. He remembered the lesson learned that day as long as he lived.[121]

Bessie had a day to herself in the woods, taking Aunt Annie's pretty basket. But soon she heard the signal that called her home. She decided to hurry home and not keep her mother waiting even leaving the basket which had just rolled down a long hill. Her mother wanted to say good-bye to her before going away on a trip. She had no chance to get the basket after her mother left, and when it started to rain she was forced to confess to her aunt that she had left her basket in the woods. Her aunt, however, was not angry, for Bessie had been *obedient* to her mother. "And you did quite right," said her aunt.

If you had stopped, your mother must have waited a whole day, or else gone without seeing you. When I write, I will tell her how obedient you were, and that will please more than anything else I can say.[122]

A bit of verse similarly suggests obedient and restrained conduct for children:

> *Why, father, Little Gracie said,*
> *Where can the birdie be?*
> *If I could sing a song like that,*
> *I'd sit where folks could see.*
> *I hope my little girl will learn*
> *A lesson from the bird,*
> *And try to do what good she can,*
> *Not to be seen or heard.*[123]

In addition to obedience, however, gratefulness and generosity are much-desired virtues to the compilers of the McGuffey readers. The story of the old man who, though very old, worked for his children, will illustrate the former. The grandfather brought up the children, though he grew older and weaker with each passing year. Finally, however, the children's father returned home from his long voyage. With a gratefulness becoming a son, the man and his children now worked to support and care for the old man who had been good to them.[124] Many of the stories involve gratefulness to parents, while others center their attention on gratefulness to wealthy merchants and rich neighbors who are kind to the poor, as we saw in another chapter.

Other lessons insist on the virtue of controlling one's temper. The story of Roger Sherman, who knew that he had a violent temper, will illustrate how, if a man makes a great effort, he can control his temper. On one occasion, the lesson relates, Sherman was trying to read his Bible, but some michievous boys played a mirror into his eyes. He controlled his temper, however, and merely put down the blinds of his study. "There is no misery so constant," the lesson informs us, "so distressing, and so intolerable to others, as that of having a disposition which is your master, and which is continually fretting itself."[125] Another lesson explains how a little boy had one big fault. To cure him of his anger the father offered him a dollar if he refrained from exercising his temper for one whole day. This seemed difficult, but the boy managed to earn the dollar. His father then asked if he couldn't restrain his anger from love of God. The boy was ashamed and promised not to get angry. "My son, for one dollar, you can do right," said the father. "Can you not do so from love to God who gives you all you have?"[126]

Some of the stories ostensibly designed to teach control of one's temper find it convenient to include other teachings as well. Such is the case of the lesson entitled "The Noblest Revenge." While walking Philip accidentally upset with his cane a pitcher of water belonging to the unpopular Robinson. Robinson, in his anger, broke the cane, disregarding Philip's apologies and pleas that it had not been an intentional act. Philip now plotted revenge, but Stephen, a friend, talked him out of it, saying that since Robinson was stronger, it was unlikely that Philip could do worse to him than he to Philip. Furthermore, Stephen reasoned, contempt alone would be revenge enough upon the ill-favored youth. As it later turned out, Philip helped Robinson with a large log, and Robinson became ashamed and repented an act he had done in haste and anger. "This," said Philip, "is the noblest vengeance I could take, in returning good for evil. It is impossible I should repent of it."[127]

The foolishness of fighting is the theme of the lesson of the fight between the hawk and the eagle over a fish the hawk had caught. In the midst of their fighting the fish was dropped and both went without their dinner.[128] Similarly, a quick-tempered boy, with only twenty minutes before the school bell rings, is blaming his slate for not getting his lessons done. His sister refuses to do the work for him, but she aids him in such a way as to make him understand that the slate is not to blame.

Now, that is the way with a great many thoughtless and quicktempered people. They try to find fault with somebody or something else, and get into a passion, and perhaps do mischief, when, if they would but reflect a little, it is their own dear selves who ought to bear the blame.[129]

Moreover, more harm is done in the world by mischief and boyish pranks than by real intenders of evil. Such is the lesson we learn from a story entitled "Never do Mischief." Two boys bent on a childish prank enter Henry's bedroom at night and try to scare him. So effective was the scare that Henry is now "a perfect idiot . . . in the night, at about the time when the boys frightened him, he will cry out with horror, 'Oh, they are coming! they are coming!' "[130] Another story of thoughtless boys tells how William and Edward didn't care how they hurt people so long as they had fun doing it. Once they tied grass together so that people passing down the path would trip and fall. Several people did fall, and the boys had a hearty laugh. One man sprained an ankle and was unable to go for the doctor he had sought for another man who was critically ill. The joke was not so funny when the boys learned the sick man was their father. "I do not know whether their father died," the story concludes. "But I am sure that Edward and William never tied the grass again, as long as they lived."[131]

On the other hand, Goldsmith, in one of the lessons of the McGuffey readers, offers us an essay on happiness of temper:

They who . . . can place themselves on that side of the world in which everything appears in a pleasant light, will find something in every occurrence to excite their good humor. . . . The world is to them a theatre, on which only comedies are acted. . . . It matters not whether our good humor be constructed by others into insensibility or idiotism; it is happiness to ourselves; and none but a fool could measure his satisfaction by what the world thinks of it.[132]

We should, then, proceed about life's business with happiness of temper, with kindness and good-will towards all. But in all this let us not do anything rashly; let us not precipitate error. Such seems to be the lesson of a wealthy Persian who took great delight in his infant son and would scarcely permit him to leave his presence. On one occasion, however, the Persian was summoned to the king, an order which he was bound to obey. The only one around to whom he could entrust his son was an old and faithful dog. Soon after the father left, the life of the child was threatened by a snake. The dog came to the rescue, killed the snake, and protected his master's fair son. When the Persian returned, the dog, still stained with blood, went out to greet his master. The latter was horrified when he perceived the blood and thought that the dog had killed his beloved son. Without thinking, he slew the dog. But when he entered the house and saw his son alive, his heart was filled with bitterness and remorse. "Shame and repentance," the lesson tells us, "are the sure consequences of precipitation and want of reflection."[133]

The epitome of thoughtfulness is reached, however, by the little boy who, in one of the lessons, wrote to Santa Claus: "I would like a gun that will shoot, and a rubber ball that will not break Mama's windows or the big glass in the parlor."[134] And the evils of boyish mischief seem to be epitomized in the case of George Norton. George always teased the girls at school and played harmful practical jokes on everyone. He one day offered to help a girl taking home a pitcher of milk, but he managed the affair so that she dropped and broke the pitcher. George's triumph was short-lived, however, for he slipped on the freezing milk and broke his leg.[135] In a similar manner, a quarrel over a nut came to a disastrous, but instructive conclusion. One boy saw the nut first; another picked it up from the ground first. While they were quarreling about who had the right to the kernel, a bigger boy offered to decide. He gave each a portion of the shell, keeping the kernel himself as a reward for his decision. "This is the way," said he, laughing, "in which quarrels are apt to end."[136]

The virtue of truthfulness is illustrated in the lesson concerning the wolf and the sheep. A boy was sent to care for some sheep. He was instructed to call for help should a wolf attack the flock. He shyly called for help several times when help was not needed and had a good laugh at seeing the farmers run futilely to the flock. On a third occasion, the wolf actually attacked the flock, and the boy's cries for help were all in vain. The wolf carried off his favorite pet lamb.

> *The truth itself is not believed,*
> *From one who often has deceived.*[137]

Truthfulness is likewise rewarded in the story of the brother who helped little Tom carry a heavy basket. Instead of deceiving the small boy by sliding the basket toward Tom's end of the pole, the boy slid it toward his own end and carried the heavier burden. "His load was now heavier than that of his little brother. Yet he was happy; for he felt that he had done right. Had he deceived his brother, he would not have felt happy at all."[138] Crime certainly does not pay, as George Washington learned in the incident about the cherry tree. "Such proof of heroic truth in my son," said George's father on this occasion, "is of more value than a thousand trees, though they were of the purest gold."[139] And the little boy who told a lie, in one of the lessons, "was told by his parents that he had sinned, not only against them, but against God."[140]

In the face of this type of exegesis, it is not surprising to find Louisa May Alcott lamenting, in one of the lessons of the McGuffey readers, that children of fourteen were dressing the height of fashion, showing a disregard for virtues which an older generation found happiness in. A little girl, fashioned in the image of the older generation than the young one about her.

In my day, children of fourteen and fifteen didn't dress in the height of fashion; go to parties as nearly like those of grown people as it is possible to make them; lead idle, giddy, unhealthy lives and become blasé at twenty. We were little folks till eighteen or so; worked and studied, dressed and played, like children; honored our parents; and our days were much longer in the land than now, it seems to me.[141]

This description of the virtues of an older generation seems almost a catalogue of the virtues the compilers of the readers sought to maintain in the face of the inevitable advance of change and progress. The appeal of Irving in one of the earlier editions had apparently less influence some decades later. Even the grave could invoke no sacred obligations to some in the Gilded Age, but the sorrowful appeal of Irving in the forties might well have had the desired effect. In viewing the grave, Irving feels called upon to say:

Console thy broken spirit, if thou canst, with these tender yet futile tributes of regret; but take warning by the bitterness of this, thy contrite affliction over the dead, and henceforth, be more faithful and affectionate in the discharge of thy duties to the living.[142]

And yet, contrasted with Irving's sorrowful appeals to virtue, are delightful and charming lessons like that of little Willie who was afraid in the dark. When Willie learns from his mother that the dark is "only a big shadow over everything," he naturally asks, "What makes the big shadow, mamma?"[143] To this simple inquiry the mother cleverly replies, "I will tell you all about that, Willie, when you are a little older. But now, I wish you would find me a brave boy who is not afraid of the shadows, to run upstairs and get my needlebook."[144] In a similar manner, another lesson delightfully explains that there are "no such things as ghosts and no one need ever expect to see one."[145] And finally, as we confront life's sorrows and fears, let us remember the people of happy tempers, to whom, in the words of Goldsmith, "The most calamitous events, either to themselves or others can bring no new affliction; the world is to them a theater, on which only comedies are acted."[146]

IV

One of the tragedies on the stage of American culture, if we are to judge by the McGuffey readers, was the treatment accorded to the Indian. In this respect the McGuffey readers clearly reflect the waves of humanitarianism that swept over the nation as tribe after tribe was mistreated and dispossessed.[147] Yet it was mostly the West that hated and distrusted the Indian, for in the West conflicting claims to land, broken peace treaties, and opposing economies and modes of livelihood brought into the open a mutual fear.[148] In all this, however, the McGuffey readers argued for justice, humaneness, and the Christian spirit of brotherly love in the treatment of the Indian.

One of the lessons goes so far as to suggest that politicians are not motivated by purely humanitarian impulses. The author laments the removal of the Cherokees and their shipment farther north. He speaks gloomily of the Indians' chances of surviving in this wild territory and of the white man's false guarantees.

To feel any solicitude for the fate of the Indians may be ridiculed as false philanthropy and morbid sensibility. Others may boldly say, "Their blood be upon us"; and sneer at scruples, as weakness unbecoming the stern character of a politician. If, sir, in order to become a politician, it be necessary to divest the mind of the principles of good faith and moral obligation, and harden the heart against every touch of humanity, I confess that I am not—and by the blessing of heaven, will never be, a politician.[149]

Another lesson carries the argument of William Penn to treat the Indians fairly, justly, and as a Christian. Part of his obligations as a Christian involve buying the land from the Indians, who are its proper owners: "Well, then," said Penn in the lesson:

How can I, who call myself a Christian, do what I should abhor even in the heathen? No. I will not do it. But I will buy the right of the proper owners, even of the Indians themselves. By doing this, I shall imitate God himself, in his justice and mercy, and thereby insure his blessing in my colony, if I should ever live to plant one in North America.[150]

The account of the speech of Chief Logan, in one of the lessons of the McGuffey readers, gives us a conception of the troubled relations between the Indian and the white man. When some Indians of the Ohio territory committed a robbery, the whites in that section decided to punish them in their own way, sending out parties to hunt for isolated hunting tribes whom they indiscriminately murdered. Among these isolated Indian groups were large numbers of women and children. After the wars aroused by these unprovoked attacks by the white man had been concluded, Logan, chief of one of the affected tribes, gave his reasons for seeking vengeance.

I appeal to every white man to say, if ever he entered Logan's cabin hungry, and gave him not meat; if ever he came cold and naked, and he clothed him not. During the course of the last long and bloody war, Logan remained idle in his cabin, an advocate for peace. Such was my love for white's, that my countrymen pointed as they passed and said, "Logan is the friend of the white men."[151]

From this friendly attitude, however, Logan passed to hatred and vengeance, because, as he said, the white man "murdered all the relatives of Logan, not sparing even my women and children. This called for revenge. I have sought it. I have killed many. I have fully glutted my vengeance."[152] With these arguments the McGuffey readers appealed for justice in the treatment of the Indian, calling attention to the Christian tenets which had been openly violated in destroying the Indian and stealing his lands. Even the lone survivor of a decimated tribe who returns to see what the white man's civilization has made of his lands cannot find the burial place of his ancestors, exclaiming, "The pale face may like it, but an Indian cannot die here in peace."[153]

A fearful story entitled "Murderer's Creek" explains how that bloody stream got its name. Naoman, the Indian, and Stacy, the white man, were great friends. Because of this great friendship, Noaman is led to tell Stacy's wife of an impending massacre of the whites in revenge for encroachments on Indian lands. The white family, is however, captured and questioned to find out who had warned them. Mrs. Stacy had promised not to reveal her secret, and does not, even when her children are to be sacrificed. Noaman, in gratitude, confesses. But all of them are slaughtered by the Indians, thus giving the fearful name to the creek that ran through the scene of the trial. Among the questions appended to the lesson is, "Which is better, to do harm, or to suffer harm?"[154]

When at last the revengeful tribes were rounded up and placed upon their respective reservations, they became the prey of unscrupulous politicians and grafters who made fortunes selling to the government and the Indian.[155] Despite all this, however, one detects the note of pathos and hopelessness in the tone of the Indian as he adjusts to reservation life, if, indeed, he can adjust. The speech of Chief Joseph dwells upon this sad note of reservation life.

The earth is the mother of all people, and all people should have equal rights upon it. You might as well expect the rivers to run backward as that any man who was born a free man should be contented when penned up and denied liberty to go where he pleases. If you tie a horse to a stake, do you expect he will grow fat? If you pen an Indian upon a small spot of earth, and compel him to stay there, he will not be contented, nor will he grow and prosper. When I think of our condition my heart is heavy.[156]

The Indian, echoed, the McGuffey readers, "will live only in the songs and chronicles of their exterminators. Let these be faithful to their rude virtues, and pay tribute to their unhappy fate, as a people."[157] And the lone Indian, who, in one of the lessons of the readers, returns to sorrow over his stolen lands exclaims, "The leaves are falling, and the clouds are scattering like my people," was not far wrong. Indeed, it is this unhappy fate of the Indian upon which the McGuffey readers dwell.

Perhaps to motivate a better treatment for the dispossessed Indian the McGuffey readers contained stories like "The Grateful Indian" which insist that kindness and humanitarianism is repaid in kindness and love. In the story of the grateful Indian, an Indian stopped at a house and asked for food, promising to pay later. The woman refused him, but a gentleman standing near-by offered to pay for the Indian. Under these circumstances the woman brought food to the Indian. When he had finished eating, the Indian thanked the man and said that he would repay him in some way in the future. Years later this same man was captured by a band of Indians while on a trip. They planned to kill or imprison their white captive. Meantime, however, another Indian crept up, freed the man, and escorted him to his home. It was, of course, the Indian whom the white man had befriended years before.[158]

In a similar manner, a white man insults an Indian who came to his house, seeking water. Later, when the white man falls into danger, the Indian saves his life by taking the white man into his house and caring for him. "If, in the future, a poor Indian, who is hungry, and thirsty, and weary, should ask for a drink of water," the lesson tells us, "do not say to him, 'Begone, you Indian dog.'"[159] On the other hand, though the Indian is generally put in the position of receiving beneficence from the white man, and though the benefit is returned in kind, the Indian is generally represented as a brave man. One warrior, for example, proudly announces at the conclusion of a war in which he, the chief, was forced to sign a treaty with the white man that, "For my country, I rejoice at the beams of peace: but do not harbor a thought that mine is the joy of fear: Logan never felt fear."[160]

In these lessons and stories it is made abundantly clear that the compilers of the McGuffey readers were motivated by impulses of brotherhood, justice, and humanitarianism. Though there is a decreasing emphasis on the Indian theme in the decades following the Civil War, it is plain enough that the humanitarianism of the readers has in no way decreased. And so to kindness, love, good-will, truth, justice, modesty, temperance, and thoughtfulness must be added another social virtue—kindness and justice to the Indian. It is in the presentation of these social virtues in interesting stories and lessons that one of the superiorities of the McGuffey readers lies.[161]

V

We have seen that the virtues emphasized in the McGuffey readers are those which may appropriately be called the social virtues, though they entered equally into the making of the good Christian and the good citizen. These virtues, however much they may have partaken of the great Hebrew-Christian tradition, were, in fact, virtues of a more secular nature. Nevertheless, the two patterns are so tightly interwoven as to defy distinctions. Kindness, truthfulness, modesty, gentleness, thoughtfulness, control of the temper, love, magnanimity, and a general spirit of happiness and good-will toward others,—these are the social virtues the McGuffey readers teach. The vices include intemperance and gambling, not to mention those like dishonesty, which we thought it more expedient to include under the discussion of the morality of the middle class.

We saw that there was very probably a close connection between the temperance crusade and the lessons on temperance in the McGuffey readers. One of the lessons, as we saw, spoke of the progress of the movement; and Dr. McGuffey himself, to whom must be attributed many of the lessons in the earlier editions, was known as a temperance advocate and friend of the great crusader John Gough. However that may be, it is clear enough that the rising tide of intemperance and gambling, all the vices of a frontier people, caused the compilers of the McGuffey readers considerable alarm. But for all this, the stories emphasize the hardship and suffering brought about by intemperance, rather than the unholiness of the vice. It is true, however, that God becomes a convenient ally of the temperance advocates, for he is apparently never on the side of the sinner.

But the point is always stressed that no one has gone too far on the path of sin to redeem himself.

Unfortunately, however, the temperance crusade became involved in the struggle for political power; and since many of the churchly advocates and crusaders were conservatives in politics, it became good strategy to call the party of Jackson a "whisky party." This strategy brought into the conservative fold unnumbered people who had nothing to gain in the conservative fold except support for their hatred of whisky. The strategy of the Women's Christian Temperance Union and other organizations in mobilizing schools and textbooks to support their crusade was noted in passing. But the important fact in this connection is that the McGuffey readers continued to stress temperance throughout all editions and revisions of the books from the earliest editions in the thirties of the nineteenth century to the latest in the twentieth century. This is a pattern, then, that receives continued and generous emphasis in the McGuffey readers.

There is a great deal said, too, about love, kindness, and sympathy for others. In this connection there seemed no direct parallel in the matrix of American culture; but the renewed humanitarianism of the thirties and forties probably had something to do with a similar emphasis in the McGuffey readers. We saw how legend had it that Grant and Lincoln disdained killing animals in the hunt, and how some people went so far as condemn cruelty to trees and fish. The pattern of humanitarianism is strong in the McGuffey readers, though it cannot be clearly distinguished from somewhat related sentiments of love, kindness, tenderness, and sympathy. On the whole, however, the lessons explicitly state the intended moral, and very few leave any doubt in the mind of the reader as to what course of action is desirable.

Finally, we noted that there was a group of miscellaneous virtues, including modesty, restraint, thoughtfulness, obedience, and happiness of outlook. The most clearly defined of the lessons in this miscellaneous group are those on modesty and obedience. Truthfulness, of course, comes in for adequate treatment; but modesty and obedience seem much more to be desired. In this connection it is important to note that obedience is of a strictly unquestioning type, in which the child obeys the requests of father, mother, relative, or employer promptly and without question. Though the stories generally show good reasons for the obedience, none are presented at the time the obedience is demanded. Children are always exclaiming that they are glad they did as they were told. Modesty, too, seems to be highly desired in children and adults. The story of the corpse dressed for a ball must have had a most telling effect upon children, and perhaps the fact that it was ostensibly taken from the diary of a physician may have heightened its authenticity. However that may be, it is clear that the social virtues were designed to make good Christians and good citizens, and that in this respect, if these ends are desirable, the McGuffey readers are much to be admired for their constancy and consistency of purpose, as well as for the charm of many of their stories and lessons.

6

The Basic Pattern

IN SEEKING TO TRACE to their source the main currents of thought in the McGuffey readers, we have been preoccupied with a heritage much older than the readers themselves. For the political conceptions of the McGuffey readers, one must turn to the broadening ideas of the middle-class apologists, to Harrington, Locke, and Blackstone; and for particular adaptations to American culture and the developing capitalist economy, to Hamilton, Marshall, and Webster. For the theological conceptions of the series, one must turn to the rigid system of John Calvin, while the morality may be sought in the middle-class Protestant ethic of thrift, industry, and hard labor; and in such canons of success were found the means which good Puritan divines could recommend to all those whose lives were devoted to laboring in the Lord's vineyard. The social virtues belong to the humane impulses of the great Hebrew-Christian tradition, with some accretions from the diverse humanitarian currents that swept through the eighteenth and nineteenth centuries. In all this we have sought to emphasize that the McGuffey readers were a product of American culture, the leading ideas of which had been passed on from older and more stable generations, and that the ideas of the readers were but the diverse manifestation of this underlying pattern. Let us now examine this pattern, without the benefit of the mass of documentation in preceding chapters, as a concluding essay in the present inquiry.

I

In the mind of Daniel Webster one might find most of the political conceptions of the McGuffey readers. For them he is a link with a Hamiltonian past and a tradition of political scholarship which would in-

clude authorities no less learned in the subtleties of economic determinism than Harrington, Locke, and Blackstone. It was the latter whom the
McGuffey readers employed as the advocate of their conception of the
origin of property, as it was the clear realism of the former that provided
the theoretical foundations of Webster's constitutional nationalism. In
the *Oceana* Webster discovered that power naturally and necessarily follows property, and in property he found the cause of the American Revolution. If the Revolution was fought for the protection and security of
property, as Webster argued, then the Declaration was no more than a
skillful piece of political propaganda whose design was to encourage our
military forces and strengthen our position abroad, as the McGuffey readers concluded.

While this position was no doubt within the tradition of political realism, it seemed to ignore the French romantic equalitarianism which so
captivated the minds and hearts of Jefferson and Paine. There was much
the McGuffey readers were willing to charge against the French Jacobin,
while the agrarian democrat of the Old Dominion was damned with
faint praise. These two gentlemen took the Declaration somewhat more
seriously than either Webster or the McGuffey readers, for both the
former and the latter had conceded that it was as an instrument of propaganda that the great document became useful. The charge against Paine
was atheism, and a similar charge was implied of Jefferson, though by
much more devious routes. But the real threat of Paine to Webster and
the McGuffey readers lay in his denial of the legal arguments of the Constitution. While Burke argued from the irrevocable nature of the contract into which the English people had entered in 1688, Paine argued
the right of revolution and the revocable nature of the social contract.
But the McGuffey readers failed to see anything in Paine's accomplishments except his supposed atheism.

One of the charges against the man who led the Jacobinical rebels of
1800, Jefferson, was his atheism, and this charge, assimilated with various
Hamiltonian projects for a Christian front in politics, was carried over
into the age of Jackson. When that great age of democracy and radicalism dawned, conservatives charged that Jackson was a tyrant and that the
democrats intended to remove the Bible from every household. The
McGuffey readers proposed a religious basis for society, and warned
darkly of the shock of exasperated parties and the revenge of implacable
demagogues. It was proposed that only religion and education could save
the nation from the horrible ravages of universal suffrage, and the Mc-
Guffey readers suggested that educational problems be set with the ob-

ject of reconciling republican institutions with universal suffrage and the terrors of undisciplined democracy. Conservatives sought refuge in the church and courts, and worked out a synthesis that identified the natural with the moral law. Some worthy divines were even willing to concede that inequalities in the distribution of wealth were the ordinances of heaven, and the McGuffey readers declared that God made the rich man as well as poor man.

The effect of this political strategy was to put the McGuffey readers wholly within the conservative tradition in American politics; and that tradition sought its basic ideas in Harrington, Locke, and Blackstone, and bandied these authorities about in the great debate over the Constitution. Unfortunately for the advocates of democracy, the authorities drawn upon in the great debate placed little trust in the wisdom of the people. The great founding fathers who created the Constitution were conscious of the ignorance and tumultuousness of the multitude, and sought refuge from the excesses of democracy in a system of checks and balances which was designed to safeguard property from the ravages of demagoguery and radicalism. Hamilton and the McGuffey readers found the justification for property restrictions on the right to vote in the writings of Blackstone, while Jefferson denounced the latter as the high tory of the conservative priestcraft.

Needless to say, the McGuffey readers were more interested in what Blackstone had to say about the origins of property than in any Jacobinical denunciations by supposed atheists. To that end the McGuffey readers adopted Blackstone's explanations for the origin of private property, and found with him that property was bestowed upon the few in order that a leisure and ruling class be created, and that time be found, freed from weary manual labor, that might be devoted by society's ruling groups to the cultivation of the arts. The primitive communism from which the rights of property grew was dissolved by ordinances from heaven, and these had as their purpose the creation of civil society for the protection and security of property. The divine right of kings was converted to the divine right of men of property to rule, and property acquired thereby not only a civil but also a heavenly sanction.

This concept of private property is the basis for the allegiance of the McGuffey readers to the conservative tradition, and is a sufficient explanation of their identification with the political concepts of Hamilton, Marshall, and Webster. But other explanations rest their case on the defense of the Constitution and the church, and in this great defensive bulwark the McGuffey readers played an important part. In patterns of patriotism and nationalism, they rallied around the flag, the Constitution, and the church. The men at Philadelphia who had constructed the elaborate legal system of the Constitution were looked upon with appropriate reverence and awe as the wisest body of assembled legislators in the history of the world. The cult of Washington strengthened the patriotic sentiment of the readers, and that sentiment was doubly blessed when the McGuffey readers discovered that Washington, Hamilton, and Marshall were good Christian gentlemen who carried in their hearts nothing but tenderness and love for all. But with all this allegiance to conservatism and the Constitution, the McGuffey readers were conscious of the horrors that war brings upon people, and denounced in the strongest terms the misery and bloodshed of the field of battle. But the pride and patriotism implicit in the appeal of Henry Clay against the impressment of American seamen was too irresistible to be deleted from an otherwise perfect record of denunciations of war, and the constitutional nationalism of Webster or the expansionist nationalism of Clay could lead alike to an implied acceptance of recourse to arms in the settlement of disputes which involved the dignity, honor, or greatness of the Republic.

Yet it was the rough libertarians of the Middle Border who seemed to threaten the snug heritage of the Republic. The best laid plans of the gentlemen at Philadelphia seemed threatened by the coonskin apostles of liberty and equality who rollicked the frontier with their laughter and came armed to every crude election. It was they who proposed to take seriously the Jeffersonian principles and sought to demonstrate the sovereignty of the public will. Democracy seemed the state of nature in the West, and backwoods democrats saw no reason to confine their natural politics to the pregnant settlements of the Middle Border.

It is against this background that the educational proposals of the McGuffey readers are clarified. By questioning the possibility of reconciling established institutions with universal suffrage, the McGuffey readers were calling before the bar of reason the principle of public sovereignty, and yet they were questioning nothing that the gentlemen at Philadelphia would not have questioned. The McGuffey readers saw the West itself as a vast Inland Empire, linked together by a series of rivers, outlined by natural barriers, but drawn to the East by the ties of blood and culture. Dr. Beecher's pitiful pleas to the East are pleas for religion, morality, and knowledge in a backwoods empire where nameless adventurers, speculators, thieves, and renegades follow their acquisitive instincts without regard for the amenities of civilization. There are no Mike Finks and Davy Crocketts in the McGuffey readers, for they are a part of the Western heritage which the compilers of the readers sought to deny.

But there were some elements of this heritage the McGuffey readers saw no reason to discard. Even the Mike Finks and Davy Crocketts, the pioneers and the outlaws, the boatmen and thieves, the speculators and renegades of the Middle Border would have applauded the economic individualism and the divine right of acquisition which seemed to lay at the heart of Middle-Western civilization. But this backwoods individualism was converted by subtle means into the middle class individualism of Henry Clay; for with all its rough equalitarianism and coonskin democracy, the Middle Border soon fell prey to the Whiggery of the post-Jacksonian reformation. Though there is much in the McGuffey readers that is Whig in origin and principle, the professed equalitarianism of Whiggery in each election could hardly gain entrance into the McGuffey readers.

With its vast land resources the Middle Border offered attractive hunting grounds for those land-hungry hordes that crossed the Appalachian barrier or followed the shifting course of the Ohio into the valley of rich and fertile farm lands. Agriculture was still the most common business when the first editions of the McGuffey readers appeared, and the speculator was still an element to be reckoned with when the lessons on private property were selected for inclusion in the series. How the accumulation of large tracts of Western lands might be rationalized on the basis of Blackstone's remarks in the McGuffey readers would not be difficult to discover. Those who had come to the valley of acquisition were armed with ordinances from heaven which approved the acquisition of private property in the building up of the Inland Empire. The real estate agent, in a sudden expansion of the lucrative business of capitalistic finance, found himself the center of an interest that bordered on mania, and the gospel of possession found safe roots in his heart.

In part the McGuffey readers must be examined against this background of Middle Western civilization, and the early editions bear mute testimony to the fact that the West was seeking to build a civilization rivaling that of the East. The great concern of the readers is not the abundant economic individualism or the cruder expressions of the acquisitive instinct; rather it is that these elements of a bustling civilization should be properly balanced with appropriate manifestations of a uniform system of manners and morals. To this end it was proposed that religion, morality, and knowledge should be encouraged by the schools, the churches, and the literature of the West, and that by this means the rough democracy of coonskin and log cabin be displaced by a more stable culture in which property could be protected by the principles of law and justice. But the Mike Finks and the renegades, the rough boatmen and the hosts of charlatans, the speculators and the thieves who swarmed to the Inland Empire, however much they may have applauded the economic individualism of the frontier, were no great respecters of private property. It was against the rougher elements of the West that the McGuffey readers struggled, and it was against the Jacobinical radicalism of the followers of Jefferson, Paine, and Jackson that they entered the arena of politics.

II

Yet the moral foundations of this approach to matters of public policy lay far back in the rigid system of John Calvin, from whom the McGuffey readers inherited a sovereign God and the theory of Christ's elect. The Genevan approach to logic and dogma, which issued in great systems of knotted argument and formal belief, was not alien to the McGuffey readers. There is sufficient explanation for political allegiances in the New England Puritanism which runs like a broad stream through numerous lessons and stories, and it is the social inheritance from the great Calvinist stewards that eventually determines matters of public policy.

It is the monarchical principle of a divine Sovereign Will standing like a despot over the petty affairs of men that generates respect for authority and awe before God's stewards on earth. If these stewards turn out to be rich merchants and men of great estate, they too are the elect of God, and it is to them that we owe our allegiance. The cosmic absolutism implied in Calvin's Sovereign Will could hardly avoid the corollary of the universality of moral law, nor could it reasonably reject the necessity of divine judgment. From the former flowed the curious allegiance that bound men of property to the priestcraft, and from the latter flowed the identification of moral and natural law which issued in the judgment that the edicts of the courts were no more than worldly manifestations of universal moral law and the divine will.

The effect of these subtleties was to hedge property with divinity and to give the courts the authority of divine will. This great clerical and judicial synthesis was worked out in detail in the middle decades of the nineteenth century, and formed the framework on which the apostles of property and conservatism rested the reactionary defense. Calvin's Sovereign Will became the Moral Governor, and the conservative philosophy was thereby given a natural as well as a supernatural basis. In the great task of converting an older body of beliefs into an effective safeguard for established institutions, the McGuffey readers played an inevitable and important role.

The foundation of this role was the recognition that religion was the most important basis of society; and its public appeal lay in the fact that Jeffersonian and Jacksonian radicalism had carried with them the hint of atheism and scepticism. The current of anticlericalism was plain enough in Jefferson's philosophy, and Jacksonian radicals did not hesitate to denounce the conservative priestcraft. The McGuffey readers portrayed the desolation that would follow the abandonment of religion; and, as it was Jackson and the democrats who were charged with this desire, the political effect of the McGuffey position could hardly detract from the conservative cause.

It was freely charged that the goal of Jackson's atheistical system was to abolish all property. Clearly the alarm of the conservatives lay not in the destruction of religious institutions, but rather in the destruction of one of the great safeguards of property. And thus it appeared that the sanctity of property, the authority of God's stewards, and the safeguards of wealth would all be destroyed should the ungodly radicals, unholy revolutionaries, and assorted sceptics of the Jacksonian regime prevail in public councils. The attack of the McGuffey readers on all those who would disturb the established order is quite pronounced, and numerous lessons carry the warning that envy of the rich is vain and idle, for the rich are God's stewards, and only the virtues of the industrious and thrifty can bring the hopeful into the house of the elect. Many were those who, in the lessons of the McGuffey readers, found God's will to be wiser than their own wishes, and reasoned that they were not among the elect of God and were thus resigned to poverty and toil.

On the other hand, the McGuffey readers clearly take upon themselves the responsibility for prodding the elect to the faithful performance of their duties. Those who are wealthy are reminded that they are so by the grace of God, and that this grace and concession implies a responsibility toward the poor that all are not willing to discharge. Many are the lessons that praise the charitable activities of the merchant, and many are those that show the kindness of the rich to the poor. Many are the proofs that all is but the working of divine will, and that in every miracle of redemption and in every example of success the hand of the Lord may be seen visibly as the worker of great things. There is cause for awe and reverence in such marvelous works, and obedience is the price of a God conceived in the image of Calvin's cosmic despot, and humble are we before the might of the Sovereign Will.

The relation of Calvin's Sovereign Will to the gospel of wealth in the Gilded Age is an easy chapter in the history of American culture. The spokesman of the new gospel sought the theological foundations of their arguments in the Puritan doctrine of the divinely elect, and found that the Moral Governor sanctioned not only the right but the duty to acquire property. To the spokesmen of this school of thought it appeared that governments had been instituted as a sort of earthly safeguard for heavenly inspired ordinances of acquisition. These bequests from the Moral Governor were not only natural rights but also moral duties laid upon the elect by the heavenly Deity. From this reasoning issued a resuscitation of the divine right of property, ever more pertinent to the maturing capitalist economy of the Gilded Age, and welcomed by textbooks like the McGuffeys readers which could see no cause to dispute the ordinances of the Creator.

But this current of thought was no more than a revival of a doctrine at least as old as Cotton Mather and the theological predecessors of all Puritan divines. However much was made of the divine right of property by the subtle metaphysicians of the Bay colony, it was left to Benjamin Franklin and the secularists of the eighteenth century to preach the doctrine to the land-hungry hordes of the Middle Border. The Puritan code of worldly asceticism in which work and thrift were sanctified could hardly exist without its counterpart in the divine right to acquire. When Mark Hopkins discovered that the acquisition of property was sanctioned by love, he was merely substituting for the older Calvinist discipline the theory of divine love.

But at its base the sanctification of acquisition by the theory of divine love was no more than a renascence of the Calvinist theory of the elect, for Mark Hopkins argued that the acquisition of property was, after all, merely a means of benefiting others. There was nothing in the newer forms of the doctrine of stewardship which the McGuffey readers could deny, for God made some men wealthy in order that He might benefit others. In both old and new forms the doctrine of stewardship appears in the McGuffey readers buttressed by numerous stories and lessons which illustrate the divine principle of benevolence as it is displayed by God's worthy stewards on earth. In the face of these arguments, it is not surprising that Bishop Lawrence should find that Godliness was in league with riches, and that material prosperity was helping make the national character more like that of Christ.

When Andrew Carnegie gave the gospel its definitive form, he was only echoing arguments and sharing beliefs that Americans had affirmed centuries before; and he could not lack support for his gospel, for everywhere the millionaire was to be but the trustee for the poor, and the McGuffey readers could declare that in man's extremity was God's opportunity. The capitalist utopia envisaged by Carnegie, a utopia in which capitalistic princes would spread their charity and benevolence throughout the land in accordance with the moral injunctions from above, was, after all, no more than that for which the McGuffey readers had argued for over half a century. If they sought to put the emphasis on benevolence, they did not neglect the proper encouragement of acquisition, and showed quite easily the virtues by which the hopeful might enter the household of the elect.

The younger secular prophets of the doctrine of stewardship were perhaps quite unaware of the Calvinist foundations of their thinking, though they preached abundantly the intimate connection between poverty and sin. The road to success was also the straight road on which the Puritan virtues were to be won, and the relation of morals to wealth seemed clear to all thinking persons. It was argued that the poor would always be with us, that the best for them was charity and benevolence, but that no one need be poor. There are, argued the apostles of acquisition, numerous avenues to success that stand open for the sober, the frugal, the thrifty, and the energetic; and they could point with pride and truth at the many examples of persons of humble origins who had risen to positions of power and affluence. The capitalistic utopia envisaged by Andrew Carnegie seemed at hand, and never before had an older Calvinist body of belief found so many appropriate uses. The success of many seemed but the living proof of a body of belief held by the overwhelming majority of Americans, and the McGuffey readers could argue with reason that the road to success lay close at hand for those who took to themselves the virtues of the middle class, pointing out that the real benefit of work lay in building a noble and beautiful character. The hand of the Lord on the ordinances from heaven was plain to all those who heeded the call to labor and acquire.

For among the ordinances from heaven was the sacred calling to labor in the Lord's vineyard in the hope not only of material but also eternal salvation. The McGuffey readers have set it down that the voice of the Almighty Benevolence calls to us to arise and labor. No more shall we partake of the sparkling pleasures of the worldly who spend their days in idleness and vanity. They have not harkened unto the Lord's voice crying out to the faithful to labor and to acquire. For the spirit of acquisition in the guise of a heavenly ordinance is in the drab ideal of laborious gain, relentless thrift, and endless toil which the McGuffey readers set before us. But labor we must, if we wish to enter the house of the elect.

This, too, is a product of an older heritage finding greater potentialities in the ethic of a rising middle class. For the medieval conception of production for consumption, of production for use, is substituted the middle-class notion of production for profit. Knowledge is not power, as Lord Bacon wanted us to believe; knowledge is gold, the McGuffey readers tell us, pushing the spirit of gain into the schoolhouse. To labor diligently in the vocation to which one is called by God, and to seek eternal salvation in the chaos of acquisition, are the commandments laid upon every aspiring son of the middle class; and to harken to the Lord's voice as he calls us to labor, and to be thrifty of the means and possessions the Lord puts into our hands, are the safest routes to material prosperity and the proper exaltation for the business of the marketplace.

By such means and such harkenings was bred the discipline of the middle class imposed by the great Taskmaster on all classes alike. By such means did the middle class capture the state and create a nation of tradesmen. The great competition is a contest of election to the calling of stewardship, and the necessities of salvation demand the eternally competitive society in which God's elect can receive notice of their proper calling. Mr. Toil is the most persistent and popular of all the lessons in the McGuffey readers, and Hugh Idle is hardly respected among the elect. Thus, not to labor diligently, whether for God or for one's employer, was the cardinal sin; work, thrift, self-denial, were the cardinal virtues. These are the lessons the acquisitive society teaches, with or without schoolhouses, and we must not be surprised to find them in the McGuffey readers; for the sign of the middle class is written large upon them, and the virtues of the middle class lie at the very core of our civilization.

However pleasing to the elect, the theory of the divinely elected gave slight consolation to the host who must fail in the acquisitive society. To them it must appear that the right to be the steward of great wealth has been denied because of some slighting of the heavenly ordinances; and as the stewardship has been denied, there is nothing left but resignation to poverty or a new resolve to labor ever harder in the hope of redemption. The successes which children could daily witness around them as the great stewards rose from humble positions to stations of affluence and power were spur enough to the laggard ambitions and reminder enough of the heavenly callings. The ideal of material success the McGuffey readers constantly put before the little ones, and, like Jonathan Edward's victims, they were stirred up horribly to seek God.

The great moral synthesis of the American middle class, though enjoined by the Puritans and Protestants, was the work of generations of Americans who achieved so striking a synthesis of Christian and middle class virtues as to put the Puritan fathers in the shade. Those New England divines were sufficiently acquainted with the heavenly ordinances to labor diligently as stewards with both personal and public responsibilities; but the stewardship of later generations, of those who read the McGuffey readers, came to mean primarily the personal duty to acquire and possess, with only an occasional gesture of charitable or public activity. The great achievement of the McGuffey readers is the complete integration of Christian and middle-class virtues; and in that respect, they are the great textbook product of American middle-class culture. Though quick enough to heed the Lord's calling to labor and acquire, they could hardly embrace any political doctrine which threatened material possessions or hindered the enjoyment of the fruits of acquisition.

It was somewhat inevitable that Calvin's Sovereign Will should issue in universal moral law erected on a kind of cosmic constitutionalism. The chief proponents of this view were substantial conservatives like Marshall, Kent, and Story who sought by subtle means to find supernatural sanctions for the opinions of the bench. Marshall declared his allegiance to the rights and duties handed down by the Moral Governor of the universe, and Story saw in our common dependence on the decisions of the Creator admirable analogies to the legal arrangements of civil societies. Even Channing and Emerson found a higher law than that which men sought to obey, and shared with many Americans the belief in the universality of moral law. The concept of a fundamental moral law was a legitimate child of Calvinist theological presuppositions, and the McGuffey readers found in the universality of the moral law sufficient grounds for the concept of cosmic constitutionalism.

It was on the concept of cosmic constitutionalism that Kent and Story tried to erect a more secular superstructure of judicial decisions sanctified and purified by its identity with fundamental moral law. Chancellor Kent found that the law of the courts was no more than a body of general principles founded on the constitution of the cosmos, and Justice Story believed that the courts were to administer justice in accordance with universal moral law. Moreover, they sought to identify moral with natural law, so that judicial interpretation would be based on both moral and natural law and gain thereby not only a heavenly but also a natural sanction. In the face of this kind of reasoning, it is not surprising that the McGuffey readers found established institutions built on unquestionable moral foundations and gently hinted that the Constitution drawn up at Philadelphia bore striking resemblances to its cosmic counterpart in heaven.

Yet Calvin's Sovereign Will could issue in quite humane impulses, as long as the universality of moral law prevailed as a conception among the devout. However much Christian ideals might be utilized by the enterprising middle class in an orgy of labor and acquisition, an older heritage from the great Hebrew-Christian tradition insisted on the dignity and worth of the individual and on his value as one of the worthies created in the image of God. In the end, it is the body of belief in the Christian code of ethics which redeems the McGuffey readers from the charge of an overwhelming preoccupation with the ideals of the middle class. Though interpenetrated with middle class ideals, the McGuffey readers were unstinting in their insistence on Christian virtues in the conduct of life.

The identity of the moral and the natural law, a conception so profitable to the proponents of cosmic constitutionalism, could also lead to the identification of the civil and the Christian virtues. From this conception came the social virtues of kindness, truthfulness, temperance, modesty, and good-will. These virtues were an important part of the catalogue of virtues in the McGuffey readers; and though they never saw in the virtues of the middle class anything damaging to the virtues approved by the Christian ethic, and do in fact intermingle them with an alarming promiscuity, they make it quite clear that profanity, gambling, intemperance, vice, unkindness, immodesty, and assorted characteristics are not desirable either for the good citizen or for the devout Christian. It is this Christian code of ethics redeemed from a mangled tradition and identified as the proper code for the good citizen that rescues the McGuffey readers from being exclusively the instrument of the middle class. For their denunciation of war, crime, and inhumanity, and for their magnificent promotion of the brotherhood of man under the fatherhood of God, the McGuffey readers must stand among the great textbooks of America; but in other respects, they are the studied and articulate reflection of a civilization dominated by middle class ideals.

Appendix:

Nature and Scope of the Problem

I

THE HERITAGE OF IDEAS which may be reckoned as distinctly American may be sought among the soiled pages of old textbooks which have captured the modes of thought appropriate to their own age. The span of years in the life of the McGuffey series makes them a provocative and promising object of study; and if they are not torn from their historical context, if they are placed with perspective against the background of thought and culture, they may aid in the recording of some hitherto untold chapters in the history of American culture. In seeking the main currents of thought in the McGuffey readers, however, we have been preoccupied with a heritage of ideas very much older than the readers themselves; and we shall, in consequence, attempt to place before those who read this work some indication of the older sources and traditions from which the ideas in the McGuffey readers are ultimately derived.

If it is true that a child is born into a culture, and that the process by which it acquires the behavior patterns, the values, and the basic ideas that constitute its culture is essentially one of learning, it is clear that a study which attempts to describe the basic pattern of ideas in a textbook series is essentially concerned to point out to educators the body of belief and idea with which the compilers of the series sought to acquaint children. In this connection, it is important to suggest that while a study of the type proposed is primarily concerned to describe the ideological content of textbooks, the resulting description, if properly carried out, may also be indicative of the commonly persuasive ideas of a given civilization.

In this respect, it is clear that a creative and positive role may be played by the compilers of textbooks; for though they doubtless attempt to reflect the commonly accepted persuasions of their civilization, they also have choices to make, and these choices are made always within a framework of the necessary, the desirable, and the possible. In this way textbook compilers may contribute to the shaping of the basic ideas and values of their culture, and their part in the educative process can be crucial and strategic.

But these are questions which the present inquiry cannot hope to decide. It is concerned, rather, to define the choices made by the compilers of the McGuffey readers by describing their basic pattern of ideas. Questions regarding the responsibility of each of the several compilers of the series are, of course, beyond the scope of this study; but it can indicate by means of the basic pattern the essential choices made and the values and ideas conserved. In this respect the study should be of value both to the students of educational history and to textbook compilers.

The problem of this study is, therefore, to analyze the meaning and significance of the basic pattern of ideas in the McGuffey readers in terms of the background of American thought and culture. If the study is properly and adequately carried out, we should be able to conclude the study with an extended statement of the social and moral foundations of the ideas described in the basic pattern, and we should be able to show, in consequence, what elements in the American heritage of ideas and values the compilers of the McGuffey readers sought to conserve, to defend, and to perpetuate. If these modest objectives can be achieved, the author will be content that he has made some small contribution to the history of education in the United States.

II

The significance of the material to be dealt with cannot be passed by without mention; for it seems entirely probable that the McGuffey readers were the most famous and influential textbook product in the annals of American educational history. In attempting to explain the fame and success of the McGuffey series, some students have been willing to accept incredible legends, and the numerous fictions concerning the life of their original compiler do, to say the least, make the serious student regret the paucity of reliable source material on so important a subject.

It is not for us here to repeat the history of the McGuffey readers, for that interesting saga has been told with relish and charm by Henry Vail in *A History of the McGuffey Readers;*[1] nor is it within our province to recapitulate the almost legendary story of the life of William Holmes McGuffey, original compiler of the series, for that story has been told with devotion in the pages of Harvey C. Minnich's *William Holmes McGuffey and His Readers.*[2] But perhaps it would be well to indicate the significance of the McGuffey series in the history of American textbook writing.

While the authenticity of some of the traditions that have grown up about the readers may, to say the least, be open to question, the social, moral, and cultural influence of the readers has frequently been praised. Many are those who announce their great debt to the compilers of the McGuffey readers, noting in tribute that much of their own characters is attributable to this early influence. Hamlin Garland, for example, notes the awakening of his literary taste in the McGuffey selections:

I wish to acknowledge my deep obligation to Professor McGuffey, whoever he may have been, for the dignity and literary grace of his selections. From the pages of his readers I learned to know and love the poems of Scott, Byron, Southey, Wordsworth, and a long line of English masters. I got my first taste of Shakespeare from the selections which I read in those books.[3]

In a similar manner Hugh Fullerton, in an article in the *Saturday Evening Post*, calls attention to the fact that the influence of the McGuffey readers in forming the taste and morals of children was, excepting the Bible, the greatest in the nation.[4] Nor can one dismiss the testimony of Herbert Quick who said of the McGuffey readers that:

These textbooks constitute the most influential volumes ever published in America. They were our most popular reading books for many generations—and for anything I know in their present form—they may be still. They had a spirit of their own, compilations as they were. And it was, in spite of much that was British in selections and illustrations, the spirit of America at its best.[5]

According to a letter from Mr. Louis Dilman, president of the American Book Company, successors to the parent companies which published the McGuffey readers, more than 122,000,000 readers were sold between 1836 and 1920.[6] This estimate is close to that of *Time Magazine*, which estimated the total number of readers sold to be 124,000,000.[7] But both estimates are in disagreement with that of Minnich, who prepared a graph of the number of copies of the McGuffey readers printed between 1843 and 1898. The high point of the graph is 1880, when, according to the information of the graph, 1,700,000 copies of the readers were printed.[8] It seems likely, however, that the estimate of the American Book Company is more nearly correct. According to the letter from its president, Louis Dilman, the sales of the McGuffey readers were as follows:[9]

1836-1850	7,000,000
1850-1870	40,000,000
1870-1890	60,000,000
1890-1920	15,000,000

These figures apparently substantiate the statements made by other observers. Between 1840-1880, writes Nila B. Smith, the McGuffey readers "outstripped all others in sales and popularity."[10] And *Newsweek* states of the McGuffey readers: "They were the basic school books in 37 states; in some they were the only ones."[11] With these statements Rusk seems to be in general agreement. "Upon the generation immediately following the pioneer period," he writes, "the influence of McGuffey may well have been greater than that of any other writer or statesman in the west. His name became a tradition, not yet extinct."[12] Though this statement would have to be modified because of the numerous contributors to the McGuffey readers, it would be substantially correct if we take the name of McGuffey as a symbol for their general social and cultural influence. "For seventy-five years," writes Hugh Fullerton,

his system and his books guided the minds of four-fifths of the school children of the nation in their taste for literature, in their morality, in their school development, and, next to the Bible, in their religion.[13]

Though this estimate seems somewhat high, the general tone of the argument is correct. A more modest and historically correct statement seems to be that of Reeder, who writes that:

The McGuffey series has probably attained the largest sale and widest distribution of any series yet produced in America. In range of subject matter it swept almost the entire field of human interest—morals, politics, literature, history, science, philosophy. Many a profound and lasting impression was made upon the lives of children and youth by the well-chosen selections of this series and valuable lessons of industry, thrift, economy, kindness, generosity, honesty, courage, duty, found expression in the lives of millions of boys and girls who read and reread these books, to the influence of which lessons were directly traceable.[14]

Mark Sullivan's survey of the McGuffey influence, though based primarily on the reminiscences of public men, is enlightening. "In a rather painstaking survey to determine the area of McGuffey's influence," writes Sullivan, "I found that apparently it had never reached any of New England except the one small southwestern corner close to New York City. Elsewhere McGuffey's was almost universal."[15] Taking everything into account, concluded Sullivan,

it would not be surprising if at least half the school children of America, from 1836 to 1900, drew inspiration from McGuffey's Readers. When America sent expeditions of school-teachers to carry American culture to the Philippines and Porto Rico, McGuffey's Readers were translated into Spanish; when Japan felt an urge to experiment with American ways, McGuffey's was translated and carried its democratic point of view into the background of a crystallized feudalism centuries old.[16]

But these bald figures hardly tell us the influence wielded by the readers in forming the tastes, attitudes, and opinions of millions of Americans. The picture sketched by Mark Sullivan is hardly overdrawn:

McGuffey's was the source of that stock of points of view and tastes held in common, which constituted much of America's culture, its codes of morals and conduct, its standards of propriety, its homely aphorisms, its "horse-sense" axioms. In this field McGuffey's embodied, of course, some points of view common to civilization everywhere; but McGuffey's also taught and accounted for mental attitudes and ethical concepts which differentiated the American from other peoples, or were more emphasized in America than elsewhere.[1]

Of course, when these evidences are examined on the principles of internal criticism and historical method, they reveal that much is to be desired in the way of authentic primary materials. But they were introduced merely to suggest the strong significance of the materials examined in this study, not as authoritative and reliable statements of fact. The most expert and reliable testimony thus far introduced, the letter of Mr. Louis Dilman, president of the American Book Company, successors to the parent publishers of the McGuffey series, however subject to the principles of internal criticism and historical method, does seem to this investigator to bear out the general tendency and tone of the other claims. And it does not seem too much to maintain, therefore, that the McGuffey readers have exercised a persuasive influence over the mind, the morals, and the manners of the American people.

III

A survey of the literature related to the problem proposed in this study will serve to orient the study with reference to other investigations and to provide suitable background materials for subsequent discussions. Several investigators have undertaken to tell the story of the historical development of school readers and reading instruction. Reeder studied *The Historical Development of School Readers and Method in Teaching Reading,* but the study contains little that is pertinent to this investigation. Smith studied *American Reading Instruction* in an effort to cover materials not dealt with in the earlier study by Reeder, and though the fame and influence of the McGuffey readers are mentioned several times in the context of her study, references to the subject-matter of this investigation are cursory. Clifton Johnson has discussed old-time reading books in an article in the *New England Magazine,* "More Quaint Readers." Rosenbach has prepared a general treatise on *Early American Children's*

Books. Rusk has uncovered some of the readers of the pioneer period in his magnificent study of *The Literature of the Middle Western Frontier.* Mahoney has discussed "Readers of the Good Old Days" in the pages of the *Educational Review.* For the history of the McGuffey readers, however, the most satisfactory reference is Vail's *A History of the McGuffey Readers,* though it may be supplemented by the numerous periodical references in the bibliography of this report.

For materials on the life of William Holmes McGuffey, original compiler of the McGuffey series, one must be content with limited primary resources. Dr. McGuffey's letters in the McGuffey Museum Collection provide an interesting insight into the temper and character of the man, though there is little of positive value for this study. His manuscript on philosophy, however, contributes to an understanding of Dr. McGuffey's religious impulses, though these are attested well enough by the early editions of the readers. In this connection, the letters of Alexander McGuffey indicate some of Dr. McGuffey's relationships with the Cincinnati literati, and his speeches before the Western Literary Institute and College of Professional Teachers are preserved in the published transactions of that association. The autobiography of Henrietta McGuffey adds a few facts concerning McGuffey's experiences at Ohio University, but contributes nothing of value for this inquiry. The records of the boards of trustees at Miami University, Ohio University, and the University of Virginia contain bits of informaton on the appointment of Dr. McGuffey.

Secondary materials on the life and career of William Holmes McGuffey abound, but they are largely of an unreliable character. The best brief statement is contained in Harvey Minnich's articles in the *Encyclopedia Britannica* and in his *William Holmes McGuffey and His Readers.* The latter publication contains a brief chapter on the social teachings of the McGuffey readers, but the material consists largely of sample lessons and stories. Philip Alexander Bruce's account of McGuffey's career at the University of Virginia in his *History of the University of Virginia* is extremely judicious and interesting, but contributes nothing to the purposes of this study. John L. Clifton's *Ten Famous American Educators* contains a brief chapter on the life and career of Dr. McGuffey. Colby's *The Grand Old Man of the Little Red Schoolhouse* and Melachon Tope's *A Biography of William Holmes McGuffey* are largely eulogy and fiction. To catch the literary and textbook spirit of the time in which the McGuffey readers had their origin, consult Rusk's *The Literature of the Middle Western Frontier,* or William Venable's *Beginnings of Literary Culture in the Ohio Valley.* These may be supplemented, however, by James Miller's *The Genesis of Western Culture* and B. W. Bond's *The*

Civilization of the Old Northwest, though the latter work covers a period somewhat earlier than that in which the McGuffey readers had their origin.

Of the mass of periodical literature that has developed concerning the life of Dr. McGuffey and the famous McGuffey readers, very little is of primary value. The article by Catherine Beecher in the early *Cincinnati Journal and Western Luminary* is valuable as a primary source in the dispute regarding the piracy of materials from the Worcester readers. The article on "Literary Plagiarisms" in the *American Annals of Education* is likewise valuable as an Eastern interpretation of the piracy dispute. The same periodical contains an article on "Movements in Ohio," which illustrates the Eastern critic's view of Dr. McGuffey's educational travels. Current articles of a secondary nature are listed in the bibliography of this study, but contain very little that is pertinent to this investigation.

Several studies of the content of school readers are, however, pertinent to this study. Tingelstad studied "The Religious Element in American School Readers up to 1830" and concluded that by that date religious content was all but disappearing.[18] Perkins studied the "Historical Development of the Moral Element in American School Readers," indicating in the graphs and tables of his study a tendency of the moral element to increase as the religious content decreased and readers became more secular in nature.[19] Hosic discussed "The Content of School Reading Books" in *School and Society,* but the discussion contains nothing relevant to this study.[20] Wood reported on "The Overlapping of the Content of Fifteen Second Grade Readers" in the *Journal of Educational Research,* but the study does not appear directly relevant to our investigation.[21] The more inclusive studies of *The Foundations of Nativism in American Textbooks* by Fell, and of *Civic Attitudes in American Textbooks* by Pierce, while they contain nothing directly applicable to this study, are certainly in the spirit of our study.[22] Robinson undertook to describe *Two Centuries of Change in the Content of School Readers* by setting up criteria against which he could tabulate the number of pages devoted to each; and while his study contributes nothing directly to this inquiry, his findings are of interest as a basis of comparison with other studies.[23]

The study most pertinent to this inquiry is Hughes' "An Analysis of the Fourth, Fifth, and Sixth McGuffey Readers." Dr. Hughes tabulated the titles of lessons and stories in the McGuffey readers in an attempt to demonstrate that certain titles had persisted throughout all the revisions of the fourth, fifth, and sixth readers and concluded, in consequence, that much of the fame of the series could be explained in terms of the persisting titles. He was able to show, moreover, that the original compiler of the series was responsible for a greater percentage of the persisting titles, and he concluded from that fact that Dr. McGuffey was entitled to the fame that history has so generously accorded him.[24] By combining the selections of the original compiler and those of his brother, Alexander McGuffey, Dr. Hughes found that they had contributed over fifty per cent of the persisting lessons in the three higher readers.[25]

Vincent Davis studied *The Literature of the Advanced School Readers,* indicating, among other items, factors in national development that had found their way into advanced readers. Using the theme-count method rather than the title-count method of the Hughes study, Davis isolated factors like economics, education, national consciousness, religion, agrarianism, war and peace, slavery, temperance, and morals, then determined by tabular count the decades during which each factor entered into the literature of the advanced school readers.[26] His conclusions with respect to literary materials and their quality are, however, beyond the scope of this study. Davis concluded with respect to the factors in national development that only religion and national consciousness seem to have been consciously emphasized.[27]

Judging from a survey of the literature related to the problem proposed in this study, then, the way would seem clear for a study of the type herein described. Though the criteria and methods, not to speak of the chronology and materials, are different for each study surveyed, it is clear that a few decades of additional research in this area will provide a valuable body of materials on the content of school readers. As for the study herein proposed, its main objective is to describe the pattern of ideas in terms of the culture which made it possible, rather than to tabulate titles or themes from a wide variety of materials. Each of the studies surveyed has its own methods and procedures to recommend it, and this study would be remiss in its obligations if it did not describe the procedures by which the research was undertaken and the conclusions derived.

IV

Perhaps it would be well, however, before turning to a discussion of the procedures of this investigation, to define the principal terms employed in this investigation. As the title suggests, the immediate problem that arose was to decide in what way the terms "social" and "moral" were delimiting. The vocabulary of this study is not far different from that encountered in the universe of discourse of the social and moral disciplines, and for that reason, the following authoritative difinitions have been more or less freely adapted from the *Dictionary of Sociology*.[28]

DEFINITIONS OF THE PRINCIPAL TERMS EMPLOYED IN THIS INVESTIGATION

attitude—an acquired or learned tendency to react toward or against something or somebody.

belief—the acceptance of a given proposition as true.

capitalism—the general economic system giving characteristic form to the present social order of the industrially advanced countries, the leading features of which are (a) private ownership of land and capital resources by individuals, partnerships, or corporations, (b) operation in competition primarily for the private profit of owners, (c) stimulation of enterprise, (d) increase of inventions, (e) specialization of finance, (f) rapid enlargement of production, (g) world-wide extension of commerce, (h) growth of powerful corporate organizations, producing (i) strong private influence in government, (j) periodic depressions, and (k) increasingly powerful labor organizations.

conservatism—the social philosophy or attitude which tends to resist change, and to adhere to and support the established order.

culture—a collective name for all behavior patterns socially acquired and socially transmitted by means of symbols.

democracy—a philosophy or social system that stresses participation in, and proportional control of, the affairs of the community by the individual member, on the basis of his personal selfhood as a human being, regardless of his qualities, rank, status, or possessions.

ideal—an imaginary or non-existential, culturally defined situation, characteristic, or behavior pattern which serves as an aim or goal for the activity of a person or group.

ideology—the aggregate of ideas, beliefs, and modes of thinking characteristic of a group, nation, class, caste, profession, occupation, party, etc.

institution—an enduring, complex, integrated, organized behavior pattern through which social control is exerted and by means of which fundamental social desires and needs are met.

middle class—a social stratum emerging in modern times between the landed aristocracy and the peasants or serfs of the feudal order; but recognized in the Roman republic by the equestrian rank, in the empire by the title of decurio, and in medieval times by various forms of the word burgher, though in modern times sometimes referred to as the bourgeoisie.

moral conduct—a form of behavior involving consideration or choice of right and wrong, appraised in terms of a standard of values or a code of morals, toward which a person recognizes a duty or feels a sense of responsibility.

moral idea—a statement or proposition relating to moral conduct.

morality of the middle class—the moral ideas or professed morals of the bourgeoisie as a social class, characterized by the cult of respectability, interest in secular education, the sanctity of wealth, the dignity and worth of labor, indefatigable enterprise, and sometimes moral inhibitions.

property—any valuable right or interest, considered primarily as a source or element of wealth.

social conduct—any behavior having to do with the reciprocal relations of interacting human beings, either as individuals or groups.

social idea—a statement or proposition relating to social conduct.

social order—the totality of human relationships and culture of any given area or time.

social thought—the totality of man's thought about his relationships and obligations to his fellow men.

social values—objects, events, or experiences to which group consensus has imputed value.

Despite the obvious inclusiveness of the qualifying terms in this report, the delimitations effected by "social" and "moral" should now be apparent. In declaring our intention of examining social and moral ideas in the McGuffey readers, we are indicating our purpose of establishing a pattern of ideas relating to social conduct, defined as behavior having to do with the reciprocal relations of interacting human beings, either as individuals or groups, and of ideas relating to moral conduct, defined as behavior involving consideration or choice of right and wrong, appraised in terms of a standard of values or a code of morals toward which a person recognizes a duty or feels a sense of responsibility. Though the terms "social" and "moral" are broad and inclusive, they do eliminate literary, esthetic, and other formal judgments.

V

Having defined tentatively the type of material to be collected, the way was cleared for the setting up of procedures by which the material of the study could be collected, organized, and reported. The primary source material of the investigation is, of course, the McGuffey readers. Most of the readers referred to in the documentation of this inquiry are to be found in the Library of Congress, the Library of the Ohio Archaeological and Historical Society, Columbus, Ohio, the Detroit Public Library, the New York Public Library, and in the personal collections of Miss Maude Blair and Mr. Henry Ford of Detroit, Michigan. These repositories contain collections that come close to being complete, though the New York Public Library has only a limited quantity of the earlier editions. Inquiries to the librarians of the collections canvassed led to other repositories reputed to have materials, but only the Cincinnati Public Library proved to have any materials that had not previously been examined.

It would be difficult, however, if not impossible, to assemble a complete collection of the McGuffey readers. For a complete collection, in the literal sense of that term, would include, as one student noted, "all imprints made from duplicate plates, all supplemental printings, all new editions, and all revisions."[29] The most that one can claim is that the readers examined in this study represent more than a judicious sampling, and the author is confident that if it were possible to have a complete collection of the McGuffey readers, in the literal sense of that term, it would not materially affect his findings. In this connection, it is particularly fortunate that the investigator was able to examine all editions known to have been printed in a foreign language, and appropriate references to the German and Spanish editions will be found in the documentation of this study. The Japanese edition, moreover, was printed with alternate pages of Japanese and English, thus obviating the necessity of mastering that tongue or of employing a translator.

The first test applied to the materials of this study was the test of external criticism of the readers. Since the compilers of the McGuffey readers had been numerous, the names of William Holmes McGuffey or Alexander McGuffey were hardly reliable tests of the genuineness of the readers, even though the name "McGuffey" appears on the title page of almost every reader. As some of the primers and readers had omitted the name from the title page, however, it was found that the name "McGuffey" on the title page could not be the final test. It was found, nevertheless, that the terms "eclectic" or eclectic series" appeared consistently on the readers examined. Even the terms "McGuffey" or "eclectic," either individually or in combination, proved in the end to be uncertain clues, as foreign editions of the McGuffey readers occasionally omitted both terms. Finally, it was determined that the adequate test of the genuineness of the materials to be examined was the imprint of one of the parent publishing firms of the series or their successors who owned the plates and copyrights of the originals. These firms are: (1) Truman and Smith; (2) W. B. Smith; (3) W. B. Smith and Company; (4) Sargent, Wilson, and Hinkle; (5) Wilson, Hinkle, and Company; (6) Van Antwerp, Bragg, and Company; (7) the American Book Company. The use of the terms "McGuffey" or "eclectic" or "eclectic series" and the imprint of the companies named are, then, the adequate tests to be applied to the materials of the study.

Shifting now from the authenticity of the materials studied to the processes of internal criticism, it was thought best to let the stories and lessons in the McGuffey readers speak for themselves; and it will be found that the study bristles with direct quotations from the readers, from the lessons and stories, in an effort to put before those who care to read this report the ideas in the language of the original. As many of the lessons and stories are from literature and well-known works and bear the name of the author, and as the lessons and stories of the McGuffey readers are the selections of numerous compilers, questions concerning the authorship of the lesson or story and questions concerning the literal or real meaning of the author in the original context of writing are beyond the scope of this inquiry. Each age, wrote a well-known educational historian, records: " (1) what it considers to be of interest or value, (2) what it has the eye to see, and (3) the will to make known."[30] In the context of this study, then, the proper question is, What attitudes, interests, values, and ideas did the compilers and editors of the McGuffey readers have the eye to see and the will to make known, and what were the social and moral foundations of those attitudes, interests, values, and ideas?

As the research proceeded, it soon became apparent that the McGuffey readers were consistently stressing a few basic ideas, playing upon a few major themes, with many nuances and variations. As the data proliferated, natural groupings of ideas manifested themselves; and the mass of data fell into rather natural chapter groupings. The continuity of the basic pattern of ideas is, despite occasional lapses into contemporaneity like the fight against the Catholic bias and the crusade for justice to the Indian, quite the remarkable phenomenon of the whole series. However, though the study seeks the main currents of thought in the readers, it has not neglected any ideas which might legitimately be qualified under the terms "social" and "moral" as herein defined. This has sometimes resulted in placing a minor theme or cluster of ideas into a larger natural grouping. The case of the American Indian, for example, has been treated under the chapter dealing with the social virtues, and the prospects of American women have been treated under the chapter dealing with the struggle for political power, though it could be argued that these clusters belong in other groupings. However that may be, the author believes that when one has read the research report he will agree that the groupings are more than merely arbitrary.

In an effort to eliminate selective bias in the collection of materials, two persons working independently but using the tentative definitions of the qualifying terms of the investigation examined nine editions of the first reader. After the statements or ideas relating to social conduct were examined and compared, a correlation of eighty-seven was found between the work of the two persons. After the statements and ideas relating to moral conduct were examined and compared, a correlation of eighty-nine was found between the work of the two persons. But in the collection of materials it was sometmies found that the differences between the two persons lay in the datum selected, rather than in what the datum expressed. It is possible, therefore, that the correlations may have been higher. The same test applied to fifteen second grade readers resulted in correlations of eighty-five for social materials and eighty-eight for moral materials. Every test seemed to indicate that the criteria of the qualifying terms of this report were reasonably accurate.

VI

One can only say, in conclusion, that in writing the research report and in interpreting the data collected an attempt has been made to present the significance of certain basic ideas in the McGuffey readers in terms of the body of belief and idea which has come to be reckoned as traditionally American. Such a study will of necessity deal with intellectual backgrounds, with the germinal ideas and the traditions of thought which go to make up the American heritage; but it will deal with them in such a way as to make the pattern of ideas in the McGuffey readers a part of that larger pattern which is the context of American culture.

The present inquiry, then, faces the problem of describing the basic pattern of ideas in the McGuffey readers in terms of the context of culture that made those ideas necessary, possible, or desirable. Its success must be judged in terms of the questions the study has set out to answer, and these questions are, as we have already noted, What attitudes, interests, values, and ideas did the compilers and editors of the McGuffey readers have the eye to see and the will to make known? What were the social and moral foundations of those attitudes, interests, values, and ideas?

Notes

NOTES FOR CHAPTER ONE

1. Daniel Webster, *Works* (Boston, 1851), III, 13-14.
2. *Ibid.*, III, 14-16.
3. *McGuffey's Newly Revised Rhetorical Guide* (Cin., 1853), 459.
4. *McGuffey's Newly Revised Eclectic Fourth Reader* (Cin., 1853), 324-326.
5. *McGuffey's New Sixth Eclectic Reader* (Cin., 1866), 319-322.
6. *Eclectic Fourth Reader* (Cin., 1837), 198-199.
7. Webster, *op. cit.*, III, 15-16.
8. Thomas Paine, *Works* (New York, 1894), III, 340.
9. *Eclectic First Reader* (Cin., 1836), 29.
10. Arthur M. Schlesinger, Jr., *The Age of Jackson* (Boston, 1945), 356.
11. Vernon L. Parrington, *Main Currents in American Thought* (New York, 1930), I, 324.
12. Quoted in Schlesinger, *op. cit.*, 358.
13. *Eclectic Fourth Reader* (Cin., 1838), 137-139.
14. Paine, *op. cit.*, III, 329.
15. *Ibid.*, 337.
16. *Ibid.*, 338.
17. *Eclectic Fourth Reader* (Cin., 1838), 137-139.
18. John Locke, *Second Treatise on Civil Government*, Chap. IX.
19. *Eclectic Fourth Reader* (Cin., 1838), 138.
20. Webster, *op. cit.*, III, 15-16.
21. Paine, *Rights of Man* (Boston, 1792), 428.
22. Moncure D. Conway, *Life of Thomas Paine* (New York, 1892), II, 4.
23. Paine, *Rights of Man*, 410-411.
24. *Eclectic Fourth Reader* (Cin., 1838), 139.
25. *Ibid.*, 139.
26. *Ibid.*, 137-138.
27. *Ibid.*
28. *Ibid.*, 138.
29. *Ibid.*
30. *McGuffey's Alternate Fifth Reader* (Cin., 1888), 299.
31. *McGuffey's Rhetorical Guide* (Cin., 1844), 203-204.
32. *Eclectic Fourth Reader* (Cin., 1838), 139.
33. *Ibid.*, 103-105.
34. H. C. Lodge, ed., *Works of Alexander Hamilton* (New York, 1904), I, 401.
35. Charles A. Beard, *An Economic Interpretation of the Constitution* (New York, 1913), 149.
36. Beard, *The Rise of American Civilization* (New York, 1927), I, 311.

37. *Ibid.*
38. Beard, *An Economic Interpretation of the Constitution* (New York, 1913), 149-151.
39. *Ibid.*
40. *Ibid.*
41. *Ibid.*, 149.
42. A. J. Beveridge, *The Life of John Marshall* (Boston, 1916-1919), I, 312.
43. *McGuffey's Rhetorical Guide* (Cin., 1844), 128-130.
44. See Beard, *The Rise of American Civilization*, I, 297-335.
45. *Ibid.*
46. Beveridge, *op. cit.*, I, 252.
47. Max Farrand, ed., *The Records of the Federal Convention* (New Haven, 1911), I, 48.
48. *Ibid.*, II, 202.
49. *Ibid.*, I, 48.
50. *Ibid.*, II, 202.
51. *McGuffey's Alternate Fifth Reader* (Cin., 1888), 263.
52. Parrington, *op. cit.*, I, 280.
53. *Ibid.*
54. *McGuffey's Newly Revised Rhetorical Guide* (Cin., 1853), 391.
55. *Ibid.*
56. *Ibid.*
57. *Ibid.*
58. *Ibid.*
59. *Ibid.*, 387.
60. *Ibid.*, 387-388.
61. *Ibid.*
62. *Ibid.*, 389-390.
63. *Ibid.*, 391.
64. Quoted in Parrington, *op. cit.*, I, 290-291.
65. J. C. Hamilton, ed., *The Works of Alexander Hamilton* (New York, 1850), II, 79-80.
66. Thomas Jefferson, *Writings* (Washington, 1853-1854), VI, 335.
67. *Eclectic Fourth Reader* (Cin., 1838), 107.
68. *McGuffey's Alternate Fifth Reader* (Cin., 1888), 185-188.
69. *McGuffey's Newly Revised Rhetorical Guide* (Cin., 1853), 460.
70. *McGuffey's Rhetorical Guide* (Cin., 1844), 222-224.
71. Quoted in Parrington, *op. cit.*, I, 284.
72. Lodge, ed., *op. cit.*, II, 51.
73. *Ibid.*, III, 207-208.
74. *McGuffey's Alternate Fifth Reader* (Cin., 1888), 51-53.
75. *McGuffey's Fourth Eclectic Reader* (Cin., 1879), 220.
76. *McGuffey's Fifth Eclectic Reader* (Cin., 1879), 75.
77. *McGuffey's New Third Eclectic Reader* (Cin., 1857), 202.
78. *McGuffey's Fifth Eclectic Reader* (Cin., 1879), 185-189.
79. Jefferson, *op. cit.*, III, 268-269.
80. *Ibid.*, III, 356.
81. *Eclectic Fourth Reader* (Cin., 1838), 143.
82. *Ibid.* (1837), 198-199.
83. *Ibid.*
84. *Ibid.*, 243.
85. *Infra,* Chapter VII.
86. Jefferson, *op. cit.*, X, 160.
87. *Ibid.*, VI, 335.
88. *Ibid.*, X, 160.
89. Parrington, *op. cit.*, II, 20.
90. *McGuffey's Rhetorical Guide* (Cin., 1844), 203-204.

91. Parrington, *op. cit.*, II, 23.
92. *Ibid.*
93. Quoted in Merle Curti, *The Growth of American Thought* (New York, 1943), 352.
94. *Eclectic Fourth Reader* (Cin., 1838), 57-61.
95. *Ibid.* (1837), 143; *McGuffey's Newly Revised Rhetorical Guide* (Cin., 1853), 349.
96. Ralph Waldo Emerson, *The Conduct of Life* (Boston, 1904), 140-141.
97. *Eclectic Fourth Reader* (Cin., 1838), 57-61.
98. *Ibid.*, 59.
99. Cited in Parrington, *op. cit.*, I, 303.
100. Lodge, ed., *op. cit.*, I, 257.
101. Quoted in J. S. Bassett, *Life of Andrew Jackson* (New York, 1928), I, 346.
102. *Eclectic Fourth Reader* (Cin., 1837), 243.
103. *Ibid.* (1838), 59-60.
104. *Ibid.*
105. *Ibid.*, 60-61.
106. William Kent, *Memoirs and Letters of James Kent* (Boston, 1898), 218-219.
107. *Eclectic Fourth Reader* (Cin., 1838), 165.
108. *McGuffey's Newly Revised Eclectic Fourth Reader* (Cin., 1853), 282.
109. *Eclectic Fourth Reader* (Cin., 1838), 59.
110. *Ibid.*, 59-60.
111. *Ibid.*
112. *Ibid.* (1837), 220.
113. *Supra*, Note 93.
114. *McGuffey's Newly Revised Rhetorical Guide* (Cin., 1853), 387.
115. *Eclectic Fourth Reader* (Cin., 1837), 221.
116. *Ibid.*, 220.
117. *Ibid.*
118. *Ibid.*, 221.
119. *Ibid.*
120. *Ibid.*, 222.
121. James Fenimore Cooper, *The Redskins* (New York, 1895-1897), 170-220.
122. *Eclectic Fourth Reader* (Cin., 1837), 243.
123. Fisher Ames, *Works* (Boston, 1809), 17.
124. *McGuffey's Newly Revised Eclectic Fourth Reader* (Cin., 1853), 261.
125. *Eclectic Fourth Reader* (Cin., 1837), 222.
126. *McGuffey's Rhetorical Guide* (Cin., 1844), 205.
127. *Eclectic Fourth Reader* (Cin., 1838), 193-197.
128. Ames, *op. cit.*, 243.
129. *Ibid.*, 181.
130. *McGuffey'sNewly Revised Eclectic Third Reader* (Cin., 1853), 183.
131. *Ibid.*, 182.
132. *McGuffey's New Fourth Eclectic Reader* (Cin., 1857), 111.
133. *McGuffey's Newly Revised Eclectic Third Reader* (Cin., 1853), 184.
134. *McGuffey's Rhetorical Guide* (Cin., 1844), 67; *Eclectic First Reader* (Cin., 1836), 51.
135. *McGuffey's Newly Revised Eclectic Second Reader* (Cin., 1844), 12.
136. *McGuffey's Rhetorical Guide* (Cin., 1844), 67.
137. *Ibid.*, 204-206.
138. *McGuffey's New Third Eclectic Reader* (Cin., 1857), 221-225.
139. *McGuffey's New First Eclectic Reader* (Cin., 1885), 77.
140. *Ibid.*, 65-66.
141. *Ibid.*
142. *McGuffey's New Sixth Eclectic Reader* (Cin., 1866), 147.
143. Charles Eliot Norton, ed., *Letters of James Russell Lowell* (Boston, 1904), II, 51.
144. *Eclectic Fourth Reader* (Cin., 1837), 209.
145. *Ibid.*

146. *McGuffey's New Sixth Eclectic Reader* (Cin., 1866), 266.
147. Harriet Beecher Stowe, *Old Town Folks* (Boston, 1896-1898), 190-240.
148. *McGuffey's New Sixth Eclectic Reader* (Cin., 1866), 266.
149. *McGuffey's Alternate Fifth Reader* (Cin., 1888), 236.
150. *McGuffey's Newly Revised Eclectic Fourth Reader* (Cin., 1853), 45.
151. *McGuffey's Rhetorical Guide* (Cin., 1844), 159-163.
152. *Ibid.*
153. *Supra*, Note 93.
154. *Eclectic Fourth Reader* (Cin., 1837), 220.
155. *Eclectic Fourth Reader* (Cin., 1837), 172.
156. Arthur W. Calhoun, *A Social History of the American Family* (Cleveland, 1917-1919), II, 49-63.
157. Carl Russell Fish, *The Rise of the Common Man* (New York, 1927), 270.
158. *Ibid.*, 271.
159. *McGuffey's New Sixth Eclectic Reader* (Cin., 1866), 76.
160. *Ibid.*
161. Fish, *loc. cit.*
162. *Eclectic Fourth Reader* (Cin., 1837), 172-173.
163. A. M. Schlesinger, *New Viewpoints in American History* (New York, 1922), 137-140.
164. *Eclectic Fourth Reader* (Cin., 1837), 172-173.
165. Quoted in Arthur W. Calhoun, *op. cit.*, II, 83-84.
166. *Eclectic Fourth Reader* (Cin., 1838), 94.
167. Elizabeth C. Stanton, *Elizabeth Cady Stanton* (New York, 1922), II, 49.
168. *Ibid.*
169. *Harper's Weekly*, II, (July, 1858), 470.
170. *Eclectic Fourth Reader* (Cin., 1838), 303.
171. *Ibid.* (1837), 70.
172. *Ibid.*
173. *Ibid.*, 71.
174. *McGuffey's Newly Revised Rhetorical Guide* (Cin., 1853), 130-132.
175. *Ibid.*, 132.
176. *McGuffey's Newly Revised Eclectic Fourth Reader* (Cin., 1853), 80.
177. *Ibid.*, 85.
178. Alexis de Tocqueville, *Democracy in America* (New York, 1855), II, 224.
179. *The Weekly Tribune*, August 21, 1847.
180. *McGuffey's Alternate Fifth Reader* (Cin., 1888), 65-67.

NOTES FOR CHAPTER TWO

1. Lyman Beecher, *A Plea for the West* (Cin., 1835), 30.
2. *Eclectic Fourth Reader* (Cin., 1838), 272-275.
3. *Ibid.*
4. *Ibid.*
5. James Clarke, *Autobiography* (Boston, 1891), 104.
6. *Eclectic Fourth Reader* (Cin., 1838), 274.
7. Samuel J. Mills and Daniel Smith, *Report of a Missionary Tour* (Andover, 1815), 16.
8. *Eclectic Fourth Reader* (Cin., 1838), 274-275.
9. *Ibid.*
10. *Cincinnati Literary Gazette*, III (June, 1825), 193.
11. *McGuffey's Newly Revised Eclectic Fourth Reader* (Cin., 1853), 313.
12. *Ibid.*, 313-314.

13. *Eclectic Fourth Reader* (Cin., 1837), 238.

14. *Ibid.*, 240.

15. *Ibid.*

16. *McGuffey's Alternate Fifth Reader* (Cin., 1888), 245-248.

17. *Ibid.*

18. *Eclectic Fourth Reader* (Cin., 1838), 59.

19. *McGuffey's Rhetorical Guide* (Cin., 1844), 458.

20. Quoted in Curti, *op. cit.*, 397.

21. *Eclectic Fourth Reader* (Cin., 1838), 66.

22. *Ibid.*

23. *McGuffey's Newly Revised Eclectic Fourth Reader* (Cin., 1853), 314.

24. Ezra S. Gannett, *A Sermon Delivered in the Federal Street Meeting House in Boston* (Boston, 1840), 17.

25. Thomas King, *Patriotism and Other Papers* (Boston, 1864), 17.

26. *Eclectic Fourth Reader* (Cin., 1837), 44.

27. *McGuffey's Fifth Eclectic Reader* (Cin., 1879), 309-312.

28. *New McGuffey Third Reader* (Cin., 1901), 189-193.

29. *McGuffey's Rhetorical Guide* (Cin., 1844), 93.

30. *Ibid.*, 94.

31. *Annual Report of the Regents of the University of the State of New York* (Albany, 1835), 95.

32. *McGuffey's New Sixth Eclectic Reader* (Cin., 1866), 447.

33. *McGuffey's Newly Revised Eclectic Fourth Reader* (Cin., 1853), 325.

34. *Ibid.*

35. *Eclectic Fourth Reader* (Cin., 1838).

36. *McGuffey's Alternate Fifth Reader* (Cin., 1888), 244.

37. *Ibid.*, 243.

38. *Ibid.*, 299.

39. *McGuffey's Rhetorical Guide* (Cin., 1844), 97-98.

40. *Eclectic Fourth Reader* (Cin., 1838), 173.

41. *Ibid.*

42. *McGuffey's Newly Revised Rhetorical Guide* (Cin., 1853), 403.

43. *Ibid.*, 402.

44. *Eclectic Fourth Reader* (Cin., 1838), 66-68.

45. *McGuffey's New Sixth Eclectic Reader* (Cin., 1866), 321.

46. *McGuffey's Alternate Fifth Reader* (Cin., 1888), 248.

47. *McGuffey's Rhetorical Guide* (Cin., 1844), 248.

48. Curti, *op. cit.*, 410.

49. *Ibid.*

50. *Infra*, Chapter IX.

51. *McGuffey's Rhetorical Guide* (Cin., 1844), 87.

52. *Eclectic Fourth Reader* (Cin., 1838), 79-81.

53. *Ibid.*

54. *McGuffey's Rhetorical Guide* (Cin., 1844), 139.

55. *Ibid.*, 140.

56. Asa Child, *An Oration* (Norwich, 1838), 18.

57. *Ibid.*

58. *McGuffey's New High School Reader* (Cin., 1857), 27.

59. *New McGuffey Fourth Reader* (Cin., 1901), 130.

60. *Ibid.*

61. *Eclectic Fourth Reader* (Cin., 1837), 190.

62. *Ibid.*, 245.

63. E. A. Hannegan, quoted in Fish, *op. cit.*, 307.

64. *Eclectic Fourth Reader* (Cin., 1837), 245.

65. Curti, *op. cit.*, 405.

66. G. F. Train, *My Life in Many States and in Foreign Lands* (New York, 1902); and Train, *An American Merchant in Europe, Asia, and Australia* (New York, 1857).

67. W. H. Russell, *My Diary North and South* (Boston, 1863), 6.

68. *McGuffey's New Fourth Eclectic Reader* (Cin., 1857), 63.

69. *Ibid.*, 99.

70. *Ibid.*

71. *McGuffey's Fourth Eclectic Reader* (Cin., 1879), 58-59.

72. *McGuffey's Rhetorical Guide* (Cin., 1844), 104.

73. *McGuffey's Alternate Fifth Reader* (Cin., 1888), 34-35.

74. *Eclectic Fourth Reader* (Cin., 1838), 107.

75. *Ibid.*, 105-107.

76. *Ibid.*

77. According to Hughes, *op. cit.*, 141-142, the lesson on Napoleon appeared in the fourth readers of 1837 and 1844, the fifth of 1844, and the sixth of 1857, 1866, and 1879.

78. *Supra*, Chapter IV.

79. *McGuffey's Newly Revised Eclectic Fourth Reader* (Cin., 1853), 239-241.

80. *McGuffey's Newly Revised Eclectic Third Reader* (Cin., 1853), 67-68.

81. *Eclectic Fourth Reader* (Cin., 1838), 230-233.

82. *McGuffey's Rhetorical Guide* (Cin., 1844), 98.

83. *Eclectic Fourth Reader* (Cin., 1838), 81.

84. *Ibid.*, 66.

85. *McGuffey's Newly Revised Rhetorical Guide* (Cin., 1853), 334-337.

86. *McGuffey's Rhetorical Guide* (Cin., 1844), 203-204.

87. *Eclectic Fourth Reader* (Cin., 1838), 103-105.

88. *McGuffey's Newly Revised Eclectic Fourth Reader* (Cin., 1853), 123-125.

89. *Eclectic Fourth Reader* (Cin., 1837), 116.

90. *Ibid.*

91. *McGuffey's Newly Revised Rhetorical Guide* (Cin., 1853), 326.

92. *McGuffey's Rhetorical Guide* (Cin., 1844), 78.

93. *Eclectic Fourth Reader* (Cin., 1837), 116.

94. *McGuffey's Rhetorical Guide* (Cin., 1844), 78.

95. *The Harbinger*, V (June, 1847), 31.

96. *McGuffey's New Fourth Eclectic Reader* (Cin., 1857), 217-218.

97. *Eclectic Fourth Reader* (Cin., 1838), 159.

98. *McGuffey's Newly Revised Rhetorical Guide* (Cin., 1853), 325.

99. *McGuffey's New Fourth Eclectic Reader* (Cin., 1857), 230.

100. *McGuffey's Newly Revised Eclectic Third Reader* (Cin., 1853), 71-72.

101. *McGuffey's Third Eclectic Reader* (Cin., 1898), 82.

102. *McGuffey's Newly Revised Eclectic Third Reader* (Cin., 1853), 69-70.

103. *Eclectic Fourth Reader* (Cin., 1838), 110.

104. *McGuffey's New Sixth Eclectic Reader* (Cin., 1866), 178-179.

105. *Eclectic Fourth Reader* (Cin., 1837), 108.

106. *Ibid.* (1838), 76.

107. *Ibid.*

108. Webster, *op. cit.*, III, 477.

109. Jefferson Davis, *The Rise and Fall of the Confederate Government* (New York, 1881), I, 104-105.

110. J. C. Calhoun, *Works* (New York, 1863), I, 132-134.

111. Davis, *op. cit.*, I, 158; Calhoun, *op. cit.*, I, 162.

112. Webster, *op. cit.*, III, 346.

113. Joseph Story, *Commentaries on the Constitution* (Boston, 1833), I, 255.

114. *McGuffey's Newly Revised Eclectic Fourth Reader* (Cin., 1853), 317.

115. *Ibid.*, 318.

116. Calhoun, *op. cit.*, I, 9-10.

117. *Ibid.*, 13-16.

118. Story, *op. cit.*, I, 340.

119. *Ibid.*, I, 244.

120. *Ibid.*, I, 246.

121. *Eclectic Fourth Reader* (Cin., 1837), 198-199.

122. *Ibid.*

123. Webster, *op. cit.*, III, 468.

124. *McGuffey's New Sixth Eclectic Reader* (Cin., 1866), 319-322.

125. *Eclectic Fourth Reader* (Cin., 1838), 188-189.

126. *McGuffey's New Sixth Eclectic Reader* (Cin., 1866), 321,

127. Calhoun, *op. cit.*, I, 28.

128. Webster, *op. cit.*, III, 333.

129. *Ibid.*

130. *Ibid.*, III, 461-462.

131. Story, *op. cit.*, I, 340.

132. *McGuffey's Newly Revised Rhetorical Guide* (Cin., 1853), 460.

133. *McGuffey's Rhetorical Guide* (Cin., 1844), 222.

134. *McGuffey's Newly Revised Rhetorical Guide* (Cin., 1853), 460.

135. *Eclectic Fourth Reader* (Cin., 1838), 188-189.

136. *Ibid.* (1837), 198.

137. *McGuffey's New Sixth Eclectic Reader* (Cin., 1866), 321.

138. Calhoun, *op. cit.*, I, 35-36.

139. Webster, *op. cit.*, III, 455.

140. *Eclectic Fourth Reader* (Cin., 1837), 198-199.

141. *McGuffey's New Sixth Eclectic Reader* (Cin., 1857), 178-179.

142. *Ibid.* (1866), 180-181.

143. *Ibid.*, 178-179.

144. *McGuffey's Rhetorical Guide* (Cin., 1844), 231-233.

145. *Ibid.*, 232.

NOTES FOR CHAPTER THREE

1. Alexander Hamilton, *Works* (New York, 1904), VIII, 598.

2. Jefferson, *Writings* (New York, 1892-1896), X, 12-13.

3. *Eclectic Fourth Reader* (Cin., 1837), 143.

4. *Ibid.*

5. Calvin Colton, *A Voice from America to England* (London, 1839), 60.

6. *McGuffey's Rhetorical Guide* (Cin., 1844), 203-204.

7. *McGuffey's Newly Revised Rhetorical Guide* (Cin., 1853), 349.

8. J. M. Wainwright, *Inequality of Wealth the Ordinance of Providence* (Boston, 1835), 6, 7.

9. Hubbard Winslow, *Oration Delivered* (Boston, 1836), 16-17.

10. *Ibid.*

11. *Boston Post*, January 26, 1836.

12. *Eclectic First Reader* (Cin., 1836), 29.

13. *Der Amerikanische Leser Erstes Buch von Germanus* (Cin., 1836), 13.

14. *Eclectic First Reader* (Cin., 1836), 13.

15. *Ibid.*, 14-15.

16. Ezra Stiles Ely, *The Duty of Christian Freemen to Elect Christian Rulers* (Phil., 1828), 8, 11.

17. *Free Enquirer*, Oct. 31, 1829.

18. *Working Man's Advocate*, Oct. 30, 1833.

19. *Sentinel*, Dec. 22, 1829.

20. *Priestcraft Unmasked,* Jan. 1, 1830.

21. R. M. Johnson, *Report on the Transportation of Mail on Sunday* (Boston, 1829), 5-6.

22. *Johnson and Graham's Lessee v. William M'Intosh,* Wheaton, 543-572.

23. Schlesinger, *op. cit.,* 16-17.

24. Joseph Story, *Miscellaneous Writings* (Boston, 1835), 74.

25. *Journal of Debates and Proceedings* (Boston, 1853), 286.

26. Schlesinger, *loc. cit.*

27. *McGuffey's New High School Reader* (Cin., 1857), 76-78.

28. *McGuffey's Newly Revised Rhetorical Guide or Fifth Reader* (Cin., 1853), 380-381.

29. *Ibid.*

30. *Eclectic Third Reader* (Cin., 1837), 60-63.

31. *Ibid.*

32. Story, *op. cit.,* II, 306.

33. C. B. Swisher, *Roger B. Taney* (New York, 1935), 202, 430.

34. James Kent, *An Address* (Boston, 1836), 6.

35. *Commentaries on the American Law* (New York, 1826-1830), II, 1.

36. *Eclectic Fourth Reader* (Cin., 1836), 29.

37. *McGuffey's New Fourth Eclectic Reader* (Cin., 1857), 73-74.

38. *Ibid.,* 74.

39. *Eclectic First Reader* (Cin., 1836), 29.

40. *McGuffey's Rhetorical Guide or Fifth Reader* (Cin., 1844), 85.

41. Story, *Miscellaneous Writings,* 30.

42. *Supra,* 395.

43. Schlesinger, *op. cit.,* 350.

44. Quoted in *ibid.*

45. James H. Lanman, "Social Disorganization," *American Monthly Magazine,* II (Dec., 1836), 582.

46. *Ibid.,* 577-578.

47. *McGuffey's Newly Revised Eclectic Second Reader* (Cin., 1844), 48-50.

48. *Fourth Reader, Eclectic Series* (Cin., 1879), 245-249.

49. *Ibid.,* 249.

50. *McGuffey's Smaller Eclectic Primer* (Cin., 1849), 27.

51. Theodore Frelinghuysen, *An Inquiry into the Moral and Religious Character of the American Government* (New York, 1838), 133.

52. Daniel D. Barnard, *Plea for Social and Religious Repose* (New York, 1845), 8.

53. *Ibid.*

54. *Eclectic Fourth Reader* (Cin., 1837), 172-173.

55. *Ibid.*

56. *Eclectic Fourth Reader* (Cin., 1837), 17.

57. *Der Amerikanische Leser Erstes Buch von Germanus* (Cin., 1853), 35.

58. *Eclectic Third Reader* (Cin., 1837), 54-55.

59. *Ibid.,* 56.

60. Frelinghuysen, *op. cit.,* 89, 92, 109, 206.

61. *Ibid.,* 133.

62. *Ibid.*

63. Barnard, *op. cit.,* 8.

64. *Ibid.*

65. Taler Lewis, "Has the State a Religion?" *American Whig Review,* III (March 1846), 273.

66. *Ibid.*

67. *Ibid.,* 286.

68. *McGuffey's New High School Reader* (Cin., 1857), 123-124.

69. *Ibid.,* 124.

70. Flavel S. Mines, *The Church the Pillar and Ground of Truth* (New York, 1838), 11, 12.

71. *Ibid.*
72. Quoted in Schlesinger, *op. cit.*, 353.
73. *Ibid.*
74. *Eclectic Fourth Reader* (Cin., 1837), 60-62.
75. Schlesinger, *op. cit.*, 355.
76. *Congressional Globe*, 25 Congress, 2 Session, Appendix 423; also in Schlesinger, *op. cit.*, 355-356.
77. *McGuffey's Rhetorical Guide or Fifth Reader* (Cin., 1848), 114-116.
78. *Eclectic Fourth Reader* (Cin., 1838), 65.
79. *Fourth Reader, Eclectic Series* (Cin., 1879), 44.
80. Schlesinger, *op. cit.*, 356; *Eclectic Fourth Reader* (Cin., 1838), 137-139.
81. *Ibid.*
82. *McGuffey's Newly Revised Eclectic Third Reader* (Cin., 1848), 123-127.
83. *Ibid.*, 124-125.
84. *McGuffey's Sixth Eclectic Reader* (Cin., 1879), 68-69.
85. *Boston Investigator*, Feb. 6, 1835.
86. Schlesinger, *op. cit.*, 357-358.
87. *Ibid.*
88. *Ibid.*
89. *Ibid.*
90. Schlesinger, *op. cit.*, 359-360.
91. *McGuffey's Newly Revised Eclectic Second Reader* (Cin., 1844), 47.
92. *Ibid.*
93. *Ibid.*, 48.
94. *McGuffey's Newly Revised Eclectic Second Reader* (Cin., 1844), 50; also in the *Eclectic First Reader* (Cin., 1836), 29.
95. *McGuffey's Rhetorical Guide* (Cin., 1844), 84.
96. Francis Bowen, *The Principles of Political Economy* (Boston, 1859), 545.
97. *Debates and Proceedings* (Boston, 1854), 131.
98. *Eclectic First Reader* (Cin., 1836), 13.
99. *Ibid.*
100. Bowen, *op. cit.*, 505.
101. *McGuffey's New Third Eclectic Reader* (Cin., 1857), 142.
102. *Fourth Reader, Eclectic Series* (Cin., 1879), 42; also in *McGuffey's Newly Revised Eclectic Third Reader* (Cin., 1853), 85.
103. *Eclectic Fourth Reader* (Cin., 1838), 85.
104. *Ibid.*, 86.
105. *Ibid.*, 88-89.
106. *McGuffey's Newly Revised Eclectic Fourth Reader* (Cin., 1853), 162-163.
107. *Eclectic Fourth Reader* (Cin., 1838), 233.
108. *Ibid.*, 236.
109. *Ibid.*, 68.
110. *Ibid.*, 69.
111. *McGuffey's Rhetorical Guide* (Cin., 1844), 290.
112. *Eclectic Fourth Reader* (Cin., 1838), 126.
113. *Fifth Reader, Eclectic Series* (Cin., 1866), 69.
114. *Ibid.*, 70.
115. *McGuffey's Rhetorical Guide* (Cin., 1844), 209.
116. *Ibid.*, 269-270.
117. Horace Greeley, *Recollections of a Busy Life* (New York, 1868), 524-525.
118. Elias L. Magoon, *Republican Christianity* (Boston, 1849), 312-313.
119. *Ibid.*
120. *New England Galaxy*, VII (June, 1842), 1.
121. James W. Massie, *An Address Delivered before the Society of Alumni of the Virginia Military Institute* (Richmond, 1857), 11-13.

122. *McGuffey's New Sixth Eclectic Reader* (Cin., 1857), 166.
123. Alexander Davis, *A Loud Call to the Citizens of this Nation* (Hanover, Pa., 1842), 104.
124. *McGuffey's Rhetorical Guide* (Cin., 1844), 67.
125. *Ibid.*
126. *Ibid.*, 203-204.
127. *McGuffey's New High School Reader* (Cin., 1857), 33-34.
128. *McGuffey's New Third Eclectic Reader* (Cin., 1857), 37.
129. *Ibid.*, 39.
130. *Ibid.*, 40.
131. Greeley, *loc. cit.*
132. *Eclectic Fourth Reader* (Cin., 1838), 74-75.
133. Merle Curti, *op. cit.* 321ff.
134. *Ibid.*
135. Diana Corbin, *A Life of Matthew Fontaine Maury* (London, 1888), 160.
136. *McGuffey's Newly Revised Eclectic Third Reader* (Cin., 1853), 173.
137. *Fourth Reader, Eclectic Series* (Cin., 1879), 103.
138. Alexis de Tocqueville, *op. cit.*, III, 89.
139. *Fourth Reader, Eclectic Series* (Cin., 1879), 151-153.
140. *Ibid.*
141. *McGuffey's Rhetorical Guide* (Cin., 1844), 316-317.
142. *Ibid.*, 77.
143. *McGuffey's Newly Revised Eclectic Fourth Reader* (Cin., 1853), 268.
144. *McGuffey's Rhetorical Guide* (Cin., 1844), 316-317.
145. *Ibid.*
146. *Eclectic Fourth Reader* (Cin., 1838), 74-75.
147. *Ibid.*, 23.
148. *Ibid.*, 24.
149. *McGuffey's Rhetorical Guide* (Cin., 1844), 206-209.
150. *McGuffey's New High School Reader* (Cin., 1857), 144.
151. *Ibid.*, 145.
152. *Ibid.*, 78-79.
153. *Ibid.*
154. *Samuel F. B. Morse, His Life and Letters* (New York, 1914), II, 36.
155. *McGuffey's Newly Revised Rhetorical Guide* (Cin., 1853), 358.
156. Schlesinger, *op. cit.*, 267-282.
157. Ralph Henry Gabriel, *The Course of American Democratic Thought* (New York, 1940), 143-160.
158. Noah Porter, *Elements of Moral Science* (New York, 1885), 362.
159. *Ibid.*, 368.
160. *Ibid.*
161. James McGosh, *Our Moral Nature* (New York, 1892), 40.
162. *McGuffey's Alternate Fifth Reader* (Cin., 1888), 87.
163. *Ibid.*
164. *Ibid.*, 88.
165. *Ibid.*, 87.
166. *Fourth Reader, Eclectic Series* (Cin., 1879), 154.
167. *Ibid.*, 155.
168. *Ibid.*, 153-154.
169. *Ibid.*
170. Daniel Gregory, *Christian Ethics* (Philadelphia, 1875), 244.
171. *Fourth Reader, Eclectic Series* (Cin., 1879), 153-154.
172. Mark Hopkins, *The Law of Love and Love as Law* (New York, 1868), 182-183.
173. Rev. William Lawrence, "The Relation of Wealth to Morals," *World's Work*, I (Jan., 1901), 289-290.

174. *Fourth Reader, Eclectic Series* (Cin., 1879), 77.
175. *North American Review*, CXLVIII (June, 1889), 661.
176. *Ibid.*, 660.
177. *Ibid.*, 664.
178. Edwin L. Godkin, "Social Classes in the Republic," *Atlantic Monthly*, LXXVIII (Dec., 1896), 725.
179. *McGuffey's New Third Eclectic Reader* (Cin., 1857), 142.
180. *McGuffey's Newly Revised Eclectic Second Reader* (Cin., 1844), 50.
181. *Fourth Reader, Eclectic Series* (Cin., 1879), 77.
182. *Eclectic First Reader* (Cin., 1836), 29.
183. *New York Times*, July 30, 1877.
184. William Graham Sumner, *The Challenge of Facts and Other Essays* (New Haven, 1914), 55-62.
185. *Ibid.*
186. Quoted in Curti, *op. cit.*, 643.
187. Schlesinger, *op. cit.*, 17.
188. Carl Russel Fish, *The Rise of the Common Man* (New York, 1926), 192.
189. Quoted in *ibid.*
190. *Ibid.*
191. *McGuffey's Rhetorical Guide or Fifth Reader* (Cin., 1844), 125-126.
192. Fish, *op. cit.*, 192-194.
193. Rev. and Mrs. O. H. Gulick, *The Pilgrims of Hawaii* (New York, 1918), 50ff.
194. *Ibid.*
195. Hiram Bingham, *A Residence of Twenty-One Years in the Sandwich Islands* (Hartford, 1849), 16-24.
196. *Eclectic Fourth Reader* (Cin., 1837), 22.
197. *Ibid.*
198. *Ibid.*, 23.
199. *Der Amerikanische Leser Erstes Buch von Germanus* (Cin., 1853), 23.
200. *Ibid.*, 35.
201. *Eclectic Fourth Reader* (Cin., 1838), 143.
202. *Ibid.*, 227-228.
203. Curti, *op. cit.*, 352; *Supra*, Chapter II.
204. Quoted in *ibid.*
205. George B. Emerson and Alonzo Potter, *The School and the Schoolmaster* (Boston, 1843), 113.
206. *Der Amerikanische Leser Erstes Buch* (Cin., 1853), 41.
207. *McGuffey's Rhetorical Guide* (Cin., 1844), 73.
208. *McGuffey's New Sixth Eclectic Reader* (Cin., 1857), 78.
209. *Eclectic Third Reader* (Cin., 1837), 65.
210. *Eclectic First Reader* (Cin., 1836), 50.
211. *Ibid.*
212. *Ibid.*, 16-17.
213. *McGuffey's New High School Reader* (Cin., 1857), 60.
214. *McGuffey's Rhetorical Guide* (Cin., 1844), 87.
215. *McGuffey's Newly Revised Eclectic Third Reader* (Cin., 1853), 180-181.
216. *McGuffey's New Second Eclectic Reader* (Cin., 1857), 80-81.
217. *McGuffey's Fourth Eclectic Reader* (Cin., 1879), 183-187.
218. *McGuffey's New Third Eclectric Reader* (Cin., 1857), 122-124.
219. *Eclectic Fourth Reader* (Cin., 1838), 146.
220. *Ibid.*
221. *McGuffey's Newly Revised Eclectic Second Reader* (Cin., 1844), 118.
222. *Eclectic Third Reader* (Cin., 1837), 54.
223. *McGuffey's New Second Eclectic Reader* (Cin., 1858), 76-77.
224. *McGuffey's Rhetorical Guide* (Cin., 1844), 81.

225. *McGuffey's Newly Revised Eclectic Third Reader* (Cin., 1848), 49.

226. *McGuffey's Newly Revised Eclectic Fourth Reader* (Cin., 1853), 166-167.

227. *McGuffey's New Third Eclectic Reader* (Cin., 1857), 58.

228. *McGuffey's Alternate Fifth Reader* (Cin., 1888), 229-231.

229. *Ibid.*

NOTES FOR CHAPTER FOUR

1. Richard Baxter, *Christian Directory* (London, 1640), 326.

2. *Eclectic Fourth Reader* (Cin., 1837), 185.

3. *New McGuffey Fourth Reader* (Cin., 1901), 51.

4. Baxter, *loc. cit.*

5. *McGuffey's Newly Revised Rhetorical Guide* (Cin., 1853), 476.

6. *Ibid.*, 477.

7. Baxter, *op. cit.*, 336.

8. *Ibid.*, 376.

9. *McGuffey's Newly Revised Rhetorical Guide* (Cin., 1853), 478.

10. Bowen, *op. cit.*, 122-123.

11. *Ibid.*

12. Freeman Hunt, *Worth and Wealth* (New York, 1856), 63.

13. *Eclectic Fourth Reader* (Cin., 1837), 185.

14. *New McGuffey Fourth Reader* (Cin., 1901), 51.

15. *McGuffey's New Third Eclectic Reader* (Cin., 1857), 216.

16. *McGuffey's Fifth Eclectic Reader* (Cin., 1879), 59.

17. Bureau of Census, *Occupations at the Twelfth Census,* lxvi-lxviii; U. S. Industrial Commission, *Reports* (Wash., 1900-1902), XIX, 917, 922.

18. Helen Campbell and others, *Darkness and Daylight* (Hartford, 1892), 356-379.

19. Edition of 1879.

20. Mark Hopkins, *op. cit.*, 104.

21. *Fourth Reader, Eclectic Series* (Cin., 1879), 155.

22. *Ibid.*

23. *McGuffey's New Third Eclectic Reader* (Cin., 1857), 211.

24. Lodge, ed., *op. cit.*, III, 332.

25. Schlesinger, *op. cit.*, 267-282.

26. *Ibid.*

27. Wainwright, *op. cit.*, 6, 7.

28. P. O. Thacher, *A Charge to the Grand Jury of the County of Suffolk* (Boston, 1834), 17.

29. Winslow, *op. cit.*, 16-17.

30. Robert Hare, *Suggestions Respecting the Reformation of the Banking System* (Phil., 1837), 28-29.

31. *Fourth Reader, Eclectic Series* (Cin., 1879), 153-154.

32. *Ibid.*, 155.

33. *McGuffey's Newly Revised Eclectic Third Reader* (Cin., 1853), 109-111.

34. *McGuffey's Fourth Eclectic Reader* (Cin., 1879), 153.

35. Calvin Colton, *Labor and Capital* (New York, 1834), 14.

36. *New McGuffey Third Reader* (Cin., 1901), 57-59.

37. *Ibid.*, 59.

38. See, for example, Catherine M. Sedgwick, *The Poor Rich Man, and the Rich Poor Man.*

39. Elizabeth Peabody, *Remiscences of Rev. William Ellery Channing* (Boston, 1880), 415.

40. *McGuffey's New Sixth Eclectic Reader* (Cin., 1866), 95.
41. *Niles Weekly Register*, Aug. 8, 1835.
42. *McGuffey's Third Eclectic Reader* (Cin., 1896), 25.
43. *Ibid.*, 54.
44. William Ellery Channing, *Lectures on the Elevation of the Labouring Portion of the Community* (Boston, 1840), 15.
45. Schlesinger, *op. cit.*, 273.
46. *McGuffey's Newly Revised Eclectic Third Reader* (Cin., 1853), 111.
47. *Ibid.*, 110.
48. *McGuffey's Fourth Eclectic Reader* (Cin., 1879), 154-155.
49. R. C. Waterston, *Addresses on Pauperism, Its Extent, and the Best Means of Prevention* (Boston, 1844), 35.
50. *New McGuffey Fourth Reader* (Cin., 1901), 21-25.
51. *Ibid.*, 25.
52. *McGuffey's Newly Revised Eclectic Second Reader* (Cin., 1844), 47.
53. Schlesinger, *loc. cit.*
54. *McGuffey's Newly Revised Eclectic Second Reader* (Cin., 1844), 47.
55. Andrew Carnegie, *The Empire of Business* (New York, 1902), 18, 109, 122.
56. *McGuffey's Newly Revised Eclectic Third Reader* (Cin., 1853), 60.
57. *Ibid.*
58. *Eclectic Fourth Reader* (Cin., 1838), 51.
59. *Ibid.*
60. *McGuffey's Newly Revised Rhetorical Guide* (Cin., 1853), 437.
61. *McGuffey's Alternate Fifth Reader* (Cin., 1888), 239.
62. *New McGuffey Fourth Reader* (Cin., 1901).
63. *McGuffey's New Fourth Eclectic Reader* (Cin., 1857), 32.
64. *Ibid.*
65. *McGuffey's Second Eclectic Reader* (Cin., 1879), 148.
66. *McGuffey's Newly Revised Eclectic Second Reader* (Cin., 1853), 29-30.
67. *McGuffey's New Fifth Eclectic Reader* (Cin., 1857), 337.
68. *McGuffey's Fourth Eclectic Reader* (Cin., 1879), 102.
69. *Ibid.*
70. *McGuffey's Third Eclectic Reader* (Cin., 1898), 147.
71. *Ibid.*
72. *Ibid.*, 150.
73. *Eclectic First Reader* (Cin., 1836), 32.
74. *Ibid.*, 32-33.
75. Gabriel, *op. cit.*, 153.
76. Hughes, op. cit., 141.
77. *McGuffey's New Fourth Eclectic Reader* (Cin., 1857), 231.
78. *Ibid.*, 236.
79. *Ibid.*, 78.
80. *Ibid.*, 151.
81. *Ibid.*
82. William Makepeace Thayer, *Tact, Push and Principle* (New York, 1881), 354.
83. *McGuffey's Second Eclectic Reader* (Cin., 1879), 36.
84. *McGuffey's New Third Eclectic Reader* (Cin., 1857), 126.
85. *McGuffey's Second Eclectic Reader* (Cin., 1879), 138.
86. *New McGuffey Fourth Reader* (Cin., 1901), 148.
87. *Ibid.*
88. *McGuffey's Second Eclectic Reader* (Cin., 1879), 106.
89. *Ibid.*
90. *McGuffey's New Fourth Eclectic Reader* (Cin., 1857), 65.
91. *McGuffey's Newly Revised Eclectic Reader* (Cin., 1848), 28.
92. *McGuffey's Second Eclectic Reader* (Cin., 1879), 72.

93. *McGuffey's Rhetorical Guide* (Cin., 1844), 172.

94. *Eclectic Fourth Reader* (Cin., 1838), 130.

95. *McGuffey's New Fifth Eclectic Reader* (Cin., 1857), 71.

96. *McGuffey's Third Eclectic Reader* (Cin., 1896), 105.

97. *Ibid.*, 106-107.

98. *Ibid.*, 28-29.

99. *McGuffey's Newly Revised Eclectic Third Reader* (Cin., 1853), 193.

100. *McGuffey's Second Eclectic Reader* (Cin., 1879), 51.

101. Eclectic Fourth Reader (Cin., 1838), 19. This story persists through all editions of the fourth reader. See Hughes, *op. cit.*, 141.

102. *McGuffey's New Third Eclectic Reader* (Cin., 1857), 218-221.

103. *Ibid.*

104. *Ibid.*

105. *Ibid.*

106. *McGuffey's Second Eclectic Reader* (Cin., 1879), 126-129.

107. *McGuffey's Third Eclectic Reader* (Cin., 1896), 123.

108. *McGuffey's New Third Eclectic Reader* (Cin., 1857), 102.

109. *Ibid.*, 103-104.

110. *Eclectic Fourth Reader* (Cin., 1838), 149.

111. *McGuffey's New Third Eclectic Reader* (Cin., 1856), 13.

112. *Ibid.* (1857), 167.

113. *McGuffey's New Fourth Eclectic Reader* (Cin., 1857), 173.

114. *McGuffey's Second Eclectic Reader* (Cin., 1879), 66.

115. *Eclectic First Reader* (Cin., 1836), 68.

116. *Ibid.*

117. *Ibid.*

118. *Ibid.*

119. *McGuffey's New Fourth Eclectic Reader* (Cin., 1857), 78.

120. *McGuffey's Newly Revised Eclectic Second Reader* (Cin., 1844), 15.

121. *McGuffey's New Fourth Eclectic Reader* (Cin., 1857), 34.

122. *McGuffey's Newly Revised Eclectic Third Reader* (Cin., 1853), 76.

123. *Fourth Reader, Eclectic Series*, (Cin., 1879), 53.

124. *Ibid.*

125. *Ibid.*, 54.

126. *McGuffey's Newly Revised Eclectic Second Reader* (Cin., 1884), 93-95.

127. *McGuffey's New Fifth Eclectic Reader* (Cin., 1857), 40.

128. *Ibid.*, 41.

129. *Ibid.*, 44

130. *Ibid.*, 47.

131. *McGuffey's New Third Eclectic Reader* (Cin., 1857), 206.

132. *Ibid.*, 62-63.

133. *McGuffey's New First Eclectric Reader* (Cin., 1885), 83-84.

134. Thacher, *loc. cit.*

135. Rev. William Lawrence, "The Relation of Wealth to Morals," *World's Work*, I (June, 1901), 289-290.

136. Curti, *op. cit.*, 647.

NOTES FOR CHAPTER FIVE

1. *Eclectic Fourth Reader* (Cin., 1837), 52.

2. J. C. Krout, *Origins of Prohibition* (New York, 1925), 119-186.

3. Fish, *op. cit.*, 262-263.

4. *Journal of the American Temperance Union,* X (March, 1837), 39.

5. *Eclectic Third Reader* (Cin., 1837), 144.

6. *Ibid.*

7. J. B. Gough, *Platform Echoes* (Hartford, 1884), *passim.*

8. *Eclectic Fourth Reader* (Cin., 1837), 56.

9. *Eclectic Third Reader* (Cin., 1837), 145.

10. Fish, *op. cit.,* 267.

11. *Eclectic Third Reader* (Cin., 1837), 145.

12. *Ibid.,* 35.

13. *McGuffey's Newly Revised Eclectic Fourth Reader* (Cin., 1848), 94-95.

14. Cole, *op. cit.,* 160.

15. *North State Whig,* Dec. 11, 1850; Feb. 12, 1851.

16. *McGuffey's Newly Revised Eclectic Fourth Reader* (Cin., 1853), 93.

17. Krout, *op. cit.,* 283-295.

18. Cole, *op. cit.,* 162.

19. *Ibid.,* 164.

20. Schlesinger, *op. cit.,* 350-360.

21. *McGuffey's Newly Revised Eclectic Third Reader* (Cin., 1853), 215.

22. *Ibid.,* 216.

23. Cole, *op. cit.,* 163.

24. *McGuffey's New High School Reader* (Cin., 1857), 56-58.

25. Allan Nevins, *The Emergence of Modern America* (New York, 1927), 336.

26. *Ibid.,* 337; E. H. Cherrington, *Evolution of Prohibition in the United States* (Waterville, Ohio, 1920), 47-59.

27. *The Nation,* XVIII (March, 1874), 13; Nevins, *op. cit.,* 338.

28. *Ibid.*

29. *McGuffey's New High School Reader* (Cin., 1857), 56-58.

30. *McGuffey's Fifth Eclectic Reader* (Cin., 1879), 259-261.

31. *McGuffey's Alternate Fifth Reader* (Cin., 1888), 203.

32. For the strategy of the moralists in politics see, G. F. Parsons, "The Saloon in Politics," *Atlantic Monthly,* LVIII (Jan., 1886), 404-414. For the story of how the W.C.T.U. used the public schools for their anti-drink crusade consult, U. S. Commissioner of Education, *Report for 1880-1890,* II, 695-742. According to two medical authorities, the textbooks of the period "fairly bristle with statements of a character to work upon the fears of the reader, and remind one in this respect of patent medicine advertisements." See in this connection the report of H. P. Bowditch and C. F. Hodge in W. O. Atwater and others, *Physiological Aspects of the Liquor Problem* (Boston, 1903), I, 33, 44. For another discussion of the same subject consult, "Temperance Text-Books," *Outlook,* LXVI (June, 1900), 706-709, 974-975.

33. *McGuffey's New Third Eclectic Reader* (Cin., 1857), 118.

34. *Ibid.,* 119.

35. *Ibid.,* 120.

36. *McGuffey's Newly Revised Eclectic Fourth Reader* (Cin., 1853), 220.

37. *Ibid.,* 219.

38. *Ibid.,* 220.

39. Fish, *op. cit.,* 160.

40. *McGuffey's Second Eclectic Reader* (Cin., 1879), 124-126.

41. *Ibid.,* 126.

42. *Ibid.,* 124.

43. *Ibid.,* 126.

44. *Eclectic Fourth Reader* (Cin., 1838), 263.

45. *McGuffey's Rhetorical Guide* (Cin., 1844), 266.

46. *Ibid.,* 267.

47. *McGuffey's Newly Revised Eclectic Third Reader* (Cin., 1853), 168-169.

48. *Eclectic First Reader* (Cin., 1836), 35.

49. *Ibid.*, 23.
50. *Ibid.*
51. *Ibid.*, 37.
52. *Ibid.*
53. *Ibid.*, 20.
54. *Ibid.*, 43.
55. *Ibid.*, 56.
56. F. P. Robinson, *Reform Movements of the Thirties and Forties* (Madison, 1925).
57. *Ibid.*, 28-35.
58. *McGuffey's Newly Revised Eclectic Second Reader* (Cin., 1849), 163-164.
59. *Ibid.*, 142.
60. *Ibid.*
61. *McGuffey's Smaller Eclectic Primer* (Cin., 1849), 28.
62. Fish, *op. cit.*, 197.
63. *McGuffey's Newly Revised Eclectic Third Reader* (Cin., 1853), 152-153.
64. *Ibid.*, 26.
65. *McGuffey's New Second Eclectic Reader* (Cin., 1857), 75.
66. *McGuffey's New Third Eclectic Reader* (Cin., 1857), 172.
67. *McGuffey's New Second Eclectic Reader* (Cin., 1857), 98.
68. *Ibid.*
69. James Bryce, *The American Commonwealth* (London, 1888), III, 498.
70. William Graham Sumner, *What Social Classes Owe to Each Other* (New York, 1882), 112.
71. *McGuffey's New Fourth Eclectic Reader* (Cin., 1857), 241.
72. *McGuffey's New Third Eclectic Reader* (Cin., 1857), 227-228.
73. *Ibid.*, 54-55.
74. *Ibid.*, 111.
75. *McGuffey's New Fourth Eclectic Reader* (Cin., 1857), 41.
76. *Ibid.*, 43.
77. *Fourth Reader, Eclectic Series* (Cin., 1879), 39-41.
78. *McGuffey's Second Eclectic Reader* (Cin., 1879), 143-144.
79. *Fourth Reader, Eclectic Series* (Cin., 1879), 62.
80. *Ibid.*, 82.
81. *McGuffey's Second Eclectic Reader* (Cin., 1879), 32.
82. *Ibid.*, 32-33.
83. *Ibid.*, 39-40.
84. *McGuffey's New Second Eclectic Reader* (Cin., 1879).
85. *McGuffey's Second Eclectic Reader* (Cin., 1879), 12.
86. *McGuffey's New Second Eclectic Reader* (Cin., 1857), 127.
87. *Ibid.*, 151.
88. *Fourth Reader, Eclectic Series* (Cin., 1879), 160.
89. *Ibid.*, 161.
90. *Ibid.*, 160.
91. *McGuffey's Newly Revised Eclectic Third Reader* (Cin., 1853), 81.
92. *Fourth Reader, Eclectic Series* (Cin., 1879), 140.
93. *McGuffey's New Third Eclectic Reader* (Cin., 1857), 117.
94. *Libro de Lectura* (Cin., 1879), 96-99.
95. *McGuffey's New Third Eclectic Reader* (Cin., 1857), 67-68.
96. *McGuffey's Alternate Fifth Reader* (Cin., 1888), 51.
97. *McGuffey's New Third Eclectic Reader* (Cin., 1857), 147.
98. *McGuffey's Second Eclectic Reader* (Cin., 1879), 37.
99. *Fourth Reader, Eclectic Series* (Cin., 1879), 253-255.
100. *McGuffey's Newly Revised Eclectic Second Reader* (Cin., 1844), 60.
101. *Fourth Reader, Eclectic Series* (Cin., 1879), 139.
102. *McGuffey's Third Eclectic Reader* (Cin., 1896), 74.

103. *McGuffey's Rhetorical Guide* (Cin., 1844), 201.
104. *Eclectic Fourth Reader* (Cin., 1838), 40.
105. *Ibid.*
106. *Eclectic Third Reader* (Cin., 1837), 31.
107. *Ibid.*
108. *Ibid.*
109. *Ibid.*, 32.
110. *Ibid.*
111. *McGuffey's Fifth Eclectic Reader* (Cin., 1879), 66.
112. *McGuffey's New Fifth Eclectic Reader* (Cin., 1857), 38.
113. *McGuffey's Rhetorical Guide* (Cin., 1844), 182.
114. *McGuffey's Newly Revised Eclectic Fourth Reader* (Cin., 1853), 66.
115. *McGuffey's Second Eclectic Reader* (Cin., 1879), 108.
116. *New McGuffey Third Reader* (Cin., 1901), 160.
117. *McGuffey's Newly Revised Eclectic Fourth Reader* (Cin., 1853), 60.
118. *McGuffey's New Third Eclectic Reader* (Cin., 1857), 133.
119. *Ibid.*
120. *McGuffey's New Third Eclectic Reader* (Cin., 1857), 88.
121. *McGuffey's Third Eclectic Reader* (Cin., 1896), 48.
122. *Ibid.*, 158.
123. *Ibid.*, 45.
124. *McGuffey's New Second Eclectic Reader* (Cin., 1857), 134.
125. *McGuffey's Newly Revised Eclectic Fourth Reader* (Cin., 1853), 49.
126. *McGuffey's New Second Eclectic Reader* (Cin., 1857), 17.
127. *Fourth Reader, Eclectic Series* (Cin., 1879), 96.
128. *McGuffey's Second Eclectic Reader* (Cin., 1879), 118.
129. *McGuffey's New Fourth Eclectic Reader* (Cin., 1857), 47.
130. *Eclectic First Reader* (Cin., 1836), 69.
131. *McGuffey's New Second Eclectic Reader* (Cin., 1857), 141.
132. *McGuffey's Rhetorical Guide* (Cin., 1844), 121.
133. *Ibid.*
134. *McGuffey's Second Eclectic Reader* (Cin., 1879), 15.
135. *McGuffey's New Third Eclectic Reader* (Cin., 1857), 77-79.
136. *McGuffey's Second Eclectic Reader* (Cin., 1879), 46.
137. *Third Reader, Eclectic Series* (Cin., 1857), 43.
138. *McGuffey's Second Eclectic Reader* (Cin., 1879), 39.
139. *McGuffey's New Third Eclectic Reader* (Cin., 1857), 236.
140. *Eclectic First Reader* (Cin., 1836), 62-63.
141. *McGuffey's Fifth Eclectic Reader* (Cin., 1879), 112.
142. *McGuffey's Rhetorical Guide* (Cin., 1844), 245-246.
143. *McGuffey's Second Eclectic Reader* (Cin., 1879), 21.
144. *Ibid.*
145. *McGuffey's New Third Eclectic Reader* (Cin., 1857), 95.
146. *McGuffey's New Sixth Eclectic Reader* (Cin., 1866), 149.
147. Nevins, *op. cit.*, 106-107.
148. *Ibid.*
149. *McGuffey's Rhetorical Guide* (Cin., 1844), 82.
150. *McGuffey's Newly Revised Eclectic Fourth Reader* (Cin., 1853), 125.
151. *Eclectic Fourth Reader* (Cin., 1838), 82-83.
152. *Ibid.*
153. *McGuffey's Rhetorical Guide* (Cin., 1844), 76.
154. *McGuffey's Newly Revised Eclectic Third Reader* (Cin., 1853), 101-104.
155. Curti, *op. cit.*, 496.
156. *North American Review*, CXXVIII (April, 1879); also in *ibid.*, 487.
157. *McGuffey's Newly Revised Rhetorical Guide* (Cin., 1853), 392.

158. *McGuffey's New Fourth Eclectic Reader* (Cin., 1857), 34-35.
159. *McGuffey's New Third Eclectic Reader* (Cin., 1857), 115-116.
160. *Eclectic Fourth Reader* (Cin., 1838), 83.
161. This does not deny, however, that other readers may have had superiorities in the same direction.

NOTES FOR THE APPENDIX

1. Henry Vail, *A History of the McGuffey Readers* (Cleveland, 1911).
2. Harvey C. Minnich, *William Holmes McGuffey and His Readers* (Cin., 1936).
3. Hamlin Garland, *Son of the Middle Border* (New York, 1917), 112.
4. *Saturday Evening Post*, Nov. 26, 1927.
5. Herbert Quick, *One Man's Life* (Indianapolis, 1925), 156.
6. Cited in John L. Clifton, *Ten Famous American Educators* (Columbus, 1933), 75.
7. *Time Magazine*, Aug. 3, 1936.
8. Minnich, "William Holmes McGuffey and the Peerless Pioneer Readers," *Miami University Bulletin*, XXVI (July, 1928), 40.
9. Cited in Clifton, *op. cit.*, 75.
10. Nila B. Smith, *American Reading Instruction* (New York, 1934), 103.
11. *News Week*, July 25, 1936.
12. Ralph Leslie Rusk, *The Literature of the Middle Western Frontier* (New York, 1925), I, 269.
13. *Saturday Evening Post*, June 14, 1941.
14. Rudolph Rex Reeder, *The Historical Development of School Readers and Method in Teaching Reading* (New York, 1903), 56.
15. Mark Sullivan, *Our Times* (New York, 1927), II, 18.
16. *Ibid.*, 22.
17. *Ibid.*
18. Oscar Adolph Tingelstad, "The Religious Element in American School Readers up to 1830." (Unpublished doctoral dissertation, University of Chicago, 1925), 145.
19. Madison L. Perkins, "Historical Development of the Moral Element in American School Readers." (Unpublished doctoral dissertation, University of Chicago, 1925), 132.
20. James F. Hosic, "The Content of School Reading Books," *School and Society*, XI (Feb., 1920), 170-180.
21. Clifford R. Wood, "The Overlapping of Content in Fifteen Second Grade Readers," *Journal of Educational Research*, II (Jan., 1928), 75-82.
22. Sister Marie Lenore Fell, *Foundations of Nativism in American Textbooks* (Washington, 1937).
23. Bessie Pierce, *Civic Attitudes in American Textbooks* (Chicago, 1940).
24. Raymond Grove Hughes, "An Analysis of the Fourth, Fifth, and Sixth McGuffey Readers." (Unpublished doctoral dissertation, University of Pittsburgh, 1943), 141ff.
25. *Ibid.*, 151.
26. Vincent A. Davis, *The Literature of the Advanced School Readers* (Chicago, 1937), 125-135.
27. *Ibid.*, 135.
28. Henry Pratt Fairchild, ed., *Dictionary of Sociology* (New York, 1944).
29. Hughes, *op. cit.*, 33.
30. H. G. Good, "The Possibilities of Historical Research," *Journal of Educational Research*, XXIX (Oct., 1935), 148.

Bibliography

I

THE MCGUFFEY READERS

McGuffey's Newly Revised Eclectic Primer (Cincinnati: Truman and Smith, 1841).
McGuffey's Smaller Eclectic Primer (Cincinnati: W. B. Smith and Co., 1849).
McGuffey's Pictorial Eclectic Primer (Cincinnati: W. B. Smith and Co., 1849).
McGuffey's Newly Revised Eclectic Primer (Cincinnati: Sargent, Wilson and Hinkle, 1867).
Leigh's McGuffey's New Primary Reader (Cincinnati: Sargent, Wilson and Hinkle, 1868).
McGuffey's Eclectic Primer (New York: Van Antwerp, Bragg and Co., 1881).
McGuffey's Alternate Eclectic Primer (Cincinnati: American Book Co., 1894).
McGuffey's Eclectic Primer (Cincinnati: American Book Co., 1909).
Eclectic First Reader (Cincinnati: Truman and Smith, 1836).
McGuffey's Newly Revised Eclectic First Reader (Cincinnati: W. B. Smith, 1844).
McGuffey's Newly Revised Eclectic First Reader (Cincinnati: W. B. Smith and Co., 1853).
McGuffey's New First Eclectic Reader (Cincinnati: W. B. Smith and Co., 1857).
McGuffey's New First Eclectic Reader (Cincinnati: Wilson, Hinkle and Co., 1863).
McGuffey's First Eclectic Reader (New York: Van Antwerp, Bragg and Co., 1879).
McGuffey's New First Eclectic Reader (New York: American Book Co., 1885).
New McGuffey First Reader (New York: American Book Co., 1901).
McGuffey's First Eclectic Reader (New York: American Book Co., 1907).
McGuffey's New First Eclectic Reader (New York: American Book Co., 1920).
The Eclectic Second Reader (Cincinnati: Truman and Smith, 1836).
Eclectic Second Reader (Cincinnati: Truman and Smith, 1837).
Revised and Improved Eclectic Second Reader (Cincinnati: Truman and Smith, 1838).
McGuffey's Newly Revised Eclectic Second Reader (Cincinnati: W. B. Smith, 1844).
McGuffey's Newly Revised Eclectic Second Reader (Cincinnati: W. B. Smith and Co., 1849).
McGuffey's Newly Revised Eclectic Second Reader (Cincinnati: W. B. Smith and Co., 1853).
McGuffey's New Second Eclectic Reader (Cincinnati: Sargent, Wilson and Hinkle, 1857).

McGuffey's New Second Eclectic Reader (Cincinnati: Sargent, Wilson and Hinkle, 1864).

McGuffey's New Second Eclectic Reader (Cincinnati: Sargent, Wilson and Hinkle, 1865).

McGuffey's Second Eclectic Reader (New York: Van Antwerp, Bragg and Co., 1879).

McGuffey's New Second Eclectic Reader (New York: Van Antwerp, Bragg and Co., 1885).

McGuffey's Second Eclectic Reader (Cincinnati: American Book Co., 1896).

New McGuffey's Second Reader (Cincinnati: American Book Co., 1901).

McGuffey's Second Eclectic Reader (Cincinnati: American Book Co., 1907).

McGuffey's New Second Eclectic Reader (Cincinnati: American Book Co., 1920).

Eclectic Third Reader (Cincinnati: Truman and Smith, 1837).

Revised and Improved Eclectic Third Reader (Cincinnati: Truman and Smith, 1838).

McGuffey's Newly Revised Third Reader (Cincinnati: W. B. Smith, 1843).

McGuffey's Newly Revised Eclectic Third Reader (Cincinnati: W. B. Smith, 1848).

McGuffey's Newly Revised Eclectic Third Reader (Cincinnati: W. B. Smith and Co., 1853).

McGuffey's New Third Eclectic Reader (Cincinnati: W. B. Smith and Co., 1856).

Third Reader; Eclectic Series (Cincinnati: W. B. Smith and Co., 1857).

McGuffey's New Third Eclectic Reader (Cincinnati: W. B. Smith and Co., 1857).

McGuffey's New Third Eclectic Reader (Cincinnati: Sargent, Wilson and Hinkle, 1865).

McGuffey's Third Eclectic Reader (New York: Van Antwerp, Bragg and Co., 1879).

McGuffey's New Third Eclectic Reader (New York: Van Antwerp, Bragg and Co., 1885).

McGuffey's Alternate Third Reader (New York: Van Antwerp, Bragg and Co., 1887).

McGuffey's Third Eclectic Reader (Cincinnati: American Book Co., 1896).

McGuffey's Third Eclectic Reader (Cincinnati: American Book Co., 1898).

New McGuffey's Third Reader (Cincinnati: American Book Co., 1901).

McGuffey's Third Eclectic Reader (Cincinnati: American Book Co., 1907).

McGuffey's New Third Eclectic Reader (Cincinnati: American Book Co., 1920).

McGuffey's New Third Eclectic Reader (Cincinnati: American Book Co., 1925).

Eclectic Fourth Reader (Cincinnati: Truman and Smith, 1837).

Eclectic Fourth Reader (Cincinnati: Truman and Smith, 1838).

McGuffey's Newly Revised Fourth Reader (Cincinnati: W. B. Smith, 1844).

McGuffey's Newly Revised Eclectic Fourth Reader (Cincinnati: W. B. Smith, 1848).

McGuffey's Newly Revised Eclectic Fourth Reader (Cincinnati: W. B. Smith and Co., 1853).

McGuffey's New Fourth Eclectic Reader (Cincinnati: W. B. Smith and Co., 1857).

McGuffey's New Fourth Eclectic Reader (Cincinnati: Sargent, Wilson and Hinkle, 1866).

Fourth Reader, Eclectic Series (New York: Van Antwerp, Bragg and Co., 1879).

McGuffey's New Fourth Eclectic Reader (New York: Van Antwerp, Bragg and Co., 1885).

McGuffey's Alternate Fourth Reader (New York: Van Antwerp, Bragg and Co., 1887).

McGuffey's Fourth Eclectic Reader (Cincinnati: American Book Co., 1896).

New McGuffey Fourth Reader (Cincinnati: American Book Co., 1901).

McGuffey's Fourth Eclectic Reader (Cincinnati: American Book Co., 1907).

McGuffey's New Fourth Eclectic Reader (Cincinnati: American Book Co., 1920).

McGuffey's Rhetorical Guide or Fifth Reader (Cincinnati: W. B. Smith, 1844).

McGuffey's Newly Revised Eclectic Fifth Reader (Cincinnati: W B. Smith and Co., 1853).

McGuffey's New Fifth Eclectic Reader (Cincinnati: W. B. Smith and Co., 1857).

Fifth Reader, Eclectic Series (Cincinnati: Sargent, Wilson, and Hinkle, 1866).

McGuffey's Fifth Eclectic Reader (New York: Van Antwerp, Bragg and Co., 1879).

McGuffey's Alternate Fifth Reader (New York: Van Antwerp, Bragg and Co., 1888).

McGuffey's Fifth Eclectic Reader (Cincinnati: American Book Co., 1896).

New McGuffey's Fifth Reader (Cincinnati: American Book Co., 1901).

McGuffey's Fifth Eclectic Reader (Cincinnati: American Book Co., 1907).

McGuffey's New Fifth Eclectic Reader (Cincinnati: American Book Co., 1920).

McGuffey's New Sixth Eclectic Reader (Cincinnati: W. B. Smith and Co., 1857).

McGuffey's New Sixth Eclectic Reader (Cincinnati: Sargent, Wilson and Hinkle, 1866).

McGuffey's New Sixth Eclectic Reader (Cincinnati: Sargent, Wilson and Hinkle, 1867).

McGuffey's Sixth Eclectic Reader (New York: Van Antwerp, Bragg and Co., 1879).

McGuffey's New Sixth Eclectic Reader (New York: Van Antwerp, Bragg and Co., 1885).

McGuffey's Sixth Eclectic Reader (Cincinnati: American Book Co., 1896).

McGuffey's Sixth Eclectic Reader (Cincinnati: American Book Co., 1907).

McGuffey's New Sixth Eclectic Reader (Cincinnati: American Book Co., 1921).

McGuffey's New Highschool Reader (Cincinnati: W. B. Smith and Co., 1857).

McGuffey's Highschool Reader (New York: Van Antwerp, Bragg and Co., 1889).

McGuffey's Rhetorical Guide (Cincinnati: W. B. Smith, 1848).

McGuffey's Newly Revised Rhetorical Guide (Cincinnati: W. B. Smith and Co., 1853).

Der Amerikanische Leser, Erstes Buch von Germanus (Cincinnati: W. B. Smith and Co., 1853).

McGuffey's New Eclectic Primer (Tokyo: 1871) in Japanese.

Libro de Lectura (Cincinnati: American Book Co., 1879).

McGuffey's New Juvenile Speaker (Cincinnati: W. B. Smith and Co., 1860).

McGuffey's Newly Revised Eclectic Spelling Book (Cincinnati: W. B. Smith, 1846).

McGuffey's New Eclectic Spelling Book (Cincinnati: Sargent, Wilson and Hinkle, 1865).

McGuffey's Eclectic Spelling Book (New York: Van Antwerp, Bragg and Co., 1879).

McGuffey's Eclectic Spelling Book (Cincinnati: American Book Co., 1907).

II

BOOKS

Adams, Rufus W., *Young Gentleman and Lady's Explanatory Monitor* (Columbus, 1818).

The American Orator (Lexington: Joseph Charles, 1807).

Bates, Elisha, *The Juvenile Expositor*, n.p., n.d.

——, The Western Preceptor (Mountpleasant, 1821).

Battin, Richard, *The New Ohio Spelling Book*, n.p., n.d.

Beecher, Catherine, *The True Remedy for the Wrongs of Women* (Boston, 1851).

Bruce, Philip Alexander, *History of the University of Virginia* (New York: Macmillan, 1921), 5 vols.

Chambers, Joseph D., *Elements of Orthography* (Zanesville: Sawyer and Chambers, 1812).

The Child's Letter-Book (Chillicothe: Pomroy, 1834).

The Child's Spelling Book (Detroit: James Miller, 1809).

Clifton, John L., *Ten Famous American Educators* (Columbus: R. G. Adams and Co., 1933).

Colby, B., *The Grand Old Man of the Little Red Schoolhouse* (Dearborn: Dearborn Press, 1926).

Dickson, Edith, *Meddlesome Mattie and Other Selections from McGuffey* (New York, 1936).

Ellis, William R., *A Mirror to Noah Webster's Spelling Book* (Ms record in copyright office for the District of Ohio, 1820).

Fleming, Sanford, *Children and Puritanism* (New Haven: Yale University Press, 1933).

Ford, Paul Leicester, *The New England Primer* (New York: Dodd, Mead and Co., 1897).

Galbreath, C. B., *History of Ohio* (New York, 1925), 5 vols.

Garland, Hamlin, *Son of the Middle Border* (New York: Macmillan, 1917).

Griffith, Etta, *Education in McGuffey's Time* (Bolboa, 1894).

Guilford, Nathan, *The Western Spelling Book* (Cincinnati: N. and G. Guilford, 1831).

Gurley, Phineas, *Funeral Sermon on the Death of Mrs. Harriet McGuffey* (Dayton, 1850).

Hall, James, *The Western Reader* (Cincinnati: Corey and Fairbank, 1833).

Hansen, A. O., *Liberalism and American Education in the Eighteenth Century* (New York: Macmillan, 1926).

James, Philip, *Children's Books of Yesterday* (London: The Studio Publications, 1933).

McDonald, James, *A New Pronouncing Spelling Book* (Georgetown: Thomas Henderson, 1815).

——, A New Spelling Book (Shelbyville: George C. Smoot, 1815).

McGinnis, R. J., *Oxford Town* (Oxford, 1930).

Minnich, Harvey C., *Old Favorites From the McGuffey Readers* (Cincinnati: American Book Co., 1936).

——, William Holmes McGuffey and His Readers (Cincinnati: American Book Co., 1936).

Pickett, Albert and John W., *Introduction to Pickett's Expositor* (Cincinnati: Josiah Drake, 1834).
———, *The New Juvenile Expositor or Rational Reader* (Cincinnati: Pickett and Co., 1831).
———, *The New Juvenile Reader* (Cincinnati: C. P. Barnes, 1837).
———, *The Reader* (Cincinnati: C. P. Barnes, 1836).
The Picture Reader (Cincinnati: Truman and Smith, 1833).
Quick, Herbert, *One Man's Life* (Indianapolis: Bobbs-Merrill Co., 1925).
Reeder, Rudolph R., *The Historical Development of School Readers and Method in Teaching Reading* (New York, 1903).
Rosenbach, A. S. W., *Early American Children's Books* (Portland: Southworth Press, 1933).
Rusk, Ralph Leslie, *The Literature of the Middle Western Frontier* (New York: Columbia University Press, 1925), 2 vols.
Ruter, Martin, *The New American Primer,* n.p., n.d.
Scott, J., *A History and Biographical Cyclopedia of Butler County, Ohio* (Cincinnati, 1882).
Scott, William, *William H. McGuffey* (Columbus, 1935).
Shoemaker, Ervin C., *Noah Webster, Pioneer of Learning* (New York: Columbia University Press, 1936).
Shreve, Joseph, *The Speller's Guide* (1824), n.p.
Smith, Nila B., *American Reading Instruction* (New York: Silver-Burdett and Co., 1934).
Sullivan, Mark, *Our Times* (New York: Charles Scribner and Sons, 1927), 5 vols.
Tope, Melanchon, *A Biography of William Holmes McGuffey* (Bowerston: Phrenological Era Print, 1929).
Vail, Henry, *A History of the McGuffey Readers* (Cleveland: Burrows Co., 1911).
Venable, William, *Beginnings of Literary Culture in the Ohio Valley* (Cincinnati, 1891).
Watson, Foster, *The English Grammar Schools to 1660; Their Curriculum and Practice* (Cambridge: University Press, 1908).
———, *The Old Grammar Schools* (New York: G. B. Putnam's Sons, 1916).
The Western Primer (Cincinnati: Corey and Fairbank, 1833).
Wilson, Samuel, *The New American Rational Spelling Book* (Lexington: W. W. Worsley, 1810).

III

ARTICLES

Beecher, Catherine, "Moral Assassination," *Cincinnati Journal and Western Luminary,* IX.
Booth, George, "William McGuffey," *Miami Student* (January, 1936), 4.
Caldwell, J. W., "William McGuffey," *Miami Journal,* I (March, 1888), 115 ff.
Chamberlain, J., "McGuffey and His Readers," *School and Society,* XXI (March, 1942), 326.
———, "Colonial Era," *School and Society,* XXI (March, 1943), 231.
Chidlaw, B. W., "William McGuffey," *Miami Journal,* I (March, 1888), 115 ff.

"Common School Advocate," *American Annals of Education,* VIII (Nov., 1838), 528.

"Death of Edward McGuffey," *Miami University Buelletin,* XXVII (July, 1929), 16.

"Eclectic Readers," *Encyclopedia Britannica* (New York, 1929), V, 476.

Edwards, George J., "Eclectic Readers," *Miami Student* (Jan., 1936), 5.

Ford, Henry, "The McGuffey Readers," *Colophon,* I (Dec., 1927), 587.

Fullerton, Hugh, "Two Jolly Old Pedagogues," *Saturday Evening Post* (July, 1941), 15.

————, "That Guy McGuffey," *Saturday Evening Post,* CC (Nov., 1927), 14-16.

Hinsdale, B. H., "McGuffey," *Ohio Archaeological and Historical Society,* VI (Columbus, 1898), 43.

Horst, John, "Presentation of McGuffey's Readers," *Ohio Archaeological and Historical Society,* XXXVI (Columbus, 1927), 157-180.

Hosic, James F., "The Content of School Reading Books," *School and Society,* XI (Feb., 1920), 170-180.

Hughes, Raymond, "McGuffey and His Peerless Readers," *West Virginia Review* (Sept., 1931).

Johnson, Clifton, "More Quaint Readers," *New England Magazine,* XXIX (Jan., 1904).

King, Edgar W., "The McGuffey Readers," *Publishers Weekly,* CXXX (Sept., 1936), 1153.

Lewis, E. S., "McGuffey and His Readers," *Classmate,* XXXV (June, 1928).

"Literary Plagiarisms," *American Annals of Education,* VIII (Dec., 1838), 563-564; 626-630.

Mahoney, J. J., "Readers of the Good Old Days," *Educational Review,* LII (Oct., 1916), 217.

"McGuffey," *Elementary School Journal,* XXIV (Sept., 1928), 8-9.

"McGuffey," *Pennsylvania School Journal,* LXXXIII (Nov., 1934), 119.

"McGuffey Building," *Miami University Bulletin,* XXII (Feb., 1924), 8.

"The McGuffey Maple," *Miami University Bulletin,* XXV (Nov., 1926), 12.

"McGuffey Memorial," *Miami University Bulletin,* XXVIII (March, 1930), 9.

"McGuffey Memorial at Oxford," *American School Board Journal,* LXXXIII (Nov., 1931).

McGuffey, William Holmes, "Letter to Chidlaw," *Miami University Alumni Bulletin,* XXVII (March, 1929), 4.

————, "Conversations in a Schoolroom," *Monthly Chronicle of Interesting and Useful Knowledge* (March, 1839).

————, "Remarks on the Study of the Classics," *Western Institute and College for Professional Teachers Transactions,* IV, 203-205.

————, "Lecture on the Relative Duties of Parents and Teachers," *Western Institute and College for Professional Teachers Transactions,* V, 129-151.

————, "Report on the Most Efficient Method of Conducting Examinations in Common Schools, High Schools, and Academies," *Western Institute and College for Professional Teachers Transactions,* VI, 239-243.

"Memorial to McGuffey," *Miami University Bulletin,* XXIX (Jan., 1931), 11-12.

"Memorials to McGuffey," *Nation's Schools,* XIII (Feb., 1934), 15.

"Miami and the McGuffey Readers," *Miami University Bulletin,* XVII (May, 1936), 26.

Minnich, Harvey C., "McGuffey Gavel Presentation," *Ohio Schools* (March, 1927), 67.
——, "William H. McGuffey," *Dictionary of American Biography* (New York, 1933), XII, 57.
——, "William Holmes McGuffey and the Peerless Pioneer Readers," *Miami University Bulletin*, XXVI (June, 1928).
Morill, Anna McGuffey, "A Daughter of the McGuffeys," *Ohio Archaeological and Historical Society* (Columbus, 1933).
"Movements in Ohio," *American Annals of Education*, VIII (Oct., 1838), 476.
Newsweek (July 6, 1936), 26.
"Ohio University, the History of the College of the Old Northwest," *Ohio University Bulletin*, VIII (Oct., 1910), 430.
Patterson, Camm, "McGuffey," *University of Virginia Bulletin* (May, 1895).
"Replica of McGuffey's Desk Given to Ford," *Miami University Bulletin*, XXX (May, 1932), 9.
Rodabaugh, James, "McGuffey, A Revised Portrait," *Oxford Criterion* (1934), 53-64.
——, "Robert Hamilton Bishop," *Ohio State Archaeological and Historical Society* (Columbus, 1935), 83-96.
Ryan, D., "McGuffey Society at Logan Elm," *Ohio Archaeological and Historical Society Publication*, XXXI (Columbus, 1922), 255-350.
Scott, William, "McGuffey," *Ohio School Journal* (July, 1904).
Spinning, Mary Louise, "Biography of Mrs. Harriet Spinning McGuffey," *Miami University Bulletin*, XXVII (Jan., 1929), 6.
Sullivan, Mark, "McGuffey's Rightful Place in America's Hall of Fame," *School Life*, XVII (May, 1932), 169.
Thorton, W. T., "The Life and Services of William Holmes McGuffey," *Alumni Bulletin of the University of Virginia*, X (July, 1917), 237-258.
Time (Aug. 10, 1936), 26.
"William McGuffey," *Americana* (New York, 1932), XVIII, 50.
"William H. McGuffey," *National Cyclopedia of American Biography* (New York, 1897), IV, 443.
"William H. McGuffey, *New International Cyclopedia* (New York, 1915), XIV, 570.
"William H. McGuffey," *Historical and Biographical Cyclopedia of the State of Ohio* (Cincinnati, 1883), 279-280.
Wood, Clifford R., "The Overlapping of the Content in Fifteen Second Grade Readers," *Journal of Educational Research*, II (Jan., 1928).
Wood, Eugene, "The Old Red School House," *McClure's*, XXIV (Feb., 1904), 390-400.

IV

NEWSPAPERS

Akron News, Sept. 26, 1930.
Baltimore Sun, May 15, 1932.
Christian Science Monitor, Sept. 18, 1935; Oct. 13, 1936.
Cincinnati Daily Gazette, Feb. 9, Feb. 27, March 3, March 31, 1837; Nov. 28, 1838.
Claysville Recorder, Dec. 10, 1928.
Cleveland Plain Dealer, May 28, 1933.
Dayton Daily News, April 19, 1926; Dec. 10, 1928.
Hamilton Journal, Dec. 7, 1934.
Kansas City Times, Jan. 26, 1932.
Los Angeles Times, April 1, 1934.
Louisville Literary Register, Aug. 27, 1838.
Martinsburg Journal, July 20, 1934.
Middletown Journal, April 26, 1936.
New York Herald, Sept. 22, 1934.
New York Times, April 29, 1923; April 17, 1927; Feb. 25, 1934.
Richmond Daily Dispatch, May 6, 1873.
Wheeling News, Aug. 30, 1931.

V

UNPUBLISHED MATERIALS

Davis, Vincent A., "The Literature of the Advanced School Readers in the United States, 1785-1900" (Unpublished doctoral dissertation, University of Chicago, 1934).
Hughes, Raymond Grove, "An Analysis of the Fourth, Fifth, and Sixth McGuffey Readers" (Unpublished doctoral dissertation, University of Pittsburgh, 1943).
McGuffey, Alexander, *Letters:* Jordan Collection, Cincinnati, Ohio.
McGuffey, Henrietta, *Autobiography:* Mary Hughes Collection, Oxford, Ohio.
McGuffey, William Holmes, *Letters:* McGuffey Museum Collection, Oxford, Ohio.
———, *Philosophy:* McGuffey Museum Collection, Oxford, Ohio.
Perkins, Madison L., "Historical Development of the Moral Element in American School Readers" (Unpublished doctoral dissertation, University of Chicago, 1925).
Rodabaugh, James, "Three Great Triumvirates and Their Quarrel" (Unpublished master's thesis, Miami University, 1928).
Tingelstad, Oscar Adolph, "The Religious Element in American School Readers up to 1830" (Unpublished doctoral dissertation, University of Chicago, 1925).

Index

VITA

Richard D. Mosier: born July 16, 1917, Toledo, Ohio; attended Long-fellow Elementary School, DeVilbiss High School, and the University of Toledo; B.Ed. degree from the latter institution in 1939; M.A., Ohio State University, 1943; Instructor in English and Head of the Department of Speech and Dramatics, East High School, Portsmouth, Ohio; Instructor in English, Ottawa Hills High School, Toledo, Ohio; Instructor in English, University of Chicago; Assistant in the Division of Foundations, Teachers College, Columbia University. Publications include, "The Spiritual Element in Education," *World Order*, V (Sept., 1939); "Our Machine Morality," *Unity*, CXXVI (February, 1941); "Literature and Prejudice," *The Personalist*, XXII (January, 1941); "Education for Morality," *Education*, LXII (June, 1942).